SUPER

SUSHI

RAMEN

EXPRESS

ALSO BY MICHAEL BOOTH

The Almost Nearly Perfect People:
Behind the Myth of the Scandinavian Utopia

Eat, Pray, Eat: One Man's Accidental Search for
Equanimity, Equilibrium and Enlightenment

Doing Without Delia: Tales of Triumph and Disaster
in a French Kitchen

Just as Well I'm Leaving: To the Orient with
Hans Christian Andersen

SUPER SUSHI RAMEN EXPRESS

ONE FAMILY'S JOURNEY THROUGH THE BELLY OF JAPAN

MICHAEL BOOTH

PICADOR

NEW YORK

picadorusa.com • picadorbookroom.tumblr.com
twitter.com/picadorusa • facebook.com/picadorusa

Picador® is a U.S. registered trademark and is used by St. Martin's Press under license from Pan Books Limited.

For book club information, please visit facebook.com/picadorbookclub or e-mail marketing@picadorusa.com.

Designed by Steven Seighman

The Library of Congress Cataloging-in-Publication Data is available upon request.

ISBN 978-1-250-09980-8 (hardcover)
ISBN 978-1-250-09979-2 (e-book)

Our books may be purchased in bulk for promotional, educational, or business use. Please contact your local bookseller or the Macmillan Corporate and Premium Sales Department at 1-800-221-7945, extension 5442, or by e-mail at Macmillan SpecialMarkets@macmillan.com.

Originally published in Great Britain in 2009 by Jonathan Cape under *Sushi and Beyond*

First published in the United States by Picador

First U.S. Edition: September 2016

10 9 8 7 6 5 4 3 2 1

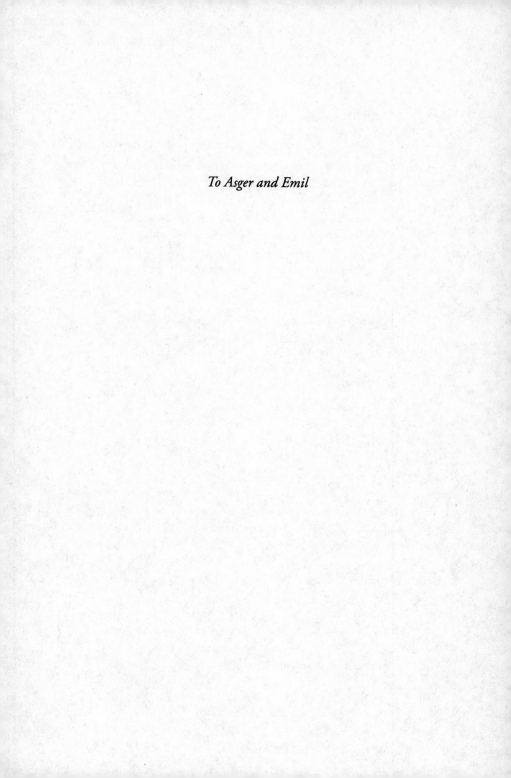

To Asger and Emil

CONTENTS

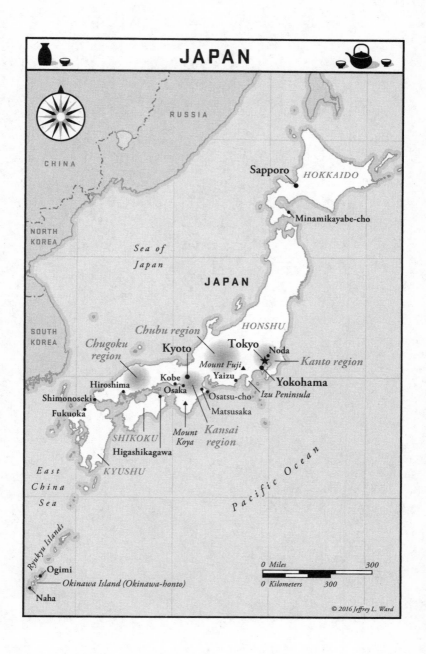

JAPAN

RUSSIA

CHINA

NORTH
KOREA

*Sea of
Japan*

JAPAN

Sapporo

HOKKAIDO

Minamikayabe-cho

SOUTH
KOREA

Chubu region

HONSHU

Kyoto

Tokyo

Noda

Kanto region

*Chugoku
region*

Mount Fuji ▲

Hiroshima

Kobe

Yaizu

Yokohama

Shimonoseki

Osaka

Osatsu-cho

Izu Peninsula

Fukuoka

Matsusaka

SHIKOKU

*Mount
Koya*

*Kansai
region*

Higashikagawa

KYUSHU

*East
China
Sea*

Pacific Ocean

Ryukyu Islands

Ogimi

Okinawa Island (Okinawa-honto)

Naha

0 *Miles*   300

0 *Kilometers*   300

© *2016 Jeffrey L. Ward*

SUPER

SUSHI

RAMEN

EXPRESS

1. TOSHI

It had started off as a perfectly temperate discussion about the relative merits of French and Japanese cuisines. I had recently had dinner at the feted French restaurant SaQuaNa, in Honfleur, on the Normandy coast. The chef, Alexandre Bourdas, was a fast-rising culinary star in France, and I had innocently remarked on his lightness of touch and the freshness of his raw ingredients, drawing what turned out to be a rash comparison between his food and Japanese cooking. I knew that Bourdas had worked in Japan for three years, so it didn't seem too outlandish to suggest that his cooking had been influenced by the food he had eaten there.

I ought to have known this would be a red flag to my friend Katsotoshi Kondo.

"What do you know about Japan food, huh?" Toshi snapped. "Do you think you know anything about Japanese food? Only in Japan! You cannot taste it here in Europe. This man's cuisine is nothing like Japanese food. Where is the tradition? Where are the seasons? Where is the meaning? *Tu connais rien de la cuisine Japonaise. Pas du tout!*" From experience, I knew that this sudden switching of languages on Toshi's part was a bad sign. He was also pouting now. I had to get my retaliation in before he detonated fully.

"I know enough about it to know how dull it is," I said. "Japanese food is all about appearance. Where's the comfort, the warmth, the hospitality? No fat, no flavor. What have you got? Raw fish, noodles, deep-fried vegetables—and you stole all that from Thailand, the Chinese, the Portuguese. Doesn't matter, though, does it? You just dunk it in soy sauce, and it all tastes the same, right? All you need to make good Japanese food is a sharp knife and a good fishmonger. What else is there? Ooh, don't tell me, cod sperm and whale meat. Mmm, got to get me some of those."

I had met Toshi while training at Le Cordon Bleu cooking school in Paris a couple of years earlier. A tall, rather severe-looking, half-Japanese, half-Korean man in his late twenties, he was an enigma wrapped in many layers of inscrutability, but he had a subversive, dry sense of humor lurking behind the gruff Beat Takeshi facade.

While the rest of us would wear our chef's whites for days until we looked like walking Jackson Pollocks, Toshi was always immaculately turned out. His plates were perfect: his food presented just so, with ample white space surrounding it; his knives were always fearsomely sharp. But he had clashed with the French chefs who taught us. They invariably marked him down because he refused to cook fish for more than a few seconds and served vegetables with bite rather than soft all the way through, as they preferred. This seeded in Toshi a lingering resentment toward the French and their cuisine, but still he stayed on in Paris, partly, I suspect, out of a sheer bloody-minded determination to single-handedly educate the locals in the superior ways of Japanese cooking.

After graduating, Toshi went to work in a Japanese restaurant in the sixth arrondissement, the kind of place—virtually invisible from the street but a haven of serenity within—that registered on the radar only of Japanese tourists. We kept in touch and met up from time to time to eat and talk food, our get-togethers usually descending into a childish rally of insults.

But this time, things ended slightly differently. "OK, just shut up, OK?" Toshi said, his head disappearing beneath the table as he fished around in his satchel. "I have something for you."

He handed me a large hardback with a blurry painting of a leaping fish on the cover. Momentarily taken aback, I promised to read it and thanked Toshi. This was embarrassing. He had never given me anything before. It had taken me some time to explain to him the concept of buying a round of drinks, for instance. It was clearly an expensive book, too, and, though it sounds ridiculous given the occasions he had ranted at me, for the first time, as I held the book on my lap on the bus home, I began to understand how keenly he must have felt the slights from me and from our teachers at Le Cordon Bleu.

The book was *Japanese Cooking: A Simple Art*, by Shizuo Tsuji, a new edition of the original, which was published in 1979. Introductions by Ruth Reichl, the former editor of *Gourmet* magazine, as well as the late M. F. K. Fisher, served notice that this was no ordinary food book. As I would later discover, it is still the preeminent English-language Japanese food reference source, the bible of Japanese cooking for a generation of Japanophile food lovers throughout the world.

"This is much more than a cookbook," writes Reichl. "It is a philosophical treatise."

There are recipes, of course, over two hundred of them, covering grilling, steaming, simmering, salads, deep-frying, sushi, noodles, and pickling—many of the dishes unfamiliar to me—but along the way Tsuji also covers everything from the spiritual meaning of rice to the role of tableware in Japanese cuisine. "No Japanese, however humble, would think of serving food on just any old plate, relying on flavor alone to please," he writes. Tsuji emphasizes the fundamental importance of the seasons in Japanese food: in Japan, ingredients with a particularly brief seasonal window are often celebrated with quasi-spiritual verve by cooks and diners. I learned, too, that the Japanese employ a number of virtually flavorless ingredients—tofu, burdock, and something called *konnyaku*, "a dense, gelatinous, dark brown to hazy gray cake" made by peeling, cooking, pounding, and coagulating a root called "devil's tongue"—purely for their texture and mouthfeel. Others, such as "steam-processed bonito fillets, dried to wood-like hardness and shaved into flakes" (referenced in the title of the John Lennon album *Shaved Fish*, I now realized), or the fearful-sounding fermented soybean breakfast dish of *natto*, were, to me, mystifying. Indeed, there seemed to be a remarkable array of fermented foodstuffs—from miso to soy to natto, not forgetting fermented sea slug entrails—all of which belied the impression I had of the Japanese as being fussy about "rotten" foods, like cheese and yogurt.

I knew that the Japanese were wary of applying heat to their food, but Tsuji writes breezily about a dish in which "chicken is tinged with pink near the bone" (in fact, it turns out that chicken sashimi—*raw* chicken—is not uncommon in Japan), and more generally of an overriding obsession with freshness and simplicity in cooking, which explained their aversion to excessive application of heat.

At times, I detected a note of condescension, albeit wrapped in a tissue of humility: "Many of our foods may seem thin and lacking in substance," he writes in his preface. "But you must learn to look for the subtle, natural aroma and flavor of ingredients." Occasionally, subsequent developments in global food trends had rendered his concern for the squeamish sensibilities of the Western palate a little outdated: "The best-loved food in Japan, sashimi—sliced raw fish—often seems unbearably exotic, almost bordering on the barbaric, and requiring a great sense of gastronomic adventure and fortitude to down!"

More troubling was the lack of desserts. There are literally none in *A Simple Art*. If this was a reflection of Japanese cuisine in general, it would be cause for more than a few moments of somber reflection. It was like hearing about a people who never laughed. *Perhaps Tsuji just didn't have a sweet tooth*, I thought to myself, and read on.

Throughout five hundred pages of what Fisher calls the "delicate pageantry" of Japanese cuisine, what struck me above all was how prescient so much of Tsuji's writing seemed. The mantra of local, fresh, seasonal food; a diet featuring little dairy and meat, more vegetables and fruit; all of it prepared with the minimum of meddling from the chef and a deep respect for the ingredients, resonated precisely with contemporary thinking in the West. Though written more than thirty years ago, this was still a thoroughly modern food book with important, perhaps critical, lessons for us all.

Reflecting on the eponymous simplicity of Tsuji's recipes, it seemed to me a colossal oversight that, while it is perfectly normal for us to cook Indian, Thai, Chinese, French, Italian, and even Mexican or Hungarian food at home, we hardly ever try to make Japanese food—and if we do, it will most likely be a poor approximation of sushi. With the recent ramen boom limited to major cities, for most of us, still, Japanese food is synonymous with the inevitable *nigiri* and *maki* with the same half dozen toppings. But, according to Tsuji, not only is Japanese food remarkably healthy and delicious but also a cinch to make. It doesn't rely on slow-cooked stocks or tricky sauces, nor does it require extensive preparation. According to Tsuji, you don't even need to mix your tempura batter properly—it is *supposed* to be lumpy.

Though, of course, I could never admit as much to Toshi, Tsuji's writing had a stirring effect on me. I had heard chefs waffle on about simplicity and "letting the ingredients speak for themselves," about how they cook only seasonal, local food, and so on—they all said the same thing. While conducting interviews for magazines and newspapers, I had spent many a glassy-eyed hour listening to them drone on—but their fussy, complicated food invariably undermined the platitudes. Yet here was a writer, and a national cuisine, who embodied all those sentiments.

There was another reason why *A Simple Art* fascinated me. Three years of committed eating in Paris had taken its toll. I had perilously high levels of cholesterol—for every Michelin star I had sampled, it seemed as if I had added one of the company's tires to my waist. A flight of stairs left me winded, and I was already beginning to worry about how, in the near future, I would be able to put my socks on in the morning. Toshi had taken to poking me in the belly, then pretending to have lost his finger. He, of course, was whippet slim and fit. His grandmother, he said, had recently turned ninety-seven and still tended her garden. Did I know the Japanese lived longer than any other race on earth? he asked. And did I know why? Diet.

"You know, maybe if you start eating Japanese food now, you might live to sixty," Toshi goaded. "I will live beyond one hundred because I always eat tofu, fish, soy, miso, vegetables, rice." He was prone to making outlandish health claims for virtually all Japanese foodstuffs: Shiitake mushrooms cured cancer, apparently, and daikon radish could prevent acne. Lotus root reduced cholesterol, he said, and, patting my barren pate, he said I really should start eating more wakame seaweed, as it was guaranteed to cure baldness. According to Toshi, soybeans were a miracle product that reduced cholesterol, prevented cancer, and helped people live forever.

I began reading more about Japanese food. Or, rather, I didn't. Because, astonishingly, even all these years since it was published, as far as serious, authoritative English-language books on Japanese cuisine go, Shizuo Tsuji's is still pretty much the beginning and the end. There are dozens of books on sushi, of course; some writing on the health benefits of the Japanese diet; and a couple on Westernized Japanese cooking, known as *yoshoku* in Japan; but precious little about the current state of Japanese food, about what they are eating in Japan right now and the direction their cuisine is going in.

Troublingly, in the late seventies, Tsuji was already observing the decline of traditional Japanese cuisine: "I am sorry to say our own cuisine is no longer authentic. It has been polluted with frozen foods," he writes, later adding that foreign influence had also had an insidious effect on the palates of the Japanese. In particular, he bemoans their newfound taste for frozen tuna, which, he says, is "ruining the tradition of Japan's cuisine."

How had things developed since he wrote those words? I wondered. Was there anything left of the authentic Japanese cooking Tsuji describes, or had his countrymen surrendered to the tyrannical allure of KFC and McDonald's with the rest of us?

Shortly after finishing the book, the same day Toshi gave it to me, I made a rash, impulsive, and, it would turn out, life-changing decision. I decided I had no other choice but to go and see, and taste, for myself; to travel to Japan and investigate the state of Japanese food today, to learn as much as I could about their techniques and ingredients and find out whether or not Tsuji's dire predictions had come true. Was there still much we could learn from the Japanese about cooking, or was *A Simple Art* now nothing more than an elegy for a lost culinary tradition? Were Toshi's claims about the longevity of the Japanese and the amazing health benefits of their diet true, and if so, would it be possible to introduce any of them into a Western lifestyle? Was Japanese cooking at all compatible with Western living? And did they really use sock glue instead of garters, as Toshi claimed?

A plan began to form. I would travel to Japan, and slowly, methodically, greedily work my way from the northernmost island of Hokkaido, south to Tokyo, then on to Kyoto, Osaka, Fukuoka, and the islands of Okinawa, eating, interviewing, learning, and exploring along the way. I wanted to sample the indigenous ingredients, learn about the philosophy, the techniques, and, of course, the health benefits of Japanese food. I badly needed to lose some weight, too, of course, and to start eating more healthfully, but had found that the options for that in the West—low-fat this, gluten-free that—held little appeal. Tsuji's book, on the other hand, had revealed a world of beautiful, healthful, simple food that I could easily envisage eating, if I could only learn to make it for myself.

Tentatively, I raised the idea with my wife, Lissen, that evening.

"God, that's a brilliant idea," she said. "I would love to go to Japan. Can you imagine how great it would be to travel there with the kids? It would be something they would remember for the rest of their lives. Imagine!"

"Wait, no. Erm. I didn't really mean . . . you know, I don't really think . . . research . . . interviews and things like that . . ." I said.

But it was too late. She was already there, and that was absolutely fine by me. Like a lot of modern fathers, I suffer from a constant nagging guilt about the amount of time I spend—or rather don't spend—with my children. I don't have a proper job, which means I never really have proper holidays either. I hadn't taken such a thing for over five years. But the idea of a poolside fortnight in some rented villa, or, worse, a trip to Disneyland, made me feel itchy and depressed. Here, though, was a way I could combine work and family, a way for me to share a passion for food with my children and perhaps plant a spore of curiosity that might grow within them and bond us over the years to come. In truth, it was a selfish decision in so many ways, which is why it feels fraudulent to dress it up as some kind of noble parenting sacrifice. I was burning to spend time in Japan, but I crumble if I don't see my family for more than a few days.

That early-August night, I booked four open tickets to Japan, instead of one, and began to map out a workable route through what Toshi had assured me were the pulse points of Japan's culinary culture.

We would take a foodie family road trip lasting just under three months. We were going to fly to Tokyo, where we would spend three weeks gently acclimatizing before hitting the roads and rails. Tokyo was, Toshi told me, the restaurant capital of Japan, with more, and more diverse, restaurants than anywhere else in the country. This was where we would find the best sushi, as well as the best tempura restaurants in Japan, along with numerous other surprises (he offered this last bit of information with a knowing smirk).

From there we would fly north to the island of Hokkaido, which would offer a contrast to the urban intensity of Tokyo, with its wide-open spaces and more relaxed vibe, not to mention stunning seafood. We would be based in its capital, Sapporo, for around ten days.

Then we would head back to the island of Honshu, where Tokyo is, but this time go farther south to Kyoto, the former royal capital and still the spiritual and cultural heart of Japan. This, Toshi said, was the home of *kaiseki*—the elaborate, multicourse formal dinner, Japan's answer to haute cuisine, yet more refined, more complex, and, according to him, leagues better. I should be sure to try the tofu there, too, which was the finest and freshest in the world.

After three weeks in Kyoto, with day trips to various other places (we should make sure to visit the sacred mountain of Koya-san,

Toshi said, and Kobe would offer some familiar Western comforts), a short train ride would take us to Osaka. I didn't need Toshi to tell me the food here would be radically different from food in Kyoto. François Simon, the esteemed restaurant critic of *Le Monde*, had enthused about it when I'd interviewed him earlier in the year; he'd gone as far as to call it the most exciting food city in the world.

A much-anticipated journey by bullet train would then take us farther southeast to Fukuoka, on the island of Kyushu. Toshi didn't say much about Fukuoka other than that we would love it and to make sure I tried the local ramen, but he became particularly animated when talk turned to Okinawa, our final destination. This wasn't really Japan, he said; it was Japan but different, with a unique food culture and way of life. If I wanted to know the secret of how to live to a hundred, this was the place to find it—it has more centenarians than anywhere else in the world, apparently. We set aside another two weeks there.

From Okinawa, we would return to Tokyo for a few more days before flying home.

I had no idea whether it was realistic to attempt such a journey with young children in tow, but I knew I wanted them to see and experience as much as possible of Japan and the Japanese.

Asger, six, and Emil, four, had never journeyed beyond Europe. Asger was as fussy an eater as I had been at his age, which meant his diet was restricted largely to potato-based foodstuffs shaped like dinosaurs. Meanwhile, Emil had a tendency to projectile-vomit foods he did not like, to the point that we had all grown accustomed to it—blasé, even. What on earth were they going to eat?

I, meanwhile, had no definable image of Japan beyond the clichéd cinematic polarities of *Lost in Translation* and Kurosawa's films, and no grasp of the language beyond the few words of polite greeting Toshi had taught me, which I suspected were almost certainly rank obscenities. (And you know what? They were.)

What was the real Japan like? Was it navigable? How did the Japanese live, and—amid the liquid-crystal canyons and the concrete, the geometric gardens and the snowcapped mountains, the Gothic Lolitas and the geishas—would there be space, let alone a welcome, for a small, curious (in both senses) family from the West?

2. DEPARTURE

We are sitting by the window on the wing of a 747. I turn idly from my video screen and look out to see vaporized liquid gushing from the far engine. My stomach somersaults.

Jet fuel.

I glance around. Asger is sitting beside me, spellbound, his mouth gaping in front of a video screen, which, I only now notice, he has somehow switched from cartoons to *Reservoir Dogs*. Emil is similarly entranced by the tray table in front of him, which he is opening and closing for the 827th time. Lissen is reading a book. Only I see the fuel. Perhaps I am imagining it. I look again. But it is still flowing. Should I alert the flight attendant?

The captain's voice comes over the speaker. "Ladies and gentlemen, I am afraid we have a small problem with one of our engines. We are having to jettison our fuel in preparation for a return to Heathrow. This is normal procedure, so please don't be alarmed. I will let you know as soon as we have made arrangements for landing."

Two hours into our twelve-hour flight to Narita International Airport and, at best, we will have to return to London and endure an interminable wait at an interminable terminal; at worst, we will end our lives in a flaming comet of death over the south of England.

You will have deduced that we didn't die, but we endured something perhaps worse: five hours in the purgatory of Heathrow Terminal 4, rummaging like strays for something edible to stave off our hunger, eventually making do with Pret A Manger sushi—wet, flavorless, and indigestible. The memory of that sushi would at least be instructive by way of comparison with the sushi we would eat during the coming months, but at the time, it really did seem as if our trip were cursed from the start.

"It's an omen," I muttered glumly as I swallowed cold, nutty rice. "If things have started to go wrong already, what hope have we got?"

"Michael, we haven't even left England yet," said Lissen calmly. "I am sure everything will be fine."

3. NO BROCCOLI

Tokyo by night rendered us dumbstruck. We stepped out of our taxi into the warm, thick, late-August air to be swamped by the ceaseless tide of people that flows from Shinjuku Station day and night. The four of us stood there for some moments, floodlit and flabbergasted, as thousands of people swarmed around us like swallows.

We had arrived in Tokyo a few hours earlier that evening, frazzled but, given the time difference, still frisky, as our brains remained convinced it was early afternoon. Before we had even cleared customs, the foreignness of Japan had become apparent in the form of a "No Broccoli" sign—a silhouette of a head of broccoli with a red line through it—at customs. Was broccoli smuggling an issue in Tokyo? Were other brassicas also prohibited? It would remain one of many enigmas from the trip.

We headed out of the airport to find a way to our hotel. Though he would graciously change his opinion over the course of our journey, Emil was not immediately taken with Japan: "It smells," he said as we waited outside for the airport bus.

"What of?" I asked.

"Everything," he said, unfurling his bottom lip.

The bus carried us forty slow miles west through treacly traffic along the ten-lane Higashi-Kanto Expressway, past mammoth sex hotels, malls, and pachinko parlors. We caught a glimpse of the Tokyo Tower, taller than the Eiffel Tower but dwarfed by the buildings around it, before we came in to land for the second time that evening, spiraling downward via several off-ramps into the center of Tokyo.

In truth, Tokyo has no real center. It is an infinite urban maze, with tower blocks and freeways stretching in all four directions and beyond. I imagine that people have driven themselves to the brink of madness looking for this city's heart, or even simply trying to make sense of Tokyo as a city in any conventional meaning of the word. Toshi told me it is better to think of Tokyo as twenty or so smaller cities, wheels within a giant wheel, all connected by the circular aboveground Yamanote train line.

Once we had opened and closed all the cupboards and drawers in our self-catering apartment in Aoyama, we realized we were hungry and decided to dip our toes into Tokyo for the first time. But neither is Tokyo a toe-dipping kind of city. Step outside your door for a moment and it will overwhelm you like no other place on earth, particularly if you choose, as we did, to alight from your taxi in Shinjuku, the largest nightlife center in Japan.

Over thirteen million people live in this city: one-tenth of the population of Japan inhabiting 2 percent of its land. Every day, two million of them pass through Shinjuku Station, said to be the busiest in the world. They were all there that night to welcome us, flowing in regulated streams, like some migration from the natural world.

Emil clung to my thigh for the first few minutes until it became apparent that the crowd was remarkably well ordered, its commuters, shoppers, and fun-seekers avoiding each other through the use of some kind of sonar as they made their way toward the bars, shops, restaurants, and home. Meanwhile, above us, a cliff face of liquid crystal broadcast the incongruous face of Tommy Lee Jones enjoying a canned coffee drink in alarmingly grizzled detail.

Emil soon retreated once more as he began to attract the attention of a group of giggling girls. Soon both boys were being cooed over and photographed by polite young women. It was our first taste of what we would come to think of as the Royal Walkabout Syndrome, the strange, thankfully benign, magnetic power our children—all Western children, from what we saw—had on a certain female Japanese demographic. If they could have given autographs, Asger and Emil would have signed hundreds over the following months.

Shinjuku Station is virtually a self-contained town in its own right, with department stores, restaurants, offices, and bars both above and below its tracks. You could spend a day there and never leave or catch a train. We soon got lost in its labyrinth of walkways, serendipitously emerging into one of Japan's largest department store food halls, known as *depachika*.

Most of Japan's major department stores have these vast supermarket-cum-multiple-takeaways in their basements, astonishing places selling just about every type of raw ingredient and processed food imaginable, and many beyond imagining, both Western and Asian. We wandered for a while, I in a pleasant food-induced trance, the others restless but impressed. There were freshly made, restaurant-quality packs of sushi; an array of tempura; *tonkatsu* (breaded pork cutlets, not to be confused with *tonkotsu* ramen); tofu; rice balls; grilled eels glistening beneath their dark basting sauce—a microcosm of modern Japanese eating preferences. We saw the famously expensive fruit: immaculately veined, orange-fleshed Yubari cantaloupes from Hokkaido tied with red ribbons and packaged in individual wooden boxes like Fabergé eggs, selling for ¥21,000 (over $150—although the record is ¥1.25 million for one melon); mangos for ¥15,000 ($134), and apples tenderly packed with little square sponges protecting their stems. There were barrels of tiny dried fish, deep-fried eel spines (well, you wouldn't want to waste them, would you?), and, in small, glassed-off kitchens, chefs busy making dim sum, fresh noodles, and mochi cakes (from rice flour, typically stuffed with sweet, red adzuki bean paste). There was a display of French cheeses almost as comprehensive as the one at my local market in Paris, and not much more expensive, and elaborate gâteaux, Swiss rolls, and macarons as good as—perhaps even more precisely fashioned than—those from Ladurée. Asger tugged on my sleeve, reminding me that we really needed to eat.

Shinjuku Station acts as a buffer between two very different parts of the city—on its west side are office and hotel skyscrapers, with more going up in the few spaces between. But we emerged on the eastern side in Kabukicho, a maze of restaurants, *kaiten* (conveyor-belt) sushi joints, shops, bars, and nightclubs.

Kabukicho and the nearby Golden Gai are about as sleazy as things get in Japan, housing lavish hostess bars with names like Vanity and Seduce, some of them hosted by young men for female clients, all crowded together over many floors of many high-rise buildings. Every single floor for several blocks around had a lit sign outside indicating the presence of some kind of restaurant, bar, or karaoke joint.

This may not seem a terribly appropriate place to take young children for an evening, but even though this is a yakuza heartland (or perhaps because it is), Kabukicho is clean, safe, and, apart from the artfully highlighted Kajagoogoo haircuts of the gigolo bar touts, fairly restrained. Even if they were older, Asger and Emil would have been none the wiser regarding the—I've no doubt hair-raising— activities in the windowless salons around us. Legend has it the city's Turkish baths all had to change their names to "soap lands" after the Turkish ambassador was taken to one by mistake and a diplomatic incident ensued (that was his story).

A fair number of Tokyo's estimated two hundred thousand or so restaurants are contained within this densely packed quarter. Many of them specialize in just one style of cooking, or even just one dish. And this is the key, I think, to the unparalleled wealth of Tokyo's dining scene. In Paris, one quite often sees individual "Asian" restaurants serving Thai, Chinese, Vietnamese, and Japanese food, all of which will be third-rate at best, but in Tokyo, chefs become attuned to every nuance and variation involved in the preparation of their chosen culinary genre, evolving over years into masters of tempura, sushi, teppanyaki (food cooked on a hot plate), soba noodles, or whatever. And their customers—of whom they need but a handful of regulars, as rents are not too high even here—know exactly what to expect and how to evaluate it in relation to other specialists in the same food (consulting restaurant review websites, such as Tabelog, when necessary).

The only problem, of course, is the choice, which is paralyzing. What's more, in Tokyo, novices can find it very difficult even to decipher what kind of restaurant they are looking at from the outside unless there are photo menus. These are not necessarily the warning signs they might be in other countries, but this was our first night, and I wanted to sample something special.

Beside the railway tracks heading north out of Shinjuku is a narrow alleyway of rather more human-scale *izakaya* (Japanese-style pub-diners), each of them with space for between six and ten diners. This is Shomben Yokocho ("Piss Alley"), a dark, shabby, downbeat remnant of late-1940s Tokyo, the kind of place Hawkeye used to go to on leave in *M*A*S*H*, a timeless sliver of old black-market Tokyo that has survived against the odds and in defiance of the developers right in the heart of one of the glitziest nightlife zones in the world.

The air was thick with the smoke and steam of charcoal grills and noodle cauldrons, and everything was covered in a thin film of transparent brown grease. In any other country, the name and ramshackle appearance of a place like this would also serve as a deterrent, but Toshi had assured me that not only was it perfectly safe and that its one-man owner-chefs and their clientele were welcoming to strangers, but that the food they served—ramen, yakitori (grilled skewers), and *yakisoba* (fried noodles)—was compulsively delicious and cheap.

We sidled up to a tiny, Formica-topped, L-shaped bar, behind which an elderly lady, bent in the shape of a question mark, with tightly permed gray hair and a red apron, was busy scraping at a hot plate with a metal spatula, tossing an unruly mound of ramen noodles (confusingly, yakisoba is made with ramen noodles, not soba) beneath fluorescent tube lighting. She barely glanced at us, though we must have been an unlikely sight, so I just pointed to the noodles, raised four fingers, and smiled. She nodded and set to work.

The place was designed for swift feeding and then departure: Kikkoman bottles and jars of chopsticks stood on the bar; the menu, written in Japanese on wooden tabs, hung around the walls; red-and-white lanterns dangled from the ceiling; and we sat on red vinyl stools. We shared a couple of piles of yakisoba with a sweet, soy-based sauce (a strain of dark, tangy-sweet teriyaki-style sauce that we would encounter in all sorts of dishes throughout Japan) topped with bright red pickled ginger and little flakes of dried seaweed. It was clinically moreish.

The other diners—salarymen in dark suits, their ties loosened at the end of the day—toasted us with brown bottles of beer as big as their forearms, pouring little glass tumblers full and offering them to me and Lissen with polite questions in disjointed English about where we were from, how long we had been in Japan, and what we thought about Japanese food. Seeing Asger and Emil struggle with their chopsticks, the owner rooted around and pulled out a couple of small forks, and we all stuffed our faces contentedly.

It is usual to hop from one izakaya to another, having a small plate of something in one and a few yakitori at another, so we settled in for a second helping in front of a smoking charcoal grill in another tiny cubicle. This time it was a young man with a wispy goatee stoking the flames and turning the skewers. We ordered by pointing at what others were having and at the raw skewers in the glass case that divided the counter from the kitchen.

The Japanese have mastered the charcoal fire better than any other nation thanks to one simple but characteristic innovation: they make the food smaller. *Yakitori* literally means "grilled chicken," but asparagus, quail eggs, tomatoes, and various vegetables are also cooked this way. Crucially, the meat is cut into bite-size pieces and skewered, three or so pieces at a time, along with short lengths of *negi*—very tender small leeks. The skewers are grilled for a few minutes over hot charcoal and basted with sauce, then put back over the charcoal briefly before being served. It is not especially healthy but is terrifically tasty and, short of administering a general anesthetic—which is hardly cost effective—there are few better ways to get children to eat vegetables.

Chicken livers, crunchy gizzards (this is the muscle birds use to break down grains before digesting them), skin, and hearts are all yakitori menu staples, but there was one skewer in the glass case I couldn't identify. I ordered one, just in case I was missing something. It had no discernible flavor beyond the sauce that covered it, but an unusual texture, like crunchy plastic.

It was cartilage—specifically the piece at the crown of the chicken's breast. It wasn't that appealing, but Emil diligently gnawed his way through the rest of the skewer before polishing off some chicken livers—true testament to the power of sugary sauces.

Each yakitori chef has his own recipe for this sauce, and guards it fiercely. Shizuo Tsuji writes that serious yakitori chefs never let their sauce run out, but instead add more when it starts to get low, which means that, as they have no water in them, some sauces can last for years. The essential ingredients are the same as for so many Japanese basting sauces: soy, sake, mirin, and sugar, in which you can also simmer chicken bones and add a thickener, such as arrowroot or *kuzu* starch, which comes in the form of rocks and, unlike corn flour, is light and flavorless. Equal parts soy and mirin, with a little less sake and sugar, make a good base.

Sitting wreathed in charcoal smoke, watching my children happily munch chicken organs on sticks, was a surreal end to a day that had begun with cornflakes and toast on the other side of the world, but also really quite wonderful. We had landed.

The next day was reward time for Asger and Emil following their stoic performance during the journey to Japan. In their minds, Japan was synonymous with just one thing, and it had nothing to do with food. They had long been obsessed with Pokémon, the bizarre, chimerical cartoon characters that inhabit the globally popular yet, to anyone over the age of eighteen, unfathomable animations. We had promised them a visit to the Pokémon store in Shinagawa but had forgotten it was Saturday. By the time we arrived, the shop was dense with seven-year-olds all clamoring for Pokémon T-shirts, figures, lunch boxes, and key rings. Asger's and Emil's eyes were on stalks, and they soon commenced their own kind of pleading chant—"I want, I want, I want . . ."—filling their baskets as if preparing for a siege.

As far as I can understand, demand for Pokémon figures is entirely predicated on the mere fact of their existence rather than any inherent practical or artistic merit. They are, then, the perfect product, placing their addicts entirely at the mercy of the corporation that churns them out, and they don't get much less merciful than the Nintendo corporation of Japan.

The next stop was Kiddy Land, the surprisingly small largest toy store in Tokyo. While we were browsing the Pokémon department there, a mother approached.

"How old is he?" she asked, pointing to Asger.

"Six," I told her. She looked aghast. I asked how old her boy was; he looked about four. "Eight," she said, looking at Asger. "Is he normal?"

"Well, depends what you mean by normal."

"Oh, *Daa-aad*."

Across the way, a small kiosk caught my eye. It was selling vinegar drinks, which I had heard were a current fad. I bought one—cherry vinegar flavor—and took a gulp. Initially, all was well: there was a sweet, sugary cherry flavor, like old-fashioned worm medicine, but, good *grief*, the afterburn was horrific—pure vinegar. It could have been worse. Another recent Tokyo drink craze I'd heard about was a zero-calorie jelly drink made with pig placenta.

In the Hello Kitty heartland of Harajuku, a short walk away, Lissen took sneaky photos of teenage girls dressed in lacy, stackheeled, puffball-skirted Gothic Lolita costumes, or as "nurses" complete with bloodstained aprons or favorite anime characters, French maids, or faux punks (like the ones you see as extras in old Kiefer Sutherland movies).

We caught a cab back to the apartment. In Paris, catching a cab is like trying to capture a wasp: it requires a great deal of patience, and you are likely to get stung. But Japanese cab drivers are a superrace of chauffeurs. Within seconds of standing by the curb with our arms outstretched (or, in Asger's case, his light saber illuminated), a boxy yellow Toyota had pulled up. The rear door opened automatically, prompting impressed gasps from the boys.

"Wha . . . wow! Did you see that?" said Emil.

"It was me! I was using the Force!" said Asger.

We climbed into the back and showed the white-gloved driver where we wanted to go on our map. He smiled, nodded, and started to drive. Ten minutes later, we paid the exact fare, the rear door opened automatically once more, and we bundled out. "Please remember to take any of your belongings with you!" he called after us.

It sounds so simple, doesn't it? A taxi driver takes you where you want to go, and you pay him the fare. But we were more used to myriad arbitrary additional charges, erratic driving, a random confrontation, and, finally, a complaint about the lack of tip.

The experience inspired me to write a list as soon as we got in the door.

GREAT THINGS ABOUT TOKYO IN COMPARISON TO PARIS, IN THE ORDER THEY OCCURRED TO ME:

There is no dog shit
No one expects a tip
There is no litter
Hold on, there are no litter bins either
I'm the tallest person here
People won't steal your stuff, try to cheat you, or be rude to
  you because you don't speak their language
How can so many restaurants make a living?
It really is great being taller than everyone for once
You can get a taxi
Even in the rain
You can be sure the driver will simply take you where you
  want to go without fuss or any funny business
People in shops act like they really want your business
I could probably have had quite a good basketball career in
  Japan

Back at our apartment complex, the concierge told us that there was a typhoon on the way. The local supermarket (slogan: "Delicious

Foods Make Us Pleasant") had set out its "Typhoon Preparedness Kits," containing blankets, food, and water for two days—surely an overreaction? By the afternoon, however, the wind and rain were bludgeoning the windows, and objects were flying through the air. The problem was, we had nothing for dinner. I would have to go out.

Outside, the rain was horizontal. The streets were empty. There were no cars, no people. *This is madness*, I thought as I leaned into the wind and battled onward. A bicycle outside a shop was blown over and began to move slowly down the street on its side. I forced myself forward like a bad mime. A single taxi drove by. A shopkeeper, his face pressed up against his window, looked genuinely alarmed to see someone on the street. By now I was soaked to the skin, but I eventually made it to the supermarket.

Inside, tinkly Muzak played as if all were normal. I stood bewildered by the unfamiliar packaging and lack of English wording and gazed at the perfection of the fruits and vegetables. The Japanese are clearly very finicky about their fresh produce. There was not a blemish on anything. The apples looked an airbrushed rosy red, the eggplants glossy and lacquered. Even the potatoes were uniform; everything looked freshly plucked.

I filled up my basket with noodles and sushi and a few other items, hummed along to a Muzak version of "Smells Like Teen Spirit," paid, and left.

Back outside, Armageddon raged. I took a deep breath, leaned into the wind again, and forged onward, but after fifty yards, it was too much for me. I panicked and dived into the first open door I passed, a ¥100 shop. Everything inside was for sale at ¥100 (less than a dollar), from umbrellas to underwear to clown costumes. I bought a Hello Kitty umbrella, but no sooner had I left the shop than it was carried off on the wind like a sycamore seed.

Eventually, I clawed my way back to the apartment, where we

watched on the news an entire house being blown away, *Wizard of Oz*–style; trees toppling like dominoes; and *Mr. Bean* in Japanese.

The concierge assured us the storm would die down by the next morning, which was fortunate, as we had rather a special lunch date planned.

4. SUMO-SIZE ME

"A re sumos people?" Emil whispered to me, his hands covering his ears as two mammoth mounds of diapered blubber collided before us with a sickening crack.

It was a fair question. Sumo wrestlers did not resemble any of the varieties of human life Emil had encountered so far in his four years on earth, particularly not in Japan, where, as his brother had already pointed out, there was "no one here as fat as you, Dad."

The Japanese could hardly have picked a national sport less suited to their physique, but sumo has been it for centuries, having emerged from the rituals of Shintoism to become an imperial spectator sport in the eighth century. Though in something of a decline these days, it is still watched by millions on TV, its protagonists unlikely sex symbols inspiring David Beckham–style mania among their adoring female fans.

I was curious to know how it was that, in a country of almost uniformly slender people with a diet so low in fat, *rikishi* ("strong men"), as the wrestlers are called, manage to turn themselves into these colossal walrus-people. If I wanted to sumo-size myself, how would I go about it? I had always assumed their diet was made up of fatty meats, ice cream, chips, and chocolate and heard that they slept after meals. It had been a strange source of comfort to know that someone, somewhere, had been living my dream life.

The Onoe stable is situated in the quiet residential suburb of Ike-gami, a dense grid of low-rise houses with tiny front gardens and no sidewalks. The stable itself is small, home to just eight rikishi, their trainer (a former wrestler of some note), his wife, and their two small sons. The building is makeshift—a single-story, corrugated warehouse with chipboard walls. From the outside, sitting amid the neat little concrete houses, each with a cigarette paper's space between them, it looked like little more than a self-storage building. Inside there was just enough room for the brown clay ring, or *dohyo*, and the raised wooden dais where we sat. In one corner were some weights, but other than that, there was no visible training equipment.

On our way there, on the crowded Yamanote line, sitting with dozens of commuters' bottoms in our faces, Asger on my lap, Emil on Lissen's, trying our best not to take up too much valuable space, I had tried to explain to Asger and Emil about sumos and their sport.

"OK, so, it's like you have two really, really fat men, you know, like Monsieur Laurent at the patisserie, but bigger."

Emil's eyes widened. "Bigger?"

"Yes, bigger, *really* fat. Basically, they throw salt around and slap their thighs for a bit. Then a bell rings, and they have to push each other over. The one who does this first, wins. Then they bow and say, 'Thank you,' to each other. Oh yes, and they are naked, except for a, well, it's a kind of diaper thing, I suppose."

This last bit of information prompted disbelieving giggles. They weren't falling for it for a minute. Dad was up to his tricks again, no doubt (like that time he said cars ran on the power of singing).

So it was with some satisfaction that I was able to present the real thing, very much in the flesh. We sat on a tatami-covered dais beneath a large flat-screen TV—the area also served as the rikishis' living room, dining room, and bedroom. Asger and Emil cowered behind us with their fingers in their ears as the wrestlers continued their training. One or two of them had noticed us and exchanged glances with one another but remained focused on their routines as the trainer, Keishi Hamasu, in a polo shirt and shorts, paced outside the ring.

"They are actually quite beautiful, in a strange way," Lissen whispered to me. I gave her a funny look. She was watching, rapt, their bending, stretching, pushing, and shadow-sumo-ing. For one exercise, called *butsukari-geiko*, one rikishi would stand still while the other tried to push him across the ring as if he were a large wardrobe. It was horribly grueling, and the pusher would invariably end up on the floor coughing up his lungs and crying out in pain.

There are no weight divisions in sumo; all sizes and shapes compete against each other. But weight superiority is no guarantee of a win, as was the case when a smaller rikishi sent his opponent, a five-hundred-pound wrestler nicknamed Sumo Monster (real name: Yamamotoyama), hurtling from the ring into the wall with a terrifying crash.

A twenty-three-year-old Estonian took his place. Kaido Höövelsen, nicknamed Baruto (a mangled Japanese phonetic interpretation of his home region, the Baltic), is a rising star of sumo and was clearly a cut above the rest of the stable, despite weighing a mere 385 pounds. He dispatched five of his Japanese stablemates without losing breath. At one point he pushed a rival all the way across the dohyo, out of the open garage-style doors, and onto the street, where a small crowd had gathered to watch the session. Asger could hardly believe his eyes. "Wow, did you see what he did?"

With the training session at an end, the rikishi washed their hands with a long-handled ladle at the corner sink and began to waddle up to introduce themselves, clearly intrigued by Asger and Emil. Emil hid behind my legs, but Asger offered his hand to the sweaty, pink giants. Baruto lifted him up onto his shoulder, and then, as Emil emerged, he lifted him with another great, meaty palm up onto the other shoulder. Sumo Monster also introduced himself. "Heaviest sumo in world," he said proudly in English.

Baruto had been in Japan for four years, he told me. "It must have been quite a culture shock to come here while still a teenager," I said.

"I did struggle when I first arrived in Japan," he said. "The food, I couldn't eat it. It is the same for all foreign sumo." It is also quite normal for young rikishi to be physically beaten by the senior rikishi. That week, the Japanese newspapers had been full of stories about a seventeen-year-old trainee, Tokitaizan, who had been beaten to death in a hazing incident that went badly wrong in a Nagoya stable. The story had given a rare glimpse into stable life, where younger wrestlers awaken at four in the morning to begin cleaning and preparing breakfast, rarely seeing the outside world throughout the day, and get to bed after midnight, their lives consumed by the duties of the stable.

Tokitaizan had died of heart failure after a prolonged training session that culminated in a half-hour butsukari-geiko. The autopsy revealed that he was severely bruised, had a fractured nose and ribs, and was marked with so-called tolerance burns from cigarettes. He had tried to escape the stable three times in the last month, but his father had sent him back.

It couldn't have been much easier for Baruto, who had the added burden of being a foreigner. The influx of foreign wrestlers—mostly from countries with a similar wrestling tradition, such as Mongolia, Bulgaria, and Greece—has been the single greatest change to sumo since the sport began, and the source of great controversy. The first to break through was a 626-pound Samoan, Konishiki, who began fighting in 1982 and achieved the second-highest rank in the sport. He was said to be able to consume a hundred beers and seventy nigiri at one sitting and retired a few years ago, suffering from gout, a stomach ulcer, and knee problems. Later, a Hawaiian rikishi, Akebono, surpassed Konishiki's achievements to earn the highest rank, *yokozuna*, but the sumo establishment still has trouble accepting that foreigners can make as good wrestlers as—or, as is more often the case, superior wrestlers to—the homegrown talent, and overseas champions can find rules mysteriously changed to prevent them from dominating. Watching sumo on TV in Japan, you notice, too, how the camera never lingers on foreign victors. That week the most famous sumo of all, a Mongolian called Asashoryu, had done little for the overseas wrestlers' cause when he had been caught on YouTube playing football in his hometown, Ulan Bator, when he should have been undertaking various duties in Japan (he had claimed he'd had to return home to treat an injured leg). But still they come, like Baruto, drawn by annual earnings of up to and over half a million dollars for topflight wrestlers.

It was lunchtime: what I had been waiting for. Each day the rikishi take turns making the food for the rest of the stable. Today was Sumo Monster's turn, and he went off to the kitchen to prepare our lunch, still wearing nothing but his *mawashi* (the "diaper").

"Come on, would you like to see where we fight?" asked Baruto, inviting Asger and Emil down to the ring. Emil scuttled behind Lissen, but Asger followed tentatively, removing his shoes. To his astonishment, Baruto squatted down into position in the ring, ready for a bout, inviting Asger to do likewise. Asger glanced nervously toward us, but I smiled and nodded that it was OK. He hurled himself at the Estonian, who fell obligingly onto the dusty brown clay, flinging his legs up in the air for good measure. Asger stood with his mouth open, stunned by his own strength, as Baruto dusted himself off, shaking his head in shock at his defeat at the hands of a six-year-old. As he sat at the edge of the dohyo, he did the splits, a reminder that suppleness is also an important trait for a rikishi. Meanwhile, outside in the street was a sight that will, I suspect, remain indelible in future years even in Emil's vague recollections of his trip to Japan: a sumo wrestler riding in circles on a bicycle, like a circus elephant.

I followed Sumo Monster's dimpled, spotty thighs into the small kitchen, most of it taken up with two fridge-freezers. Amused at my interest in his lunch plans, Sumo Monster explained that he was making a *chanko nabe*, the traditional sumo hot pot. "There are lots of different kinds," he said. "Maybe as many as ten. We all take turns to make it, and each of us has a specialty. This is a chicken and soy sauce one." As if sharpening a pencil, he chopped daikon radish and then carrots into a pot of simmering water seasoned with soy (a cut known as *sogi giri*). He then added half a ladle of salt. Did he have a recipe? "No, this is man's cooking; we don't really worry about the details. The important thing is that there is enough—this is how the chanko nabe developed. Sumo stables used to be much larger, up to a hundred wrestlers, and they needed a dish that could be cooked in one pot but feed many."

With Sumo Monster engrossed in his chanko nabe, I took my chance to sneak a look into the fridges. Instead of the cakes and chocolates I was hoping to find, they were full of sweet corn, tofu, chicken, and other vegetables—a veritable showcase of healthy eating. I was a little crestfallen.

Sumo Monster had been studying economics before becoming a pro sumo, he told me. I asked him if there were riches to be made in the ring. "Only seventy or so rikishi make much money out of nine hundred. I still worry about the money." He chopped some chicken pieces and added them to the pot. They cooked for a few minutes before he threw in some Chinese cabbage and then the tofu. "You must cut tofu in your hand like this," he said, using his broad palm as a chopping board, before swiftly adding shiitake and enoki mushrooms. "It is the only way; otherwise, it falls apart. You cook the hardest things first, and then work your way to the softer things."

Back in the training room, Lissen had gotten us all an invitation to lunch from the stable master, Keishi Hamasu, and his wife. As we sat down on the floor by the low dining table, Oyakata-san, as Hamasu is addressed at the stable, beckoned for me to sit with him.

"They are kind of like my sons," he explained, gesturing to the rikishi who were milling around the room. One was watering the dohyo; the others were waiting, I later realized, for us to eat so they could come to the table and eat themselves. "Expensive sons! We live like a family, my wife does their washing, they sleep right here, my own children are like siblings to them. I tell my [actual] sons that we eat because of their work."

I told him I was disappointed not to see more chocolate in the fridges. He laughed. "For us, carbohydrate is the best way to make our size, along with meat and fish, but it has to go hand in hand with training. We have got to build muscle that won't get damaged, not fat. But the sumo diet has changed. We get many more imported things now, like sausages. It used to be more fish-oriented."

Rikishi begin their careers in their teens and tend to finish in their early thirties, although it has been known for some sumos' careers to last into their forties. Oyakata-san had retired only three years ago, aged thirty-six, but already seemed relatively slim. He told me he had lost almost seventy pounds since he'd stopped. Only a cauliflower ear betrayed a lifetime of combat at the highest level. How had he lost all that weight? "When I stopped, I just ate less, particularly less carbohydrate; my appetite died down naturally because I was using less energy. But I have diabetes from the time when I was a rikishi."

Diabetes is just one of the illnesses to which rikishi are prone, along with high cholesterol, high blood pressure, and heart problems. In the nineties, the sport's governing body implemented a regime of medical checks to try to control wrestlers' health, and things have improved. Many of the problems rikishi suffer from in later life arise through the use of performance-enhancing drugs: there is no testing in the sport, and use of steroids and similar drugs is apparently rife. As with pro cyclists, rikishi will, it seems, put their bodies through almost any stress to achieve success. They used to have a similar life expectancy to normal Japanese, but as the rest of the population started living longer, their average life expectancy remained at around the midfifties to early sixties. That said, recent studies have shown that wrestlers don't have *absurdly* high body-fat levels and are remarkably fit, with fairly normal levels of uric acid and glucose—usually high among us bona fide fatties.

The lunch spread, though relatively healthy, was on an impressive scale. As well as the protein-rich chanko nabe, there was omelet, rice, cocktail sausages, and, of all things, fried Spam. Traditionally, sumo wrestlers don't eat four-legged animals, because a rikishi on all fours is a loser, but processed pork apparently doesn't count. We barely made an impression on the amount of food at the table and left them to enjoy their well-earned feast and afternoon beauty nap.

The training at the Onoe stable had been particularly intensive that day, as the September Grand Tournament was starting the next day, the first week of the month. We rose early and took the train across the river to Ryogoku, in eastern Tokyo, for three hundred years the traditional sumo quarter and home of the national sumo stadium, Kokugikan. Outside the stadium were rows of flagpoles with multicolored banners. Crowds of fans swarmed over the rikishi as they arrived. As we queued for tickets, four wrestlers climbed out of a visibly sagging taxi, dressed in kimonos with bold floral patterns, their hair heavily oiled and perfectly arranged. They looked like a Hawaiian welcoming committee of silverback gorillas.

I had never been especially taken by the sumo I had seen on

TV—the small screen seems to render sumo even more ridiculous somehow. But watching real, live bouts inside the stadium, sitting cross-legged on red cushions, it all made sense. The preamble was the best bit, as the wrestlers waddled into the ring, clutching the sticks that dangle in front of their crotches, slapping imaginary mosquitoes on their thighs and belts and cocking their legs. Next comes one of the most bewildering rituals in sport: the pre-bout jockeying for psychological advantage, during which each wrestler will start to bend down as if readying for action. The knuckles of one hand might even touch the clay, but just as you think the other is about to touch down, signaling the start of the fight, one of the wrestlers will apparently have second thoughts, feign indifference to the whole affair, stand up, turn his back on his opponent, and launch into the whole face-wiping, salt-scattering, thigh-slapping rigmarole once again. They can go on like this for minutes, with five or more false starts, during which a knowledgeable audience will applaud eagerly at a particularly audacious sumo tease.

Though the bouts themselves usually last mere seconds, there are few more thrilling moments in sport. Two great fatties slapping each other, then tumbling on top of each other in a great blubbery heap? Bring it on! (Although I can't help thinking some stout ropes around the ring might be a good idea.) Techniques for winning varied from frenzied, girly slapping to locking horns and standing in stalemate until one began to flag. One sumo, who would go on to win the tournament outright, simply picked up his opponent and dumped him out of the ring as if he were a large barrel.

Afterward, Asger, Emil, Lissen, and I retired to a sumo restaurant around the corner for lunch. Yoshiba is housed in a former sumo stable—much larger than the one we had visited the day before—and staffed by ex–sumo wrestlers, some of whom were engaged in what seemed to be sumo stand-up comedy when we arrived. Several diners shoved thousand-yen notes into their mawashi belts as if they were lap dancers. Our still-simmering chanko nabe arrived within minutes. It was a more refined version of the one we had tried the day before, with shiitake mushrooms, prawns, red snapper, scallops, pork, chicken, tuna dumplings, potato noodles, fried tofu, and omelet. It was terrific, though, in the manner of all *nabemono* and *suimono* dishes (Japanese "one-pot" and "soups"), screamingly hot. Long after the others had eaten a seemly amount, I was still forcing down mouthfuls, my stomach stretched like a haggis skin. I was determined to finish the lot, but as I did, the waitress arrived with a vast mound of noodles, which she added to the pot before giving it all a quick stir with her chopsticks.

Reluctantly, I had to draw the line. That was enough for me. I was as sumo-sized as I was going to get, for now.

5. WORLD FAMOUS IN JAPAN

I am shaking hands with one of the five most famous people in Japan. His name is Takuya Kimura.

No, me neither.

Close by, in the same TV studio, designed in a kind of Disney-baronial style with fake stone walls, pastel colors, extravagant floral displays, and stained-glass windows, are the four other most famous people in Japan, known to every schoolchild, parent, and grandparent from Hokkaido to Okinawa. Their names are Masahiro Nakai, Goro Inagaki, Tsuyoshi Kusanagi, and Shingo Katori. Ring any bells?

This was the day after the sumo championship. To a Japanese contact with connections in the TV world I had expressed a vague interest in trying to get to the bottom of the Japanese food show obsession, which—to judge by the sheer volume of programs about food, cooking, restaurants, or food producers—surpasses even that of the British and Americans. According to some estimations, over 40 percent of all Japanese television output can be categorized as "food TV"—whether it is serious programs in search of obscure artisanal producers or the crazy campiness of the world-famous cook-off *Iron Chef* (sadly no longer in production but still replayed).

Certainly, my own empirical research during our first few days in Japan had confirmed that, if you turn on the TV, you will come across something to do with food within two or three clicks of the remote.

My friend had arranged for me to sneak into the studio during the recording of Japan's most popular TV show of the last decade. I had heard neither of SMAP—for "Sport, Music, Assemble, People"—nor its constituent elements: five former boy band singers, now in their early thirties, turned TV interviewers, cooking show hosts, and actors, but they are, without rival, the biggest TV stars in Japan. Over the last dozen years, these five young men have conquered every entertainment sphere, whether it was J-Pop (Japanese pop music aimed at teenage girls), TV, or, latterly, individual film careers. Along the way, they have amassed unfathomable fortunes; millions of devoted, obsessive fans; and a level of fame that exceeds even that of the Hollywood stars who make sure *Bistro SMAP*, as their food show is called, is the first stop on their Japanese publicity junkets (recent guests had included Matt Damon, Madonna, Cameron Diaz, and Nicolas Cage). *Bistro SMAP* is not just the number one food program in Japan; as a segment of the band's main variety show, *SMAP×SMAP*, it is the number one TV show in Japan, period, with up to thirty million viewers tuning in most weeks—a position it has held on and off for over ten years. We had already seen the band's faces around Tokyo promoting the unappealingly named "sports" drink Pocari Sweat on the metro; Japan Airlines, on a four-story billboard beside the Mori Tower; and their latest movies and TV series just about everywhere.

I always think that domestic-only stars reveal far more about a country's tastes and aspirations than those who go global—like Johnny Hallyday in France or Andrew Dice Clay. So what does SMAP tell us about the Japanese? Most obviously that they like pretty, polite, and apparently wholesome young men who conform to just about every boy band stereotype, right down to their hurt-puppy faces during ballads and Bronx-pimp moves in the rap bits. But SMAP have done more than just polish their Backstreet Boys moves in their bedroom mirrors. Through *Bistro SMAP* they have done nothing less than overturn centuries-old conventions about who wears the aprons in Japanese households. Thanks to this show and its seven spin-off cookbooks—which, I should add, are the bestselling celebrity cookbooks in the world—these five performers have managed to convince the Japanese male that it is OK to cook at home, that there is no shame in a man frying noodles or taking time to slice sashimi and present it just so on a bed of grated dai-kon. Today more Japanese men than ever cook at home, and the boys from SMAP are one of the main reasons. Indeed, you could argue that they are the most influential people in contemporary Japanese food culture.

So what is the televisual magic that has almost a quarter of the Japanese population glued to their TVs every Monday night at ten? I was about to find out.

Band member Masahiro, the "maître'd" of *Bistro SMAP*, enters through the upper floor of the horseshoe-shaped, two-story, faux bistro set, dressed in black waistcoat, white shirt, and black trousers. The rest of the band, wearing Western-style chef's uniforms and toques, take their places in the kitchens below, two per team. I take a step backward behind the central camera and trip over some cables, prompting a look from the stage manager. Shingo, the "funny one," waiting in the wings, shoots me a quizzical glance—I am the only Westerner in the studio—but then winks and waves as the stage manager starts his countdown. I smile back. Even though I had no idea who he was until fifteen minutes earlier, celeb whore that I am, this contact with Japanese light entertainment royalty makes me unaccountably happy.

Masahiro introduces this week's guests, a Japanese husband-and-wife actor couple, who enter through the upstairs door and are shown to their table. Masahiro's opening remarks prompt exaggeratedly loud laughter from the crew. (There is a man standing next to me whose job, it seems, is to laugh as loudly as he can at every comment or gesture.) It turns out that the host is friends with the couple and has visited their house. "I remember when we were just getting famous," he says, "and we came round your house to watch porn!" Everyone laughs; the wife giggles coquettishly. Following the same routine as every week, Masahiro asks the guests what they want to eat. "We have no menu, so you can order anything you like!" They order "Chinese food with lots of vegetables." All the ingredients have already been prepared and set out in the kitchens below for the other four SMAP members to cook.

More hard-hitting questions—"Do you love your wife?"—are interspersed with shots of the boys cooking. Offstage professional chefs prompt them from time to time, but I can exclusively reveal that the SMAP boys really do cook the food and with impressive confidence and skill.

"Well, they have made over 6,500 dishes over the last twelve years," the show's producer tells me as we chat in the studio canteen after recording has finished, adding that the band members themselves create the menus.

"What do the American and English guests make of it?" I ask (the show is very much in the tradition of wacky Japanese TV).

"They love it. Nicolas Cage said the food was better than Wolfgang Puck's. Cameron Diaz has been on twice; she was singing and dancing! Madonna loved Shingo's shabu-shabu. When we started, none of them could cook, but they wanted to challenge themselves. They'd done singing and dancing; now they wanted to do cooking. At the beginning, they just learned how to wash the rice and cut the cabbage. They weren't trying to impress anyone; they just wanted a challenge. But now they are really involved in creating the menus;

they love to make new dishes. They have shown the same type of creativity they did with their music. We didn't know it at the time, but this was the beginning of a whole new trend of getting boys to cook. There used to be a Japanese proverb about how a man should never enter a kitchen. SMAP changed all that."

So what is the secret of their success?

"First, they are like the Beatles. They each have distinct characters that everyone can relate to [the boy next door, the class clown, the older brother, the rebel, and the pretty one]. The second and most important thing as far as the show is concerned is the energy of hospitality they show to the guests in the studio. They really want the guests to enjoy it, and the audience can sense that. This is the real secret of the program. SMAP communicates though food, and that is becoming a bigger and bigger way of communicating around the world."

Back in the studio, Masahiro, the host, takes the guests on a walkabout downstairs in the kitchens, where the other four are busy cooking. More anodyne banter ensues. Returning upstairs, the food—a cream lobster chow mein with pork-bone broth from the Red Team, and fried rice with tofu, beef tongue, shark fin, onion sauce, spinach, and lettuce from the Yellow Team—is brought up for the guests to judge. Everything is pronounced *oishii* (delicious), but the Yellows are this week's winners.

Suddenly, Shingo appears in drag, wearing a short tartan skirt and long wig and singing a song that, apparently, the wife once sang in her days as a young pop star. Everyone laughs hysterically, and I must admit, he is funny, even though I understand nothing of what he is saying. He has touches of Buster Keaton about him, a great face-puller. Masahiro is also charismatic, a wiry ball of energy who reminds me of a young Billy Crystal, but as for the other three's talents, they seem limited to either smoldering, scowling, or looking blank.

As usual with TV cookery shows, the minute the cameras stop, the crew descend on the leftovers, and the talent leaves as quickly as possible. All except Tsuyoshi, the boy next door, who sits quietly in a corner finishing a bowl of rice as the crew begin to clean up around him. I approach and introduce myself, and he smiles warmly. "Great show," I say. He smiles again. I am not sure he understands English and, anyway, I feel guilty about interrupting his meal, so I leave him be. (A few months later, Tsuyoshi will be arrested for being drunk and naked in a Tokyo park; always the quiet ones you've got to watch, isn't it?)

I squeeze through the hundred or so fans waiting outside the Fuji TV studios that evening and make my way back to the apartment. Lissen, Asger, and Emil, who have spent the afternoon playing in Yoyogi Park and visiting temples, are underwhelmed by my new celebrity name-drops, but I can't help thinking Japan could have worse teen idols than these. Can Justin Bieber make shabu-shabu? I very much doubt it.

6. TEMPURA MASTER CLASS

The business district of Tokyo is a maze of corporate canyons buzzing with salarymen, traders, deal makers, captains of industry, glossy black limos, and money. At least it is on weekdays. On weekends it is desolate. There might as well be tumbleweed. There actually *are* giant jungle rooks, wheeling in the sky like vultures. All of which means there is no one to ask for directions. When you get lost. And can't find what you have been assured by your friend Toshi is the best tempura restaurant in the city. And your wife and children are wilting in the midday heat. And you have been walking for an hour promising them that it is "not far now . . ." or "just around this corner . . ." and for the last half hour you have been buckling under the burden of a drowsy four-year-old who weighs roughly the same as an air-conditioning unit and is sitting on your shoulders.

Street numbers in Tokyo do not appear to be arranged according to any logical order, so that 1 Yoko Ono Avenue will not necessarily be at the beginning of the street but might just as easily be next to number 302 and across the street from number 25. How anything gets delivered is one of the great inscrutable mysteries of the East, but I do know that if you are trying to find the anonymous doorway of a small, one-room, local restaurant that has no external number or sign, not even a kanji character that you might match to the one on a crumpled piece of paper in your hand, or indeed any evidence that it is a restaurant of any kind, then you might as well go whistle.

We were about to give up hope when, suddenly, seemingly from nowhere, a tiny, wizened old man, bent almost double, with close-cropped gray hair and a knobby walking stick, appeared in front of us. Quickly, I shoved my crumpled note under his nose. He took it with a shaky hand, spent some minutes examining it from all angles, then eventually turned and beckoned us to follow. A left turn, a right turn, and across a street, he stopped in front of a doorway concealed by various potted plants and a beaded curtain and gestured toward it with an open palm. Holding my breath, for I dared not believe this was our tempura Valhalla, I parted the curtain and waved the piece of paper at a passing waiter. He nodded confirmation and handed me a menu. Lissen and the kids had started to follow me into the restaurant. I turned to thank the old man, but he had completely disappeared from view. Had he been a phantom? A mere apparition, a Fata Morgana somehow conjured by our collective desperation? Had we *willed* him into existence?

No. I looked down, and there he was, smiling. I thanked him, attempted to bow even lower than he, and invited him in to join us. He shook his head vigorously, waving his hands as if I had invited him to an opium den, and we parted.

We had just made the end of the lunchtime service and were shown to a small side room, where we sat down on the tatami floor, accompanied by what would over the next couple of months become my customary crescendo of clicks, pops, and crunches from my aging bones.

We ordered whitebait, squid, eel, and shrimp, the latter's heads served separately, much to Asger's and Emil's consternation. It was exquisite, all of it: the crunchy, gnarled batter glistening yet virtually greaseless; the fish cooked to moist, still-steaming perfection within. The meal ended with a lip-smackingly savory miso soup with minuscule clams floating on the surface and a crispy-sweet, raggedy fritter of scallops each the size of Emil's fingernail, called *kaki-age tendon*, held together with a nut-brown batter and served on rice to indicate the end of the meal. Even Asger and Emil agreed it had been worth the walk.

Toshi had assured me that if I mentioned his name, the chef might talk to me.

This seemed generous of him, but I had learned to be wary of Toshi's assistance. Back in Paris he had helped me to write a Japanese business card, a *meishi*, as I knew that they were essential for almost any kind of social interaction in Japan. It was only when another Japanese acquaintance of mine had chanced to see the dummy of the card, a day before I was due to take it to the printer, that I learned that, instead of "Michael Booth, Journalist, England," Toshi had in fact written "Please help me, I have learning difficulties."

Still, I took the chance and mentioned his name to the waiter, who passed it on to the chef, who soon appeared by the entrance to our room. Some more diners had arrived; would I like to come and watch him work in the kitchen?

I was dying to know the secret of great tempura with that chiffon-like carapace, craggy with nodules of light brown, deep-fried batter, with just-cooked vegetables or fish within. Why was it so different from British fish-and-chips batter, which tends to be smooth and heavy with oil, its interior often overcooked?

"It is all about your knowledge of the fish," the chef explained in his cramped open kitchen, our faces burning in the heat from the shimmering oil. "And the vegetables. And the seasons. And the oil. And the batter. I trained for ten years. It was one year before they allowed me to mix the batter."

Clearly, I was going to struggle to master this during a lunch sitting. As Shizuo Tsuji writes in *A Simple Art*, "Although the technique of deep-frying was originally introduced to Japan centuries ago by Europeans and Chinese, the Japanese have elevated it to its very apogee of refinement." He then offers elaborate instructions on how to fold the paper on which you present the tempura. Quite. But the chef did let me in on a few secrets: first, the batter. This was made from just flour, water, and egg, but the water was ice-cold; he used his own special blend of tempura flour, which included a little baking powder and rice powder, and the eggs were ultrarich, as Japanese eggs usually are. You add them to the bowl in the order of flour, water, and egg, so that the food gets coated with egg first and flour last, and use it immediately (there is no resting in the fridge as you do with traditional beer batter). The next secret is that you must, at all costs, resist the urge to overmix the batter, or *koromo* (literally "clothing" or "enrobed"). The chef used chopsticks to give it the most cursory of swirls.

"But you've got great lumps of flour sticking around the side of the bowl," I said. This unmixed batter made me feel tense. I wanted to give it a good whisk.

He smiled enigmatically. "Yes. Lumps are good. Now, you need one pair of chopsticks to mix and cover with the batter, another to fry. Next, test the oil." Most books say tempura oil should be at around 350°F, but an expert tempura chef will modify the temperature depending on what is being fried. He explained why: though the oil is 350°F, most of the items within the batter have a large water content, which means they won't cook beyond 212°F—the water sets a ceiling on the temperature, which is also why the items you are frying should be as dry as possible before you start. The skill of the chef—and it is a highly specialized skill; good tempura chefs don't cook anything else—is to know when the tempura is cooked to perfection inside. This depends on the ingredient being fried, of course, and on the batter, but also on how the batter is applied.

With eel, for instance, the chef showed me how, after coating it with batter, he scraped the skin side so that the batter was thinner where the heat has to penetrate the skin.

I made an exasperated face, and the chef conceded that 350°F is fine for home cooking. In other words, a piece of bread should come fizzling to the surface almost immediately when you drop it in (although, should you find yourself cooking tempura for Japanese people, be warned that those from eastern Japan—the Kanto region—like theirs golden brown, while those from the west—Kansai—prefer their tempura pale and interesting).

He deftly lifted a shrimp with his extra-long chopsticks, placing it in the ceramic batter bowl, which was tilted at an angle for ease of access, before lowering it into the oil. After a few seconds he moved it around in the oil, then took it out again. "Is that it?" I asked. He nodded. "What exactly is the oil? Just vegetable?"

"Well, in Kanto, we put a little sesame oil in, but in Kansai they don't. The important thing is not to put too many vegetables into the oil at the same time, or it will cool the oil and the batter won't crisp."

I have learned to my cost that such impatience is my most common failing, that and the fact that I usually get carried away and cook too much. After all, the human body can take only so much deep-fried food. The Japanese always serve tempura with grated daikon mixed in with the dipping sauce (made from a base of dashi, the Japanese "stock" made from seaweed and dried bonito fillet shavings, with mirin and light soy added—although tempura purists dip only in fine salt), because it is said to help the digestion of oily foods. The so-called Father of Japan, the legendary shogun Tokugawa Ieyasu, is said to have died from eating too much tempura, and the Japanese remain wary of overindulgence to this day.

I tried to describe to the chef the concept of a deep-fried Mars bar. He squinted skeptically. I drew a picture in my notebook; he looked more dubious and called another chef over. They conferred and looked at me expectantly, awaiting further clarification. "In Scotland—you know, haggis? Sean Connery?"

"Besides guns and the Bible, they brought tempura," writes old Japan hand Donald Richie of the European missionaries who came to Japan in the mid-sixteenth century.

Clearly, thankfully, there were no Scots among them.

7. A TALE OF TWO COOKING SCHOOLS: PART 1

There is a vacancy at the pinnacle of the Japanese food scene. Since the death of Shizuo Tsuji, in 1993, there has been no obvious figurehead, no unimpeachable authority on culinary matters, someone to whom everyone turns for a definitive answer on what to dip your soba in if you live in Fukuoka, the correct expression to adopt when grilling eel, and suchlike. No one has managed to replace Tsuji, though several have tried.

Today, there are perhaps two clear contenders, who, fittingly, represent the two main rival culinary regions that divide Japan: Kanto, the area of eastern Japan with Tokyo at its center, and Kansai, in the western part of Japan, centered in Kyoto and Osaka.

As we continued on our travels through Japan, it became increasingly apparent that virtually every type of Japanese food has a Kanto and a Kansai method of preparation, and needless to say, each group devoutly believes theirs is the superior method, the other's barbaric. This great Japanese food schism encompasses everything from how to fillet an eel to whether to eat your noodles hot or cold to how sweet you prefer your sushi rice.

Each of these two rival regions boasts a large, state-of-the-art cooking school—bastions of their respective culinary traditions: In

Osaka, there is the Tsuji Culinary Institute, which Shizuo founded in 1960 and which is currently run by Yoshiki Tsuji, his son. In Tokyo, the Kanto school of cooking is championed by the Hattori Nutrition College, founded in 1939 and currently run by Dr. Yukio Hattori, also the son of the founder.

Today, if any two men can claim to be the torchbearers for Japanese cuisine, it is Yukio Hattori and Yoshiki Tsuji. As I would discover, there is little love lost between these two: Each of them is wealthy, highly educated, urbane, and, in person, not a little intimidating. Each is vying for the papacy of Japanese cuisine, a position of obvious cultural, quasi-spiritual significance in a country that venerates its food to such a degree as Japan.

The future of Japanese food in the early twenty-first century is, then, encompassed by a tale of two cooking schools. Hattori's first.

Of the two men, Dr. Yukio Hattori is by far the better known in Japan. He is a major-league celebrity thanks to his starring role on Japan's—and my—favorite cooking show, *Ryori no Tetsujin*, or *Iron Chef*, in which a professional chef challenges one of the in-house panel of Iron Chefs, each of them experts in French, Japanese, Chinese, and Italian cooking. Hattori, nicknamed "Doc" (he is a qualified medical doctor), helped to develop the series, devised the menus, and acted as on-screen commentator each week, passing judgment on the gladiatorial goings-on from a balcony above the lavish set, like a one-man Statler and Waldorf. Sadly, the Japanese version of *Iron Chef* finished in 1999 (although the U.S. version continued until 2001 and made a star of, among others, Matsuhisa Nobu), but Hattori remains very much in the public eye, appearing regularly on a number of Japanese TV food shows, including the evocatively titled *Apron of Love*, as well as in major advertising campaigns for a variety for food products (his face is almost as common on Tokyo's trains as the boys from SMAP, on whose show he has, of course, also appeared).

In a recent profile, *The Japan Times* called Hattori "Japan's busiest man." As well as running his media career and the school (which has over 1,800 students), Hattori writes regular food columns in the press and has written dozens of food books. Also, for the last fifteen years or so, he has been at the forefront of the Shokuiku food and health education program run by the Japanese government designed to reverse the national trend toward the Western diet. All of which made him the perfect man to give me an insight into contemporary Japanese eating habits.

The Hattori school is based in a large office-style building in a well-to-do district of central Tokyo, close to Yoyogi Park. Outside is a large poster showing Hattori shaking hands with a beaming Joël Robuchon, the celebrated French chef, currently the holder of more Michelin stars than anyone else, and in whose Paris restaurant I had worked a couple of years earlier (though he is probably less well-known for this).

Hattori himself met me in reception, a dapper man in a Mao suit made from the deepest black, seemingly frictionless silk. His silver hair was oiled and combed in a meticulous arc above his rimless glasses. His shoes alone looked like they cost more than my annual clothing budget, as did his tan.

He led me through the school to a large door decorated with the cartoon bulldog logo of El Bulli, the famous Spanish restaurant, which led into the kitchen-boardroom atelier overlooking tree-lined Meiji Avenue. Within seconds of us sitting down, two cups of green tea and a small plate of cookies had arrived on the table.

I wanted to know where it had all gone wrong for the Japanese diet. Though the situation isn't nearly as bad as in the West, I had been reading in the local English-language press that the Japanese are getting fatter, eating more processed foods, more dairy, more sugar, more fat, and fewer vegetables and fruits, and the popularity of traditional foods is on the wane. Even consumption of rice, that most sacred of Japanese foodstuffs, is down, from 330 pounds per person a year a century ago to 132 pounds today. Meanwhile, their consumption of fish has more than halved, and their meat intake has more than doubled.

Hattori blames the Americans.

"The Japanese had huge respect for Americans after the war. They saw their physical strength, saw that they ate bread and potatoes and steaks as thick as the soles of their shoes, and copied them," he told me. "They felt a huge pressure to be physically stronger, so they started eating more butter, milk, and flour to be like Americans. The lunch menus at school changed from rice to bread overnight; out went the balance of Japanese food, the soy, seaweed, cooked vegetables, rice, and fish; in came the fat and the diabetes and heart problems, which are all increasing. We had the ideal diet. We got our protein from soy, fish, and tofu, but young people today eat junk food; they buy ready-made meals, bad-quality food."

Hattori explained that the problem was compounded by the physical differences between the Japanese and Westerners. Many believe that the Japanese intestine is on average twenty-three to twenty-eight inches longer than Westerners'. This has obvious implications. Genetically programmed to maximize the nutritional yield from healthy foods due to a historical paucity of domestic produce and frequent famines, the Japanese are now paying the price for holding all the fat, additives, and sugar from their newly adopted Western diet in their bodies that bit longer. "We have a long history of starvation and harvest crises in Japan," Hattori said. "Deep in our DNA is the fear that we may not eat again within the next week or month, so we hold food in our bodies longer." Which is why, when the Japanese move to, say, Hawaii, and adopt the local diet, they actually get fatter than the locals. No mean feat.

Hattori was not terribly impressed by the younger generation.

"Young people are not prepared to work as hard in the kitchen," he told me. "The quality of cooking is declining. If you work so hard, so that you are almost dying, you learn a lot, but when you look at Japan today, discipline is running out at school and in the home. People give up too easily; they get too much praise and can't take criticism. My students here in this school, they can't take criticism." (According to *The Japan Times*, Hattori advocates a good smack on the hand or behind for disobedient children. "Leave it too late and their character will be fixed!" he told the paper.)

Clearly, Hattori's attitudes toward discipline and education were a product of immediate postwar Japan—when we first met, he was in his midsixties—which made it all the more surprising that he had chosen to be involved with populist shows like *Iron Chef* and now *Apron of Love*.

But he was proud of *Iron Chef*. "Before *Iron Chef*, young people were not so interested in becoming chefs. *Iron Chef* created the superstar chef. Young people saw that, and it motivated them. Before *Iron Chef*, the job of chef was ranked thirty-fifth most popular in Japan among elementary schoolchildren. After *Iron Chef*, it became number one, and even now it is number five."

Hattori had just returned from a trip to the UK. I asked him what he thought about British food and about the Japanese food available in the UK. "Japanese food in other countries is getting better," he said diplomatically. I knew that he had been involved in a recent move by the Japanese Ministry of Agriculture, Forestry, and Fisheries to award authenticity certificates to Japanese restaurants overseas, but I suspect he was too polite to tell me what he really thought. "I loved the Fat Duck," he continued, referring to the British Michelin-starred restaurant of chef Heston Blumenthal.

"Why has molecular cuisine not caught on in Japan?" I wondered. "Especially in Tokyo, where they seem to love innovation and play."

"Ha!" Hattori laughed dismissively. "We have had molecular cuisine for forty years or more. You know the fake caviar they make with tomato juice, or whatever? That was in Japanese markets forty years ago [he is right; a similar gelling agent is used to make tofu]. Ferran [Adrià, the head chef of El Bulli] loves it here; he buys so many things when he comes. When I introduced him to yuzu, he really went crazy for it, and miso, fresh wasabi, and *katsuobushi* [the smoke-dried, fermented fillets of the bonito fish, shaved on a special plane]." Many of the other clever thickening compounds used in molecular cuisine are Japanese, such as kuzu and agar-agar.

Hattori was now glancing impatiently at his watch; the interview was clearly drawing to a close. There was one last, crucial question I wanted to ask him. What was the best restaurant in Japan?

"Ah, the best restaurant? Regular people can't go there. It is not open to the public." A beatific smile spread across his face. "You cannot make a reservation; it is not even in the phone book. You have to know someone who is a member. I am a member. Every year the chef sends me a reservation card, and I can choose one day a month to eat there, and he sends me back a confirmation. I took Ferran there. He cried when he ate the food. I took Robuchon there; he cried, too. You should see the faces of people who eat there. They just smile naturally when they taste the food. The chef makes the most of each ingredient; he is amazing. A master of dashi. I have been going there for fifteen years."

"Wow," I said. "It is now my greatest ambition to eat at that restaurant."

Hattori looked me in the eye and then looked down at his hands for a moment, considering. He looked back up.

"You will come with me," he said.

"What? You mean to see the restaurant?"

Hattori took out a small black notebook. "No. To eat. October 30, six thirty in the evening. Meet me outside the Sony building in Ginza. The restaurant is called Mibu."

"Thank you, thank you so much. I will look forward to it." I could scarcely believe what I was hearing. Japan's leading food authority (clearly this swung it for Hattori as far as I was concerned) was inviting me to dinner at the restaurant he held to be the finest in all of Japan, a dinner date with destiny.

Meanwhile, Hattori had another invitation to extend—the reason he had been looking at his watch. That afternoon, the school would be hosting the Tokyo round of the first-ever national Chef of the Year competition, founded by the Japanese Culinary Association to find the best professional chef currently working in Japan. Hattori was the head judge of the competition. Would I like to come along and watch?

I arrived back at the school a couple of hours later to find the dozen contestants, all men (female chefs are even rarer in Japan than they are in the West), already at work in two vast and sparkling kitchens. I was the only Westerner among several Japanese journalists covering the event, and I seemed to be the only one allowed to roam freely among the chefs—or perhaps it was just that no one could pluck up the courage to stop me. Either way, I took full advantage of my stupid-foreigner status. I love watching chefs work; their dexterity, speed, and commitment are hypnotic to me.

Each chef had three hours to complete three dishes for four people—one each for the three judges and one for the display table. The chefs ranged in age from thirty to fifty, and each had a minimum five years' professional cooking experience. Only one would go through to the finals in Kyoto, where the winner would receive ¥1 million ($8,000) and, more important, go on to represent Japan in the Culinary Olympics in Frankfurt the following year.

The tension in the air was palpable, as was the rich aroma of dashi. I was slowly coming to appreciate that dashi is one of the major elements of Japanese cooking, in the same way that veal stock or tomato sauce is the basis of much classical French or Italian food. But dashi and *fond de veau* are very different substances, not least because dashi takes just a few minutes to make, as opposed to the six hours or so that it takes to roast and then simmer veal bones.

In the basic recipe for *ichiban*—or number one—dashi, you slowly bring a postcard-sized piece of dried konbu seaweed almost to the boil, remove it before the water actually boils (otherwise the smell can be off-putting), add a handful of katsuobushi flakes, leave them to infuse for a minute or so, then strain. And that's it. There are many other optional ingredients—other dried fish, different varieties of seaweed, dried mushrooms—but this basic dashi is the foundation for a vast array of Japanese dishes, from miso soup to tempura dipping sauce.

I watched one competitor make dashi with several handfuls of katsuobushi. He let it infuse for some minutes, which seemed a little long based on what I had read; another was using chicken wings and spring onions for a more French-influenced stock, which smelled heavenly.

The rest chopped, stirred, primped, and fried with intense focus beneath the watchful gaze of the kitchen-based judges, who were observing how well the contestants organized themselves as well as their processes and hygiene. "To be a good chef, you must have the entire process in your mind from the beginning," one judge whispered to me. "You have to be clear about your goals. We have different judges for tasting because we don't want them to be influenced by having seen the chef working in the kitchen. If you see really good process you can become a fan of them, but if you go to a restaurant you don't see the process."

One chef took a small sheaf of raw wheat and deep-fried the whole thing—the seeds exploding like popcorn—which he used for decoration. Clearly of an avant-garde bent, he also left the scales on a fish fillet before grilling it so that, beneath the heat, the scales threw spectacular shapes, like quartz crystals.

Some ingredients were unfamiliar to me. One chef was cooking with mugwort; another was working with konnyaku, the flavorless, jelly-like substance made from the "devil's tongue" tuber, said to be good for the digestion. Another had cape jasmine seeds, lily root bulb, sake lees (a by-product of sake brewing), and wood ear mushrooms on his countertop.

I asked contestant number thirteen, Yusaku Kodama, if he had practiced for the competition. "Not really," he replied. "It is the menu I cook at my restaurant." He had entered the competition because his boss had told him to. "But it is much more difficult than I thought working in a different kitchen with limited space. I wish I had thought about how to use my space better. The big problem is the time. Often I let things sit overnight, but here I am having to boil them, then put in ice, then boil again, and cool in ice to extract the flavor."

One of the contestants' bamboo steamers caught fire, setting off the alarms and prompting a flurry of activity from the assistants. Tension was mounting along with the mounds of dirty pots and pans. The chefs were moving more quickly now; the noise was increasing; there were signs of panic.

The competitors had staggered finish times. When each was done, their dish was sent downstairs to a small, windowless hall where Hattori and two other judges, both leading chefs, sat at individual tables waiting to taste. The fourth identical dish was placed on a trestle table near the far wall of the hall for the contestants to inspect later.

Downstairs with the judges, all was deathly quiet but for the occasional clink of chopsticks on porcelain, the scratch of pens on scorecards, and gulps of palate-cleansing water.

Hattori was sitting at the center table. He looked up and raised his eyebrows at me as I tried to sit as quietly as possible in a corner. But as he tasted the different dishes, I could tell something was not quite right from the occasional slight shake of his head and heavy sigh every time a new plate was brought forward. After one dish, he shot me an exasperated glance. What could be wrong?

After an hour or so, the judging was complete, and Hattori stood up to leave the room. I followed him into the elevator with one of the other judges. As soon as the elevator doors closed, his demeanor changed completely.

"Did you see that! Good grief, I don't know what they were thinking of. It was a disgrace!" he said.

I was stunned. "But the food looked terrific to me," I said.

"No, no. No one knows how to make dashi anymore. They were terrible!" he said. "It was an amazingly low standard. The same level of my students. Too salty, too strong tastes."

An hour later, we reconvened in the Red Room, the school's flag-ship demonstration kitchen. The contestants were now in civvies. Some were making small talk; others sat nervously fidgeting with ties and pens. Little did they know they were about to face an execution.

Hattori entered together with his fellow judges and the assistants. One of the process judges spoke first, saying how well the chefs had done considering the time limitations, even though they had obviously been nervous. Hattori rose to address them, stony-faced.

"I have a feeling there are many among you who are just not qualified in the basic skills—things like using salt, making dashi, and controlling heat. These are very important things, but many of you put too much salt in your food, and too few of you seem to know how to make a basic dashi. In some cases, the level here was like home cooking. To tell you the truth, I asked myself, *Are these people professionals?* I want you to go back to the basics of Japanese cooking. I want you to master dashi, salt, and fire. I want you to master the real tastes of Japan that the world will respect!"

None of the chefs had been expecting a tirade of this kind, and I felt sorry for them. It was a national holiday, the Day of the Dead, usually spent visiting cemeteries with family. It was probably their only free day of the week. They had slogged their guts out for three hours to be told their careers had amounted to nothing. They looked shell-shocked, even the winner, who accepted his plastic medal to muted applause.

Afterward, I asked a couple of the contestants what they thought of Hattori's speech. "He stabbed my heart," said one, pounding his chest. "But he was right."

8. THE MOTHER OF ALL FISHMONGERS

On reflection, if you are traveling through Japan with two fussy children who are refusing point-blank to eat a number of foodstuffs—in particular, raw fish—a trip to the parasite museum in western Tokyo is unlikely to assuage their fears. Frankly, coming face-to-face with a twenty-nine-foot-long tapeworm, as we did the next day, almost put me off sushi myself.

There are said to be over fifty different types of parasites that live in fish; some of them, judging by the photographs of swollen, distended, and just plain scary body parts on display at the museum, are very nasty indeed. Some boast festering larvae that induce relentless vomiting. Others just kill you. One photograph from the museum, which haunts me to this day, was of a man with testicles each swollen to the size of a duffel bag. How does a parasite do that to a man? And to what end? They don't even get to see the photographs.

Perhaps deliberately, the museum is hidden well away from squeamish eyes, on the second and third floors of an anonymous residential block in a humdrum Tokyo suburb. It was founded in 1953 by Dr. Satoru Kamegai, who, appalled by the number of patients he saw in his clinic suffering from problems caused by parasites, set about trying to educate the Japanese about food hygiene. He collected forty-five thousand parasite samples during his career and, if you ask me, developed a rather unhealthy fixation on microscopic bugs, effluent, and toilets.

Oddly, most of the visitors to the museum the day we visited seemed to be couples—a curious date destination—all of whom were studying the various models and diagrams of parasitic cycles in worms, cats, mice, and insects with solemn interest. There were gruesome specimens in formaldehyde, as well as three-dimensional cutaway models of the parasites themselves: hideous extraterrestrials with multiple limbs and spiny faces.

Other unsettling displays at the Meguro Parasitological Museum included arrestingly lifelike models of dog waste and illustrations of the parasitic chain of invasion from river to fish to man. And then there was the mega tapeworm—removed from the body of a man who had acquired it after eating trout—hanging like a sacred relic in a glass case. "If I had one of those, I could use it as a rope," said Emil, channeling MacGyver.

Wild salmon are particularly risky fish to eat raw because they travel between fresh and salt waters, picking up the worst of both worlds. They carry tapeworms as well as the larvae of the anisakiasis parasite, which, if eaten, will give you severe stomach cramps and make you very sick (farmed fish are less prone to parasites, not least because most are pumped full of chemicals). They can live in the host human for decades. Of course, either cooking the fish to 285°F or deep-freezing kills the parasites, but dead parasites aren't a whole lot more appetizing, are they? What's more, if you want to minimize the risk of eating fish raw, the chances are your freezer won't reach the required −5°F to kill the larvae, anyway, so home freezing isn't going to help. And if you think salmon is iffy, you should run a mile from mackerel, which spoils even quicker—the reason that, in the early, pre–frozen food days of sushi, in the eighteenth century, it was typically pickled in vinegar before consumption.

After stopping off in the museum shop on our way out to stock up on parasite key rings and celebrity tapeworm T-shirts, I felt that we all needed to commune with nature a little, particularly the sea. We couldn't very well continue our travels through Japan with two of our party refusing to eat fish on the grounds that they might themselves be eaten by worms. I had a solution.

The thing that strikes you—but not until *after* you have left the greatest fish market in the world—is that it doesn't smell remotely fishy, despite the fact that 4.4 million pounds of seafood pass through its gates every day, and the cobblestones are awash in fish blood, guts, and seawater.

If you had told me that all the oceans in all the world had been dredged that day and their contents brought to the Tokyo Metropolitan Central Wholesale Market—better known as Tsukiji, after the district in which it is located—I would have believed it, but all of it is so twitchingly fresh—in many cases the creatures are still very much alive—that the only smell is of the sea itself.

We were exceptionally fortunate in that we had the chance to tour the market with a brilliant young sushi chef called Osamu. Osamu runs a local sushi restaurant far out in the eastern Tokyo commuter belt and visits Tsukiji virtually every morning to buy fresh fish and vegetables. He had generously agreed to act as our guide.

Tsukiji is the largest seafood market in the world, feeding twelve million people a day; less well-known is its outer market, Jogai Ichiba, which sells everything apart from fresh fish and is a fertile hunting ground for authentic Japanese ingredients, such as whole katsuobushi fillets and myriad types of dried seaweed. One of the open-fronted shops was selling a stuffed panda as well as crocodiles, leopards, and objects recognizable with considerable effort as penises, albeit too dried and wizened to identify the donor species. There was coral, too, just to tick off the final box on the environmental outrage checklist.

Just outside the market, we passed the Namiyoke Inari Shrine, where some of the sixty thousand people who work at or visit the market every day leave offerings of sake to protect against the volatile oceans. Among the Tsukiji regulars are most of the better restaurateurs of Tokyo; Chinese and Korean stevedores; middlemen from such companies as True World, part of the Reverend Sun Myung Moon's organization and one of the largest wholesalers of tuna in the world; bargain-hunting housewives; shopkeepers; and, of course, the 1,677 market holders, four of whom can trace their businesses back four hundred years, long before the Great Kanto earthquake of 1923 destroyed the original market in Nihonbashi.

The fresh seafood market is the heart and soul of Tsukiji. You enter at your own risk, which is considerable given that at any moment you could be mowed down by one of the hundreds of turret trucks, whose drivers stand upright at their helm to scout a path through the market's narrow alleyways, transporting piles of white polystyrene boxes of fish slopping about in seawater, at breakneck speed. "Don't take your kids there," Toshi had warned me. "No one ever takes kids there. They'll fillet them and sell them as swordfish!" Pedestrians give way to diesel at all times, Osamu warned us, eyeing the boys nervously. I clasped Asger's and Emil's hands and wrists firmly, and we followed Osamu as he dived into the warren of stalls to find his regular contacts.

It was as if we had entered the world's greatest aquarium. Before us was an endless parade of the most extraordinary marine life—in tanks, boxes, or laid out on vast mounds of icy scree. Every species was represented and priced by the kilo, from chunks of vampish red whale meat to tiny brown shrimps the size of an eye-lash, still twitching on delicate beds of soft wood shavings. The market was indoors and artificially lit, the rows of stalls tightly packed, making it tricky for two people to pass, let alone turret trucks and stevedores with carts. The glistening cobblestones were treacherous.

Tuna is, of course, the star of Tsukiji, and much has been written about the early-dawn tuna auctions here—the absurd prices paid for the fish (although, actually, pound for pound, whale meat is more expensive); the extraordinary lengths wholesalers will take to pre-serve it (carbon dioxide keeps the raw flesh red); and the precision filleting by master fishmongers. It takes four men to divide up a tuna the size of a man, weighing up to 661 pounds, using yard-long, thin "samurai" blades. Osamu explained that of the seven spe-cies of tuna, the most sought after is the bluefin, whose most delectable cut is *o-toro,* the fattiest part of the belly, closest to the head. But as recently as the 1960s, all tuna, and *o-toro* in particu-lar, was considered fit only for cat food. The Japanese postwar fond-ness for fat changed all that, of course, as did the explosion in the popularity of sushi in the West, where tastes also leaned toward rich, fatty meats.

In the summer, the best wild bluefin comes from the seas around Hokkaido, in northern Japan, because the tuna here feed almost ex-clusively on squid. In the winter, the best come from the eastern coast of the United States. Mostly, though, it is ranched from young fish caught in the wild and raised in pens from the Mediterranean to North America and Mexico—often in breach of quotas and to the great detriment of wild stocks, which are perilously low, some say on the brink of extinction. Advances are being made in tuna farming in Japan—that is, breeding from eggs in captivity, once thought impossible for fish that swim so far and fast in the wild—but the process remains controversial and, currently, very expensive.

The record price paid for one bluefin was ¥155 million (around $1.76 million) for a 489-pound example caught off the coast of Aomori, in northeast Japan, in 2013, which, though it may well yield ten thousand nigiri toppings for Kiyomura—the Tokyo sushi chain that bought it—was still ludicrous. (The record price was as much a political statement; the rival bidder was Chinese. A price of ¥6 million to ¥10 million—$53,000 to $90,000—is more typical.)

We were at the market early enough to catch the end of the auction, which takes place at the rear of the main market in a hall the size of a football field (and has since, sadly, been closed to tourists). Men in blue galoshes and overalls were using hooks and torches to inspect scarlet divots cut in the tails of frozen tuna (in this case, from Mexico) lined up on pallets on the floor like frosted, black neutron bombs. The auctioneer was making a bizarre noise: a Muslim call to prayer as read by a steeplechase commentator. Osamu explained that experienced buyers were looking for oiliness, color, and any sign of parasites in the fish, but he admitted he had no idea what the auctioneer was saying.

We followed Osamu, stopping to inspect prehistoric-looking barnacles; oysters the size of my hand (from Tsuruga Bay, on the Sea of Japan); a type of scallop as big as my forearm from Aichi Prefecture, south of Tokyo; and crabs of all shapes and sizes, foaming disconsolately at the mouth. There were soft-shell turtles, popular as a soup base, and piled hugger-mugger in barrels, their feet sold separately in tubs beside them; gigantic abalone; sea cucumbers resembling freaky sex toys; horseshoe crabs that looked like living fossils; and scallops sneaking a peek at the passing world through tentatively opened shells. Emil stopped dead in his tracks beside some trays of giant fish eyes, each the size of a small saucer. "Sea monster!" he said, pointing open-mouthed.

"Tuna," said Osamu.

I spent most of my time simply pointing and raising my eyebrows at Osamu. What were those? Sea pineapple, or *hoya*, gnarled and purple like subaquatic dragon fruit. And those? "Octopus beaks." What was *he* doing? "That's an eel; he's filleting it." The fishmonger had pinned the eel to a wooden chopping board through its eyes, while it was still alive, with a short, stubby wooden-handled knife and was swiftly dividing it into tassels of meat and bone as it breathed its last. And, oh my god, what on earth were *those*? "*Mirugai*, sea squirts," said Osamu, smiling. It was the most extraordinary sea creature I had ever seen: a geoduck clam with, well, an oversize squirting appendage protruding, writhing, from its shell.

Asger and Emil spent some time bent over a large black bucket filled with wriggling elvers. Asger was goading Emil to stick his finger into the morass and, after a few aborted attempts, he did. "It tickles!" he squeaked. The fishmonger laughed and gave them two stickers each with fish logos, which made their day. The elvers were not the only live produce, by any means. Everywhere we looked there were bubbling tanks with mournful sea creatures staring out at us—squid all lying in the same direction; octopus, their suckers pressing against the glass of their tanks; and flatfish stacked up one above the other. Asger pointed in horror at a ferociously ugly stonefish, mottled and droopy-mouthed; not as notorious as the poisonous fugu, it also carries a nasty toxin concealed in its dorsal spines.

Emil squealed as a jet of seawater squirted onto his arm from some unidentified shellfish. He stepped back, setting off a chain of events that would have been comical had I not been directly related to their instigator. Emil's sudden movement forced a turret truck to brake, which caused one of its boxes to fall onto a nearby stand, scattering large gray-pink prawns on the cobblestones. Lissen hastily bent down to help pick them up, then immediately dropped one as it started to wriggle in her hands.

"Come and see this," said Osamu calmly as if he went shopping with the Four Stooges every day. He took us to meet a wholesaler

friend who was wearing waist-high rubber waders. His stall was surrounded by tanks full of live fish, best described, for lack of more
thoroughgoing marine knowledge on my part, as "kind of sea bream–
ish." Osamu pointed at one fish in a tank, and the wholesaler
grabbed it from the water, carried it over to a well-worn, blood-
soaked wooden chopping board, and brought a cleaver down
cleanly onto the back of its head, only partially severing it from its
body. Swiftly, he lifted the fish from the board, took what looked
like a straightened wire coat hanger, and thrust it down its spine,
right through the heart of the marrow. "It kind of freezes it," said
Osamu, turning to see four faces looking like something from an
Edvard Munch painting. "It isn't dead; it is suspended." Asger and
Emil didn't know what to make of this. How could a fish still live
after having its head half chopped off and its spine kebabed? This
was *ikejimi*, a method of preserving fresh fish by stopping brain and
therefore muscle activity instantly, preventing the release of sour-
tasting lactic acid. It was invented decades—if not centuries—ago
by the Japanese, and its use is becoming more widespread.

A little farther on, I turned my nose up at some small wooden
trays of perfectly arrayed *uni*, or sea urchin eggs (actually, these frilly
little yellowy-pink morsels aren't roe but gonads—sea urchins are
hermaphrodites). "Tastes like toilet cleaner," I said to Osamu, re-
calling the only other time I had tried sea urchin, at a market in
Paris. "Wait till you try these." He smiled, pointing to the still-
twitching spines of the uni.

We ate like kings at Osamu's restaurant that evening, and along
with the live shrimp, whose flesh moved in a most unnerving manner on our tongues as we ate them, the uni were a highlight. He
prepared the sea urchins whole, also while still alive, chipping open
their spiny black shells with the square end of his knife as if they
were boiled eggs and plucking out their furry "tongues." The shell
fragments continued to twitch like antennae on his chopping board.

The gonads were delicious—not a phrase I ever imagined myself writing—rich and creamy and, with no time for the ammonia taste, which had put me off in Paris, to mature, a transcendentally sweet flavor of the sea.

Tsukiji is scheduled to move any moment now from its current site to a new, purpose-built facility just across the bay. All I can say is, take out a new mortgage, sell the car or your neighbor's kidneys, just make sure you visit the old one before you die. It contains what is, in my eyes, the greatest man-made wonder of the world, the ultimate symbol of our courage, ingenuity, and greed as a species. There is no greater food-lover's sight on earth.

9. MSG: AN APOLOGY

I do my best to give my children pure, healthy food. I use as much organic produce as I can; cook fresh meals every day; check for food additives, palm oil, maltodextrin, artificial flavors, and trans fats on ingredients lists; and know my saturated from my polyunsaturated fats. But there is one ingredient I have been more vigilant about than any other: monosodium glutamate, or MSG. You find MSG in the most abhorrent foodstuffs known to man: ready-made sandwiches, ready-made sauces, supermarket pizza, low-fat this, diet that, and Pringles, whose manufacturer, Procter & Gamble, in 2008 won a petition to have them declassified as potato chips, thus avoiding sales tax, on the grounds that they were almost entirely an industrial product that had virtually nothing to do with potatoes.

In other words, MSG is the neon arrow alerting me to foodstuffs I consider toxic for my kids. If I see it, I don't buy it. And that goes for autolyzed yeast and hydrolyzed soy protein, which are MSG in disguise.

We have known about the evils of MSG for decades. In 1968, a doctor called Robert Ho Man Kwok wrote to *The New England Journal of Medicine* to share an observation that Chinese food made his neck go numb, among other troubling symptoms. He coined the term "Chinese Restaurant Syndrome" to describe it and speculated that MSG was the cause. Others soon wrote in to add palpitations and headaches to the list of symptoms, and since then, MSG has been blamed for everything from Alzheimer's to childhood asthma to attention deficit disorder.

The world's largest producer of MSG is a Japanese company called Ajinomoto, which makes 2 million tons of the stuff every year and exports it around the world. Ajinomoto—it means, literally, "essence of taste"—was founded by Professor Kikunae Ikeda, who discovered MSG in 1908. He realized that konbu seaweed was a natural source of the particularly delicious amino acid called glutamate and that if he could manufacture it, he would have a powerful flavor enhancer. He patented it in the form of a white crystalline powder, stabilized with salt, the following year. As frozen foods and canning changed the domestic culinary landscape in the decades that followed, MSG played an important role in adding flavor and mouthfeel to processed foods when these were lost during their industrial preservation—which is why it is particularly prevalent in diet foods.

And that's not all. Back in Paris, Toshi had told me, actually looking over his shoulder to make sure we weren't overheard as he said it, that a few years ago Ajinomoto had made the hole in the top of the MSG shaker larger so that people would use more. Now if that's not a scandal right there, I don't know what is.

As a serious journalist, I could hardly go to Tokyo and not see it as my aim—nay, my *duty*—to infiltrate Ajinomoto and expose their corporate mendacity. But how could I sneak behind the forbidding walls of their Nihonbashi HQ? What cunning ruse could I employ to gain access to the hidden, high-security world of this sinister, cultlike organization?

I rang their press office and asked if I might pop by and ask them a few questions. They said they would be delighted. When would I like to come? I said: But isn't it supposed to be harder than this? You mean you're just inviting me along? They said: Yes, see you tomorrow at eleven o'clock. I said: All right.

I arrived five minutes early—all the better to catch them off guard—and stood taking in the grand marble entrance hall of the Ajinomoto tower. I took a sneak look at some of the company's products—soups, powdered dashi, pure MSG—while I waited for my contact (although, looking back, maybe it wasn't such a sneak peek, as they were, like, you know, on display).

My contact turned out to be a friendly young PR lady who welcomed me to the company and showed me to a meeting room on the fifth floor. There, already waiting (damn!), were Shigehiro Yamamoto, the company's PR associate general manager, and Kumiko Ninomiya, the company's scientific affairs spokeswoman, smiling and friendly. As if they had done nothing wrong.

I settled into a chair across the table from them, took out my questions, pen, and notebook, and commenced the interview, trying to keep thoughts of the Pulitzer from my mind.

Official Transcript of Interview Recording

MB: [*Clearing throat and rustling papers*] So, MSG. It's really bad stuff, isn't it, or what?

YAMAMOTO: [*Laughing politely*] No, it is no more processed than sugar or salt. It originally comes from konbu, seaweed. It is just a basic seasoning.

MB: [*Pauses, looks down at notes*] So what about all these headaches and numbness, then?

YAMAMOTO: That was disproved years ago. Have you never read the essay by the American food writer Jeffrey Steingarten, "If MSG Is So Bad for You, Why Doesn't Everyone in China Have a Headache?" The World Health Organization, the U.S. Food and Drug Administration, and the United Nations have all concluded that it poses no health risks.

MB: Steingart . . . erm . . . it doesn't say anything about that in my notes. Wait a minute. [*More rustling of papers, the sound of a seat squeaking, nervous coughing*] OK, but what about umami? You say your product enhances the umami in food, but no one has actually proved that umami exists, have they?

NINOMIYA: Actually, since the Miami research group discovered the umami receptor, in 2000, I don't think there has been any doubt in the scientific community that it exists and that it is one of the basic tastes. It is not really questioned now that umami has a physiological function.

MB: [*Long pause, a deep sigh*] But isn't it true that Ajinomoto wants to conquer the world with MSG? I have evidence that you deliberately made the hole in the top of the dispenser larger so that people would use more of your product. What do you say to that?

YAMAMOTO: [*More polite chuckles around the table*] We did make the hole larger about thirty years ago, it's true, but that was simply because when people added MSG to their miso soup, the steam from the soup was clogging up the hole. It is true that MSG is our company's original product, but we only want to explain more about umami. We don't want to destroy anyone else's food culture or get everyone using MSG, but we want to spread the word about Japanese food as a whole. We want people to learn more about how to make Japanese food. We want people to know about dashi, but even in Japan it is difficult for people to make dashi from scratch with seaweed and katsuobushi. Restaurants can do this, but MSG is, in my opinion, a really good product for home use.

MB: Well, if all that is true, how come America has been so hostile to MSG?

YAMAMOTO: Because it is a Japanese discovery, I guess. Perhaps they didn't want to eat something that looked like a chemical and was made abroad.

MB: That's as maybe, but no chefs in the West believe in umami, do they? I mean, we've managed without it for centuries. It isn't exactly a hot topic of conversation in Europe and America, is it?

YAMAMOTO: Do you know a chef called Heston Blumenthal of the restaurant the Fat Duck, with three Michelin stars? He wrote to us some years ago, a very simple letter asking for more information about umami and later came to an umami workshop we ran in Kyoto in 2004. He said to me, "My heart belongs to umami." He uses dashi and konbu in his cooking now, as does Ferran Adrià. Do you know it? Thomas Keller of the French Laundry is coming to our next symposium, too.

So: the truth about MSG.

To set the record straight, MSG does not make mice's heads explode. Nor is it in any way toxic, at least no more than, say, salt. The U.S. Food and Drug Administration has indeed given it the all clear, as have the UN and the European Union. It turns out that the studies carried out in the sixties purporting to show that MSG had adverse side effects had involved giving mice absurd quantities of the stuff, equivalent to an adult eating a pound. So, while even Ajinomoto concedes that some people might have an adverse reaction to MSG, it is no more than are allergic to eggplants, say, or sofas. MSG is merely a man-made glutamic acid produced by fermenting carbohydrates and sugars—nothing more, nothing less.

Now, to umami. Umami and MSG are inextricably linked but

are by no means the same thing. Umami is usually referred to as the fifth taste, after salty, sweet, bitter, and sour (although some neuroscientists claim there are fifty or more tastes, but let's not get into that; it has taken long enough for the Japanese to convince the world that umami exists). When Ikeda identified it in konbu, he wrote: "An attentive taster will find out something common in the complicated taste of asparagus, tomatoes, cheese, and meat, which is quite peculiar and cannot be classed under any of the well-defined four taste qualities, sweet, sour, salty, and bitter." It is not confined to Japanese foodstuffs. Cheese—parmesan in particular—and tomatoes have a powerful umami flavor, as do air-dried ham, veal stock, and Worcestershire sauce. Mother's milk is rich in umami (far more than cow's milk), as is the crust on grilled or fried meat. In fact, it is often easier to describe what umami is by listing the things that are full of umami flavor, as people do tend to tie themselves up in knots on this subject—*savory* and *meaty* are the words most frequently employed, but often the Japanese resort to translating it as *delicious* or *tasty*.

The other four tastes serve a clear purpose. Salt identifies whether there is salt in a food—obviously; sweet tells you if there is sugar (and that the food is therefore an energy-giver); while bitter and sour are useful as warnings of toxins or unripeness. So why does our body need an umami detector? Because the flavor of umami indicates the presence of glutamates, which indicate protein in food. Protein is essential to our survival, so it makes sense that our tongue has a receptor to identify it in food. Glutamates are one of the key compounds that make food tasty to humans, but unlike salt or sugar, there are no obvious go-to foods to get your hit. The nature of glutamates and umami is that they support other flavors, add body, and enhance them, which is why it has been so difficult to identify. Umami is also an indicator of ripeness and therefore tells us when vegetables and fruits are at their most nutritious—tomatoes are at their most umami-ish when they are at the peak of ripeness, for instance. What MSG does is artificially replicate the naturally occurring flavor of the amino acid glutamate, which makes things taste umami-ish.

Umami has actually been identified in over forty compounds, but it is most strongly present in glutamate and certain ribonucleotides, chief among them inosinate and guanylate. No, me neither. But the most important thing to know as far as Japanese food is concerned is that the Japanese are the world masters at maximizing the umami in their cooking. This is best exemplified by one dish: miso soup. As Professor Ikeda discovered, konbu has more glutamate than any other foodstuff on earth, while katsuobushi, the other main base ingredient of the dashi used to make miso soup (along with water), is one of the richest natural sources of inosinates. Meanwhile, shiitake mushrooms happen to be extremely rich in guanylate and are often added to miso as well. That's quite an umami triple whammy as it is, but the combination of these three ingredients generates far *more* umami flavor than the mere sum of their parts. When the glutamate of konbu meets the inosinic acid in katsuobushi and the guanylate of shiitake, the umami profile is multiplied by a factor of eight. Apparently, it drives one's left lateral orbitofrontal cortex quite batty.

The Italians aren't too bad at generating this so-called synergistic umami effect either, having long ago figured out—albeit intuitively—that parmesan, which has the second-highest amount of glutamate (1,200 milligrams per 100 grams to konbu's 2,240 milligrams per 100 grams), and tomatoes pack a tasty punch when combined. The French, too, have been maximizing their umami intake for centuries by reducing veal stock to a meaty, savory, amino acid–packed essence. The British, meanwhile, found their umami in a more prosaic source: Marmite, or yeast extract.

There is also a clear connection between foodstuffs that are fermented or aged in some way and an increase in umami-ness, as these processes tend to break down proteins, turning them into tasty amino acids. Katsuobushi is fermented, for example, as are sake, miso, and soy, and all of them have rich umami flavor profiles. To that list we could add bottarga and other dried or smoked fish roe; the fish sauces of Southeast Asia, which have much in common with the ancient Roman anchovy sauce *garum*; and, of course, aged cheeses. I would guess that Roquefort and Stilton are mightily glutamate-rich.

And a big fat "So what?" I hear you say. So what if there is a fifth flavor? We've been eating it all this time; now we just have a name for it. Big deal. But it is a big deal because, first, if we know what "tasty" is, then we can learn to make things tastier. Heston Blumenthal makes a dish at the Fat Duck called Sound of the Sea—it is the one where diners sit listening to sounds of the ocean on an iPod—with seaweed, edible sand in the form of tapioca, powdered konbu, miso, abalone foam, and wakame stock with oyster juice, along with dashi. Sounds terrific, doesn't it? And what a combination of umami-rich foods. I bet the synergistic effects are off the scale.

But there could also be significant health benefits to learning how to maximize the umami in your cooking. Umami brings extra depth and savory flavor to dishes, which allows the cook to cut back on salt, fat, and sugar—all the things that are killing us in the West. Umami gives flavor without the calories or other health risks.

It would also appear that the human body has a kind of automatic umami limiter. Once you've had enough umami, your appetite slows markedly, so you don't want to eat so much umami-rich food and favor something blander. The very latest information from the Umami Information Center—which is, admittedly, funded by Ajinomoto and is trying to alert people to what umami is so they can sell them MSG and get it into their food quickly and easily—suggests that there are umami receptors in our stomachs as well as

our mouths and that they are important for the digestion of proteins. In other words, we also taste with our digestive tracts. Apparently, these receptors, upon getting wind of some glutamates on the
way from the umami receptors on the side of our tongue, prepare
the stomach to better digest food—in particular, meat. Something
similar happens in the pancreas, too. And the simple fact that we
enjoy food laden with umami, that we are more content when eating it, makes it easier to digest.

Adding MSG is one way of bringing extra umami tastiness to
your cooking. Sure, if you throw great fistfuls of it into the pot, there
may be some unpleasant side effects and your food will taste awful,
but used sparingly, it genuinely does make food taste better and gives
it more mouthfeel and flavor length. That said, as always, if you can
generate umami from the primary ingredients in a dish, all the
better—after all, neat MSG does taste like bacon-flavored potato
chips, which is not the most refined of flavors. A dashi made with
dried konbu and fresh-grated katsuobushi will always taste better,
deeper, more satisfying than one made from a powder, in the same
way that fresh stock tastes better than a Knorr cube.

10. THE BUSIEST FISH IN THE OCEAN

wanted to find out more about the two key, umami-rich ingredients used to make dashi: konbu and katsuobushi. Konbu would have to wait until we headed north to Hokkaido the following week (this was now late September), but I wanted to see how katsuobushi was made while we were still in Tokyo.

Katsuobushi are dried and fermented fillets of the bonito fish, as hard as wood and dusty brown in color. In their whole state they look kind of like fossilized bananas but are usually sold preshaved in airtight bags. They crop up either as shavings, dancing bewitchingly in the heat atop various dishes, or steeped and then strained in dashi to add a deeply satisfying savoriness to soups and sauces. The shavings are fantastically moreish just eaten on their own from the bag, too, with an addictive smoky-citric flavor and a mildly fishy aftertaste. Fishiness aside, the closest comparison I can think of is the salty meatiness of a really good, paper-thin slice of *pata negra* ham. It really is that delicious.

Soon after my visit to Ajinomoto, I took the Shinkansen south from Tokyo to Yaizu, a fishing port midway between Tokyo and Nagoya (to my eternal gratitude, Lissen again agreed to entertain the children—this time with a trip to the Mori Art Museum and the aquarium). Yaizu is Katsuo Town, built on the money from processing bonito. Yaizu katsuobushi is famous throughout Japan; it's a brand in its own right, with some of its output still made the traditional way, by drying the fillets in the sun.

The town was more prosperous than other rural communities I would see in Japan. The price they'd had to pay for that prosperity was apparent as soon as I got out of the taxi. The air was heavy with the smell of smoking fish. To me it was deliciously tangy, but I could imagine one might grow immune to its charms if one lived with it all the time. The smell was accompanied by a cacophony of machinery and diesel engines, forklift trucks, and conveyor belts. As I approached the factory gates, there was an almighty rubbery clattering noise behind me as a truck tipped a load of silver-black, glistening torpedoes, together with a large quantity of bloody seawater, into a tank. My first sight of a real, whole bonito.

The Yaizu Fish Manufacturing Park is a town within a town made up of corrugated warehouses housing twenty-four factories. Each is in some way involved with processing every scrap of this dense, oily, red-fleshed fish, making everything from super-fresh sashimi to canned bonito. One company takes the guts and salts, pickles, and ferments them to be eaten as a delicacy; another makes calcium supplements for school meals from the dried, powdered bones. Even the essence from the liquid used to cook the bonito is recuperated and used to flavor instant ramen, and, of course, several make the katsuobushi itself. It is an incredible fish.

"Nothing is wasted here," a spokesman for Yaizu explained as he showed me into the boardroom. "Even the guts and hearts are processed for fertilizer. Quantities of bonito are declining, and the number of ships catching them are decreasing, too. Even though the government [which controls prices] says the number of fish in the ocean is stable, we don't agree. There are fewer fish to go after, oil costs mean it is more expensive to go after them, yet demand is rising, so we have to maximize the yield from every one we catch."

Yaizu processes around thirteen thousand tons of *katsuo* each year—that's about sixty thousand fish per day—but as recently as 2004, that figure was as high as eighteen thousand tons. I learned all this from what was about the tenth corporate video I had endured since arriving in Japan, all of them opening with the same shaky, synthesized strings and a portentous voice-over. As well as informing me that they "make the most of our blessings from the sea," it did explain the bonito's migration pattern: *modori* is the name given to katsuo returning from the north (specifically the southeast coast of Hokkaido) in the autumn, which are fatter and richer and mostly eaten raw or lightly grilled (bonito is considered a lower-grade fish to eat than tuna); while in spring the fish come from the south on the so-called Black Current, mostly from the Philippines, and are leaner and better for making katsuobushi. The migration is changing, however, with fish traveling farther north to spawn while the Black Current itself is changing, too.

I asked if they had tried ranching or farming bonito. "It has not yet become economically viable to farm bonito like tuna; they are too small and are even more active than tuna," explained the spokesman. Apparently, bonito even swim in their sleep: especially industrious Japanese are said to "work like a katsuo."

I was curious to see the process that takes the fish we had seen being tipped out of their tanker as we arrived and turns them into the dried fillets, like glockenspiel keys, that I had seen for sale in the shops in the outer part of Tsukiji.

We headed outside to take a look. The spokesman explained that the fish are defrosted and their heads and internal organs removed. After boiling, an army of local women fillet every one of those sixty thousand fish by hand—after cooking, the fish are fragile, and this is the only way of removing the spine and other bones while retaining the perfectly shaped fillets the aesthetically conscious Japanese demand. We visited one of the processing halls, a dark, strip-lit factory, smelly and steamy, its every surface coated in brown fish grease. Around fifty women in blue hygiene hats, wearing rubber gloves, with their sleeves rolled up, stood as the cooked fish passed by on conveyor belts. I watched one as she swiftly picked a fish up and turned it over in her hands a couple of times, dividing the four fillets from the skeleton, perfectly, in seconds. The bones disappeared down a hole to be taken off and ground up, while the fillets were placed carefully on a wire tray beside her.

Smoking and fermenting come next. Obviously, different types of wood will affect the final flavor. Some companies use konara oak, others cherrywood, but the flavor of the finished katsuobushi can also change according to how many times it is smoked: between ten and twenty is the norm to dry the flesh thoroughly until only about 20 percent of the water remains. We saw the vast smoking kilns, again caked in old fish goo, treacly and brown. The finest bonito of all, however, are cured in the sun for two days. There are records dating back to the Middle Ages of bonito being mold-cured in this way, and one company in Yaizu still prepares its bonito this way—weather permitting.

Next, the fillets are placed in a hot, humid storage area, like a huge oven, that has been impregnated with the *Aspergillus glaucus* mold. Some of the storage chambers are decades old and imbue the fillets with a unique flavor, each identifiable to a true katsuo connoisseur. As with miso, soy, and sake, this fermentation contributes greatly to the deep, complex flavor and umami power of katsuobushi. The mold creates flavorsome enzymes that turn the fish protein into amino acids, in particular a compound called inosine monophosphate (IMP). The process takes up to six weeks, during which the fillets will be taken back out into the sun to kill off the mold—perhaps several times—each time being returned to the chamber to grow a new layer, which deepens the flavor further. By the end, the fish fillets are hard as wood, ready for the final stage: shaving.

This is done using a *katsuobushi kezuriki*, an upside-down carpenter's plane with a container underneath to catch the shavings. The best chefs will shave the katsuobushi fillets by hand, literally moments before they go into the dashi, as they start to lose flavor and aroma the moment they are shaved. Many use airtight bags of pre-shaved fillets, which you can buy in all Japanese supermarkets. Most home cooks, however, will use some kind of powdered form of instant dashi, most likely with an Ajinomoto label on it.

We ended up in a small shop selling some of the produce made nearby. The Yaizu spokesman showed me how to pick good katsuobushi fillets by gently tapping two together—the denser the fillets, the better their quality and flavor, and the sound they make should be almost metallic. (Also, should you find yourself out shopping for katsuobushi, Shizuo Tsuji, in *A Simple Art*, says that if there is a green tint to the mold, the fillet is too watery, and if it is yellow, too acidic.) He broke one in half to show me the rings, again, just like wood, the color ranging through its center from dark purple to brown. Apparently, I was the first Westerner ever to visit Yaizu, and, overcome by the honor, I rashly bought two whole fillets for a few thousand yen, not really thinking ahead that I didn't have anything to shave them with, later realizing that a proper katsuobushi grater costs around a hundred dollars or so.

I still have the fillets. They remain at the bottom of my "too good to use" drawer, as yet unshaved. From time to time I take them out, sniff them fondly, and imagine how great they will one day taste.

11. THE CAMPAIGN FOR REAL WASABI

I t is rare to find *Wasabia japonica* served outside of Japan. I had only ever seen the Kermit-green, sinus-scorching paste, usually made from dyed horseradish served—quite incorrectly, it turns out—as a blob on the side of a sushi plate. But as I was about to discover, fresh wasabi root has about as much in common with that substance as snow from a spray can does with the real deal.

Lissen, Asger, and Emil had chosen to spend the day at KidZania, an indoor theme park where children take on proper jobs, such as fireman, dentist, or graphic designer, and earn fake money, which they can then exchange for chocolate and fizzy drinks: designed, I think, to prepare Japanese children for a life as diligent taxpayers.

Meanwhile, I traveled about sixty miles south of Tokyo to the Mount Amagi area on the Izu Peninsula, in Shizuoka, a forested area south of Mount Fuji. This is a popular *onsen*—or hot spring—area, but for the Japanese, it is also synonymous with wasabi: over 60 percent of Japanese wasabi is grown here—worth ¥2.5 billion ($22 million) a year.

I hired a car for the final drive up into the hills. My first stop was for a meeting with Yoshio Ando, head of the local wasabi growers' association, in the small shop and wasabi processing center he runs with his wife. Yoshio, in his late fifties and sporting an over-size baseball cap with a cartoon wasabi character on it, explained that he was one of 355 wasabi growers in the region.

Wasabi is one of the most temperamental plants in the world, he said, requiring precise climactic conditions and fresh water, lots of it. "Wasabi needs very clean, fresh-flowing water to grow," Yoshio explained. "The water is the key; it needs to be around 53°F to 55°F [never more than 60°F, never less than 50°F] and flow at 4.7 gallons per second to keep a constant depth of half an inch. We have wonderful mountain springwater here, but the climate is also crucial. You need a cool summer and water throughout the year."

He offered me a real wasabi root to inspect. "This one will sell for more than ¥3,000 [$25] in Tokyo," he said. "It is only for the rich. It is very limited quantity." Although we had passed several giant fiberglass replicas on the roads (the Japanese are fond of pro-moting their local specialties in oversize roadside model form), I had never seen a whole wasabi root before. It was knobby, green, and rather phallic, with floppy leaves at the top end, tapering to a point at the other. This one was roughly the size of a banana. The roots can grow larger, but the ones you see in Japanese supermarkets tend to be more Mars bar–sized. "They are harvested throughout the year when the plant has reached between fifteen months and two years, during which time it grows progressively hotter in flavor," Yoshio told me.

The Japanese have been cultivating this enigmatic plant—a rhi-zome and distant relative of the horseradish—since 1744. It was originally used as a sterilant to kill bacteria on fish, among other things, which is how it came to be associated with sushi and sashimi. It is also believed to stimulate the appetite.

I asked about the difference between fresh wasabi and the wa-sabi you buy in tubes. Yoshio shook his head dismissively. You couldn't compare them, he said. Good, fresh wasabi is hot, but not burning hot, and much sweeter, more fragrant than the industrial stuff. And, needless to say, Japanese is best.

They do grow wasabi in Taiwan and China, but when I asked about this, Yoshio shook his head even more vigorously. "They grow in soil in Taiwan. No running water, lots of chemicals. The same in China." But surely there must be other places in the world with similar water supplies and climate, and with a crop as desirable as wasabi, others must have tried to cultivate it the correct way. "Yes, I have heard they grow it in Canada and New Zealand. Maybe that's better." But the look on his face suggested he thought otherwise.

I was finding it difficult to visualize how wasabi grew. Was there any chance Yoshio could show me? He looked dubious and conferred with his wife in a low murmur for a while. They didn't usually do this, he said finally, and he did like to keep his fields secret for obvious reasons—implying, intriguingly, the existence of wasabi rustlers—but seeing as I had come all this way, he agreed to take me to see his fields, higher up the mountain.

I followed his raggedy Toyota pickup for over an hour up into the forests of pine, cedar, and bamboo, far from the tourist onsen towns. It was thrilling to imagine that, somewhere in the trees around us, wild wasabi—as opposed to Yoshio's cultivated variety—was growing in fresh flowing streams.

We came to a deep, dark, forested river valley, open at one end with a spectacular view to the landscape below, narrowing at the other end, where the river that gives life to the wasabi descended from the summit. As I followed Yoshio along a narrow, overgrown path to the wasabi paddies, dragonflies and butterflies bright as Hermès scarves flapped up from the undergrowth. Lizards scattered every which way, and bright green spiders hung from webs in the trees. I had a sense of being shown something secret and precious, for here Yoshio grows what is not just the best wasabi in Japan (and therefore the world—he's won every prize going), but, according to a recent prime-ministerial pronouncement, one of the best items of produce in the country.

The entire valley floor had been terraced rather like a rice paddy, but instead of the bright green, grasslike rice plants, it was carpeted with the broad, rhubarb-like leaves of wasabi. The sound of running water was deafening, although there was no river in sight. It was all flowing beneath the plants, which were packed, Yoshio told me, in a six-inch-deep bed of sand. The plants themselves were covered with black netting to keep them from sunlight and falling leaves. "The angle of the slope is very precise; otherwise, the water would flow too fast. The other problem we have is with the local deer. They love the leaves," Yoshio said. I tasted one. It was a little like arugula, but with a sweet, burning wasabi aftertaste.

I asked if he had any tips on using wasabi. "Ooh, you've got to try the stems pickled in sake lees; that's lovely." When I left Japan, I was planning to take some roots home with me. How long would one keep? "Keep it dry and it will last a month, but if it gets damp, it will turn black."

"You know," Yoshio said later, after our hour-long tour of the wasabi fields and as we were about to leave, "if you really like wasabi, there is someone you should meet."

Shirakabeso, or the "white wall inn," was back down in the onsen region of Shizuoka. It is a traditional onsen guesthouse with two communal outdoor baths run by a husband-and-wife team, Haruyoshi and Ikuko Uda. Ikuko, Yoshio's contact, is obsessed with wasabi and has spent years studying it at the University of Shizuoka under Professor Naohide Kinai, a specialist in the various medicinal properties of this miraculous root.

As we sat on the floor in a simple room with a tatami-covered floor in the traditional manner, overlooking an immaculate garden, Ikuko explained the basic principles of using wasabi. "You grate it on sharkskin," she said, "because that is fine and gentle but tough.

And you must grate it in a circular motion. When the oxygen mixes with the wasabi, it increases its hotness. The top end is sweeter than the bottom end." She showed me how to do this, making gentle circles with the root on the sharkskin board.

She could see I was looking a little anxious about consuming the entire wasabi root—it was a large one. "Don't worry. Real wasabi warms the throat; it doesn't burn or go up your nose like the artificial stuff. And you know what? If you eat wasabi and drink, you don't get a hangover, because it is antibacterial and detoxifying."

As well as various minerals and vitamins, wasabi contains around twenty different types of isothiocyanates (compounds it shares with mustard and broccoli), which have anti-inflammatory properties. This makes wasabi a useful treatment for allergies and eczema. Its antimicrobial qualities also mean it works against tooth decay, and apparently, it can even calm diarrhea. Most interesting of all, the isothiocyanates are thought to stop the spread of cancers at the metastasis stage. Wasabi is, then, a bona fide superfood.

The real thing did indeed taste very different from the paste. The isothiocyanates give wasabi a pleasing pungency when grated, and as they evaporate, they release a brief, pleasurable sinus heat. Sometimes chefs will add a little sugar to real wasabi to enliven the pepper flavor.

Ikuko began to present the dishes we would be eating that afternoon: pickled rhododendron, chrysanthemum, and jellyfish (surprisingly crunchy) to start. I noticed a beautiful abalone shell on the table and turned it over; inside, the creature was still writhing. Ikuko placed it on the hot plate for a minute or so and served it sliced with a small mound of wasabi as accompaniment. It was sublimely tender. As well as wasabi, this region is famed for its wild boar, which I had a chance to taste next. It had been marinated and tenderized in miso and *koji* (the fermenting agent added to sake) for ten days, which helped make the flesh spoon-tender. Its deep, gamy richness went superbly with the sweetness of the wasabi, again neatly placed in a small mound on the plate.

I asked Ikuko how she grew to be so obsessed by wasabi. "I started seven years ago. I wanted to make the most of our local produce and surprise people." She had certainly done that, although, in doing so, she had probably ruined my enjoyment of wasabi paste and sushi forever. How could I ever go back to artificial wasabi? By the end of the afternoon, I had consumed half an entire wasabi root by myself, with no ill effects. In fact, it had been a stunning and surprisingly delicate meal. It finished with the juiciest, sweetest melon I had ever eaten, together with wasabi ice cream, of course.

12. KITCHEN STREET

Clearly, my life would be two mockeries of a sham wrapped up in a disgraceful fallacy without my own wood-backed sharkskin grater on hand in my kitchen for all my future wasabi-grating requirements.

It didn't take too much research to find out the best place to buy one. In fact, Kappabashi-dori had been second only to Tsukiji on my list of must-sees while we were in Tokyo.

Some people like to shop for shoes or clothes or, if they have given up on life entirely, soft furnishings. My biggest retail vice is kitchenware. Give me a good kitchen store and I will browse happily until they kick me out at closing time. I stalk the kitchen stores in Paris—rarely buying anything but tormenting myself with various electric gadgets that I know full well I will use once before abandoning them to the wilderness of the bottom kitchen drawer, along with old washing machine guarantees and freezer bag ties; or expensive, posh versions of things I already have, like walnut chopping boards, or pro-standard food processors; and, best of all, those little steel or chrome thingamabobs for zesting, balling, paring, coring, and all those other rarely encountered tasks that can usually just as well be dispatched with a small knife and some concentration.

My real fetish, however, is reserved for the restaurant supply stores, the places the pros go to buy catering-sized rolls of plastic wrap and silver foil, or giant tubs of mustard and salt, at a fraction of the price you pay in the supermarket.

Paris has just a few of these shops, most of them close to Les Halles or in Chinatown, and in New York there are still a few on the Bowery, but for kitchenware addicts like me, the one true global mecca is Kappabashi-dori: a whole street, plus side streets, full of shops selling every conceivable piece of equipment needed to create every conceivable cuisine in the world.

It is not the most attractive of thoroughfares: four lanes of traffic lined with a motley assortment of low-rise shops, none of which pays the slightest heed to contemporary retail convention regarding presentation or promotion. But just as with the city's restaurants, the shops of Kappabashi-dori leave the rest of the world's kitchen stores for dead because most of them specialize, with an obsessive zeal, in one specific type or area of kitchen equipment.

I spent some time and far too much money in a shop that sold only cookie cutters in thousands of shapes, for instance; another had what must be the world's largest range of rice steamers; and in another I stood in silent awe before giant vats of tempura oil and sinks as big as sofas. Next door to that was a shop that sold only menus and menu holders, and another had only cash registers and order pads. This was just across the way from one of the famous plastic food shops, used for the displays outside restaurants. From a distance it looked like a candy store with its brightly colored nigiri models. Back in the nineteenth century, the models used to be made out of wax, the woman in the shop told me. I wondered how they made it through with Tokyo summers without melting.

I was having no luck with the sharkskin wasabi grater, although, admittedly, the mime I employed when asking directions probably confused as much as it clarified. I was happily distracted by a shop devoted entirely to trays and one that sold different sizes of otherwise precisely the same shape and color of lanterns that hang outside izakaya restaurants. Asger and Emil were out of their minds with boredom by this point. Reminding them of the hours I had spent patiently following them around various Disney stores held no sway.

Time, then, to visit the stars of the kitchen strip, the knife shops: dark, somber, dusty places, their walls lined with glass cases displaying an extraordinary array of knives, each with blades like razors, forged from dozens of layers of high-carbon steel. As I explained to my suddenly more interested sons, the oldest knife makers are direct descendants of samurai sword makers who turned their skills to making kitchen knives when carrying swords was banned in Japan in the late nineteenth century. After weighing a rectangular *usuba*, for vegetables, and a triangular *deba*, for filleting fish, I bought two—one kitchen knife, pretty much a standard Western variety with two beveled edges, and one *yanagi*, or sashimi knife, ten inches long. The two cost less than one Global knife would have back home.

Sashimi knives are made with only one beveled edge, as this causes less damage to the fibers of the fish's flesh, the elderly salesman explained. The flat side doesn't push against the main block of fish in the way that a blade with a double bevel does. Frankly, I don't suppose I could tell the difference between sashimi cut with one or the other type of knife, but a Japanese chef could, and that is all that matters. (I did later find mine was also good for cutting slabs of ganache into squares before dipping in tempered chocolate.) They are persnickety fellows, sushi chefs. According to Shizuo Tsuji, the best keep two sets of knives for working with fish: one to use while the other set is "cooling down" after being sharpened. This isn't quite as ridiculous as it might sound to someone like me, who sharpens his kitchen knives roughly once a month. Japanese knives

may be the sharpest in the world, but they are very high mainte-
nance; their blades damage easily and require sharpening daily.
Otherwise—as I was to discover—they go blunt quickly. Yet they
heat up under sharpening and, of course, the last thing you want
near fresh, raw fish is something with even vestigial warmth.

The shopkeeper also recommended that I buy a heavy, brick-sized
whetstone, called a *toishi*, for sharpening. He showed me how to use
it, telling me to soak it in water for five minutes, then to sharpen the
knife by pushing it away against the surface of the stone, pressing
with some force, then dragging it gently back, pouring more water
over the stone every few strokes. He threw in a fish scaler for free,
too, which was nice, as I was hardly likely to be a return customer.

But what of the wasabi grater? Eventually, I found a policeman.
Not only was this sharp-witted constable able to interpret my humming of the theme from *Jaws* together with a washboard-grating
action, but he knew where I could buy one and led us there himself.

And there it was, a small piece of square wood, one surface covered with what felt like extra-coarse sandpaper, for ¥2,000, or just
under $20. Later, when I got it home, following one of the most
protracted and bitter luggage-contents-selection battles of our mar-
riage (I had to lose the packaging for my air guitar toy *and* my
tubes of sock glue to make room for it while Lissen was somehow
allowed to keep *all* her Japanese hair-care products), its purpose
and the materials used in its manufacture would prove satisfyingly obscure to all my friends. Apart, of course, from Toshi, who
pointed out, quite accurately, the folly of buying an implement for
grating fresh wasabi and then transporting it halfway around the
world to a continent where such a vegetable is unheard of.

13. SUSHI FOR BEGINNERS

doubt whether even the Japanese feel that a sharkskin wasabi grater is an essential element of their kitchen arsenal. There was certainly no evidence of one in the kitchen of Mrs. Shinobu, with whom I had a lunch date the next day.

Sixty-year-old Etsuko Shinobu is doing her shopping. "A small tin of 'sea chicken'; that's what we call tuna," she says, dropping one into her basket. "Some eggs—we prefer brown eggs in Japan; taro root; and some Kyoto sake." She shuffles around the aisles in a violet kimono, and I follow right behind.

I had found Mrs. Shinobu on the website for Japanese travel company H.I.S., which offered some interesting food-themed experiences in Tokyo, so I signed up for three cooking lessons: one at the home of a "typical" Japanese housewife, Mrs. Shinobu; the second with a Japanese chef; and finally a sushi-making class.

After Mrs. Shinobu had paid and collected her reward points, we trooped out of the shop to her nearby house: a well-manicured two-story concrete box overlooking a railway line (as most homes seem to do in Tokyo), where she lived with her husband and grown-up daughter. I removed my shoes at the door in exchange for some undersized red vinyl slippers and followed her upstairs to the kitchen–living room. She was going to cook us lunch, and I was going to help, Mrs. Shinobu announced. She invited me to put on a *tenugui*, or head scarf, and set me to work chopping daikon into matchsticks.

Meanwhile, Mrs. Shinobu set the rice steamer in motion, rehydrated some dried mushrooms, and made some dashi with Ajinomoto instant powder. She made a paper-thin omelet with egg, salt, sugar, and a little mirin in a pan, which she first heated, then removed from the heat before adding the egg, letting it cook in the residual heat only. She lined a bowl with strips of the omelet, then filled it with rice and the tinned tuna, which she had heated with some soy sauce.

"They recommend that you eat thirty different ingredients every day," she said, gently adjusting my knife grip (she had given me a sashimi knife, which works only if you slice by pulling it toward you in individual strokes). "So I try to do that. My motto is 'a little of everything.' The difficult thing is that my husband is rarely home from work before eight, and my daughter sometimes doesn't come home until midnight. I learned how to cook from my mother, but my daughter isn't interested. I do worry how the next generation is going to learn this."

Lunch was ready, and we moved through to the tatami living room. As I stepped onto the mat, I felt something grabbing me from behind. It was Mrs. Shinobu, looking aghast. "No, no, you must take your slippers off before you go on the tatami mat," she said.

More etiquette: it is rude to hover with your chopsticks over food; don't use chopsticks to move bowls and dishes around; never lick your chopsticks; never leave your chopsticks sticking down into rice; and never, ever pass food from your chopsticks to another person's—that is a funerary tradition.

I attempted all of these during our lunch. But to her credit, my Japanese host didn't bat an eye. Afterward, we adjourned downstairs to Mrs. Shinobu's tea ceremony room. It takes years to learn how to orchestrate a tea ceremony, and the correct procedure has been the subject of controversial debate for centuries. To give you an idea of the Olympian levels of pedantry involved, the tea ceremony schism starts as you enter the room—one school of thought believes it should be left foot first, the other the right. Both agree that there must be no excess of movement, and so each motion is strictly choreographed and laden with meaning, most of which was lost on me as I knelt at a point exactly sixteen ridges of tatami mat from the wall, beside the *tokonoma*—the display alcove—occupied by a vase holding a single peony, watching Mrs. Shinobu purify, brew, swirl, pour, and sip. This went on for a good forty minutes, during which time I initially lost all sensation in my legs, before the numbness was relieved by a million agonizing pinpricks.

Finally, after some frothing with a delicate little bamboo whisk, Mrs. Shinobu handed me a bowl of perfectly warm tea, instructing me to turn it twice counterclockwise before drinking from it, then to turn it clockwise before replacing it on the mat. The tea itself was thick, frothy, a vivid bright green, and awfully bitter, with notes of soil. Each of our two bowls was different, I noticed. Though beautiful, mine was slightly asymmetrical. Mrs. Shinobu spotted me examining it. "You know," she said, "this may be the only time you will ever meet that bowl; you should cherish this moment. The Japanese have a phrase for making the most of fleeting encounters: *ichigo ichie*. It means 'one encounter, one chance.'"

I cherished my tea ceremony encounter and my morning with Mrs. Shinobu. How many visitors get a chance to see inside the home of a Japanese person, let alone make and eat lunch with someone as wise and dignified as my gentle, smiling host?

Next stop on the H.I.S. food experience tour was Hifumi-an, a traditional restaurant and cooking school in Kagurazaka, a former geisha neighborhood of central Tokyo, now renowned for its top-quality but elusive restaurants. Our chef for the afternoon was Takamitsu Aihara, a welcoming but stern man with twenty-four years' experience and a recently earned Michelin star. It was his mission to impart to us the techniques and etiquette of traditional dining.

"The color of food is very important to the Japanese," the chef began. "It reflects the seasons—spring is green, then dark green for summer, autumn is orange and brown, winter is white. It is all reflected on the plate."

The half dozen students and I took some cold mashed potato, which we patted out into discs on plastic wrap. On top of this we placed a minced chicken filling, then pulled up the dough to form something the size of a tennis ball. Next, the chef gave us a dashi master class.

After showing us how to make ichiban dashi—in much the way the chefs had at the cooking competition at Hattori's school in Tokyo, though with less katsuobushi—the chef went on to explain how you can use the same katsuobushi and konbu to make a number two, or *niban*, dashi by boiling them gently for another ten minutes. "Ninety-nine percent of Japanese stock is water," Aihara said, adding just a dash of sake, some light soy sauce, and, finally, arrowroot flour to thicken it as a sauce for the potato-chicken bun.

Next came a sashimi lesson. "You cut the fish as if you are drawing a line on the board toward you with your index finger," the chef said, carving up a fresh bonito fillet, black-skinned with dark red flesh. He set a torch to the bonito to char the flesh slightly, then placed the slices on top of a bowl of rice, sprinkled a fine julienne of Japanese ginger over them, and in the middle placed an egg yolk that had been marinated in soy sauce until it had firmed up. We all had a go and ended up with a meal that was original and pretty.

The final part of my cooking lesson trilogy was the sushi class, which took place in a rather down-at-heels local sushi restaurant in southwest Tokyo, our session squeezed in between the end of lunch service and the start of the dinner rush.

Chef Eiji Hayashi had the face of a boxer and the physique to match. He was a tough, no-nonsense sushi chef, with over two decades' experience on the front line serving the most discerning sushi eaters in the world, in the city where nigiri was invented.

"There are no female sushi chefs," he announced gruffly, eyeing a couple of female students. "Their makeup and perfume taint the fish and rice. Also they have a higher body temperature, which warms the fish." (This is not actually true, but I wasn't about to contradict him.)

He showed us how to mold the rice for nigiri by using two bowls of cold water, one for washing our hands after each molding, the other for wetting them to stop the rice from sticking. He formed his hands into a *ninjitsu*—so named because it resembles the secret ninja hand signal—by placing the index and middle fingers of the right hand across the palm of the left hand, where they press a bite-size block of rice into a small rectangular box.

The rice had been steamed with a small piece of konbu and some sake, the chef explained, then tipped out into a *hangiri*, a traditional, round, shallow cedarwood tub. "It doesn't have to be cedarwood, but metal bowls might react with the rice," the chef said. "The tub must be wet, though; otherwise, it will soak the moisture from the rice." In the tub, the chef cut through the rice—now slightly cooler, but not too cold—with a wooden paddle, cooling it further and mixing in the vinegar, salt, and sugar. This rice seasoning—typically seven parts rice vinegar to five parts sugar with a half teaspoon of salt—is the real reason, I suspect, that sushi has caught on to such a degree in the West: it consists, after all, of essentially the same flavors that keep us coming back for Big Macs—sugar, salt, and vinegar. The rice for making sushi should be neither too hot nor too cold—according to Eiji-san, around 77°F is optimal, although others say it should be warmer, ideally body temperature. The main thing is it should act as a contrast to the chilled fish.

The better restaurants use expensive, short-grain rice, the best being *koshihikari*, which is dried naturally in the sun, but most use medium-grain japonica, often grown in the States (domestic Japanese rice production can't meet demand). Many also add an MSG-laced flavoring to their rice called *miora*. "When I was training to be a sushi chef, I had to spend a year just making rice before I was allowed near a fish," Eiji-san said, adding that the total period of his training had been six years, average for a sushi chef in Japan.

He invited us to try to make our own nigiri as he had shown us. We each held the lumps of unformed rice in the palms of our up-turned hands, curled the fingers of the same hand up to form a coffin-shaped hollow, closed the thumb over one end of the "coffin," and then pressed the rice into shape with the index and middle fingers of our right hands. Then the chef did something odd. He showed us how, once he had made what looked like a perfect oblong-shaped block of rice, he took his index finger and pressed down in the center, spreading the rice out once more, before re-forming it again. He did this "to air out the rice," before adding with the care-free chauvinism common to chefs the world over, "Like treating a woman. You don't want the rice packed too tightly; you want it to just hold together long enough to get into the mouth, where it should fall apart easily. And the top of the rice should be slightly pointed so that the fish stays on better." Though how this equates to "treating a woman," I still don't understand.

But this "airing" just made my blocks of rice look even more ragged and shapeless, like lumps of clay randomly squeezed by a five-year-old child, prompting open laughter from the chef and the six other students, most of whom were Japanese. I tried again, this time with more success.

I asked the chef if it was true that the best sushi chefs can get all the grains of rice in a nigiri pointing the same way. He dismissed the idea. No, that wasn't possible, he said. You should try instead to be "natural," a word he repeated several times during our demonstration.

Next we made *gunkan maki* (*gunkan* means "battleship," which they vaguely resemble), in which the block of rice is wrapped with a sheet of nori seaweed and topped with, say, sea urchin or crab. Nori is a type of algae. In its natural state, it is a reddish brown, but it turns green when it is dried. In the better sushi restaurants, the chef will briefly wave the sheets over the grill to get them really crisp before using them. Shizuo Tsuji points out that one side is rough, the other smooth, and that you should be sure to make your maki rolls with the smooth side pointing outward. The trick with gunkan maki, the chef explained, is to anchor the nori with a single grain of rice.

That was quite straightforward, but I made an almighty hash of my *ura maki*, or inside-out rolls. The trick here seemed to be to spread the rice evenly and thinly over the large sheets of nori, summon all the courage you have, and then lift the whole thing up, turning it over on your maki mat, or *makisu*. When I lifted mine, the rice avalanched inelegantly onto the table.

The best sushi chefs don't provide soy sauce for dipping, the chef continued, but make their own milder blend of dip, called *nikiri*, with dashi, mirin, sake, and soy (6¾ ounces soy; 8 teaspoons dashi; 4 teaspoons sake; 4 teaspoons mirin, briefly heated together). And they don't provide extra wasabi either—the wasabi they add within the nigiri or maki should be enough. Anyone spotted mixing wasabi in with his or her soy will immediately be marked down as a novice—after all, how can you expect to have any sensitivity left in your taste buds if you blitz them with artificial wasabi? I had already noticed that many Japanese don't use chopsticks to eat sushi; they just pick it up with their hands, and so Japanese chefs will generally pack their nigiri more densely for foreign diners who insist on using chopsticks, believing it to be correct. Sashimi, on the other hand, should always be eaten with chopsticks.

One of the other students asked the chef which was his favorite nigiri topping. Was it toro? she wondered. No, he said, he preferred uni or *engawa*, the frilly bit from the edge of flatfish (which Western chefs often discard).

The chef gave us some other useful tips: If you want really great service from a Japanese sushi chef, it requires just one word: *omakase*, which means, "I'll let you decide." And if you want to really piss a sushi chef off, just keep ordering tuna, which many restaurants sell as a loss leader. If they bring you miso soup to start, the place is probably run by Koreans or Chinese. Miso soup should come at the end of a sushi meal, as it is thought to aid digestion of the fish. Meanwhile, if you are picking from a conveyor belt, choose white fish or lighter fish to start before working your way to the salmon and tuna. Ignore spiced-up maki rolls, often employed to disguise the taste of aged fish.

In her introduction to *A Simple Art*, M. F. K. Fisher recalls how "fish leapt from glass tanks to the cleavers and pans and then into our mouths, in a ballet of accumulated motions and flavors," but in truth, fresh fish is not always desirable for sushi and sashimi. As with meat, fish needs to be left for some time—days, even—after being caught in order to reach its peak flavor. There are some exceptions, of course: eel, shellfish, and squid are worth keeping alive until the point of preparation and shouldn't be left too long after, and mackerel is notoriously perishable, but with most fish the enzymes in the flesh need time to break down the proteins and connective tissue and produce the all-important and very tasty inosinic acid that goes so well with the glutamate in dashi or soy. The bluefin tuna, for example, is better a week after it has been defrosted—kept well chilled, of course; sea bream needs a day; fugu, or blowfish, apparently is best aged between half a day and a day. The world's greatest sushi chef, Jiro Ono, now ninety-one, the subject of the famous documentary *Jiro Dreams of Sushi*, and who still works every day in his Ginza restaurant, will wrap tuna in ice for ten days until it reaches the ultimate flavor; with white fish, he might leave it for three days.

Some final sushi advice: if you enter a restaurant and see fish with what Tsuji describes as "the flaccid look of hospital patients," turn and flee, pausing only to make a quick call to your local health authority. Instead, he offers this useful advice: "When I enter a sushi restaurant, I can tell at a glance by the texture of their skins—like the bloom of youth on a young girl—whether the fish is really fresh."

14. THE "SPECIAL STUFF"

Tsuji offers no advice on evaluating whale meat. Ordinarily, this wouldn't have been a great loss as far as I was concerned. As an especially self-righteous teenager growing up in the UK in the seventies and eighties, there were two indisputable certainties in my world. The first was that Margaret Thatcher was evil incarnate; the second was that killing whales was as bad as, if not worse than, killing human beings.

Star Trek IV: The Voyage Home, in which, you'll recall, Kirk and his crew kidnap a pair of humpback whales to communicate with aliens, merely bolstered my argument with hard facts. I can remember marching on Downing Street at some point in the early eighties to protest some unspecified Nordic people who were either harpooning whales or clubbing seals, and working myself up into a right old lather. So I hesitated for a brief moment when Emi, a Japanese friend who had been helping me set up some meetings and interpreting, popped by our apartment to plan the next week's activities (it was now late September, and we were about to leave for Hokkaido) and asked if we would all be interested in grabbing a bite of whale for lunch. Admittedly, it was only a brief pause. Like all foodies, I am prone to silly boasting about eating rare or exotic foods.

("Kangaroo? Pah! Of course I've tried it. But have you tried crocodile? Oh, but you must; it is rather like chicken, you know.") I am always looking for the next food thrill, and the more it makes girls squeal, the better. Nevertheless, I still had qualms about eating a creature that makes soft, mournful noises and could outthink me in a plankton-herding contest.

In the end, I said yes, but Lissen wrinkled her nose. Asger and Emil looked at me as if I had taken leave of my senses, and, I have to admit, their horror did make me hesitate once more. But who was I to judge the Japanese? In my time I'd eaten a fair few battery chickens, drugged-up cows, and plenty of cute bunnies, tiny, fragile quails, and frogs whose legs had most likely been rendered from their bodies without anesthetic. I know whales are supposed to be really smart, but pigs are no fools either.

Of course there are rather more chickens, cows, frogs, and quails in the world than there are whales. Japan, Iceland, Greenland, and Norway stand alone as whale-eating nations these days, circumventing or simply ignoring the recommendations of the International Whaling Commission. Of the three, Japan is by far the most rapacious in its consumption of all kinds of fish, eating around a tenth of the world's catch overall. On average, a Japanese person will consume almost 154 pounds of seafood per year, compared to a global average of 35 pounds. Much of the whale meat harvested by Norwegians and Icelanders goes straight to Japanese tables.

Wherever fish are being caught in the world, there will be Japanese middlemen waiting with their wallets open and a large box of ice. In remote parts of the southern Philippines, I have seen huge Japanese fishing harbors supporting entire local economies with their demand for tuna and bonito, while over half of the tuna ranched in the southern Mediterranean ends up at the end of Japanese chopsticks. Wild Mediterranean and Atlantic tuna stocks are at perilously low levels, perhaps as low as 10 percent of the levels they were at in the sixties, a state of affairs for which the Japanese must take a good portion of the blame.

But if you ask ordinary Japanese about either the threat of tuna extinction or whales, they will regard you quizzically. This is genuinely news to them and certainly not a pressing issue in the domestic media. What is an issue, from time to time, is foreign interference in what they see as the essential traditions of Japanese cuisine. The Japanese usually claim that they only really started eating meat as a nation in 1872, after the emperor casually announced he had eaten beef for dinner—signaling a Liberty Hall for Japanese carnivores. Until that point, it was technically illegal, and although the law was widely ignored, it is true that the Japanese historically ate far more fish than meat—they still obtain more than a third of the protein in their diet from fish. It is one of the reasons, of course, for their general good health.

Today, the Japanese still kill around seven hundred to eight hundred whales a year "for scientific research," a figure surpassed only by the Icelanders, who kill around a thousand, many of them, as I've said, ending up in Japan anyway. The Japanese have long been calling for more quotas following reported gains in the populations of some species, such as southern right whales and humpbacks, which have now been removed from the endangered list. Every year at the annual assembly of the International Whaling Commission, Japan presses to be allowed to commence unrestricted hunting again. "We've been eating whale since 300 B.C.," they complain. "This is culinary imperialism."

Despite the national conversion to Buddhism in the eighth century, consumption of whale was always permitted because whales were categorized as fish, not mammals (this pragmatic approach to food classification saw wild boars renamed "mountain whales"). By the 1820s, whale cuisine had become so refined that there were recipes for up to seventy different cuts—the Japanese even cooked with whale feces. Mmm, no? With the food shortages following World War II, whale became a vital source of nourishment for the Japanese, providing an important protein and omega-3 oil source. Indeed, today most adult Japanese remember whale meat with nostalgia from the time when it was a regular item on school lunch menus. The Japanese continue to eat whale, albeit in smaller quantities, rather like we might eat venison. They claim—and to be fair, I don't think this is a disputed point—that its meat is extremely healthy, with proven antiaging properties.

So I accepted Emi's invitation and met her outside Shinjuku Station. From there, she led me deep into the shimmering maze of girlie bars and karaoke joints of Kabukicho to a doorway at the side of a shop. Up some flights of stairs we climbed until we came to the entrance to Taruichi, the whale restaurant.

The room was packed. Countless paper menus hanging from the ceiling, each decorated with large kanji characters, some with delicate pen-and-ink drawings of fish, lent it a festive air. Aside from the beautiful illustrations of frolicking whales on the screens and doors, it could have been any normal Japanese restaurant, assuming one could ignore the giant dried whale penis hanging from the ceiling like some obscure alpine wind instrument. Which I couldn't.

We set about the menu with Emi translating. There was whale bacon, tongue, ovary, brain, skin, testicles, penis, internal organs, and various cuts of meat, but sadly no droppings. You could have whale raw as sashimi, on sushi, deep-fried, or as a steak. We ordered a little of everything, and soon the plates began to arrive from the dark, hole-in-the-wall kitchen behind us. First was a bowl of glistening, chewy, beige blubber, not unlike tripe. Not nice, although Emi, who had grown up on whale meat at school, tucked in happily. A tinfoil-covered plate came next. Underneath the foil was a large, stiff, brown leaf, as big as half the table, covered with thin cuts of whale bacon and sashimi, all slightly different, with a smudge of mustard and yellow chrysanthemums for decoration. Some were edged with pink, others looked like air-dried ham, some were gray and quite unappetizing (this was skin, Emi said). The sashimi looked similar to Japanese beef, with rampant marbling and purple-red flesh. Some was challenging to chew, most of it had a fatty mouthfeel with a not-unpleasant, faint beefy flavor. I wouldn't rush to sample any of it again, particularly the deep-fried cubes of whale meat, which I struggled to break down into digestible chunks, but neither did I gag, and some of it, like the sashimi, was very good indeed. The whale ice cream was green with small chunks of whale where you might ordinarily hope to find chocolate chips. I wouldn't care to revisit that.

On our way out we met the chef, Hiroyoshi Gota. I asked what breed of whale we had been eating. He pointed to a wall chart depicting all the different types of whale, singling out the minke, caught mostly in the Antarctic. Which was the best eating? This one: he pointed with a sigh at the picture of the blue whale, not, I suspect, out of pity for its plight, but because he had no ready supplier. As we made to leave, he gave me a whale's tooth, like a giant, brown, frilly fingernail, to take with me as a souvenir.

Whale might be the largest sea creature eaten by the Japanese, but fortunately it was by no means the tastiest. This we would encounter at our next destination, the northern island of Hokkaido, famed for its abundant fish and shellfish.

15. CRABS

We flew from Haneda Airport, Tokyo's domestic terminal. Though I am not exactly phobic about flying, I have now reached the "bored" stage of what experienced fliers tell me are the three acts of air travel: at first it's exciting, then becomes tedious, and then comes the Fear. I find the whole getting to the airport, checking in, going through security, getting to the gate, queuing to get into the gate lounge, then queuing again to get on the plane—at each stage being asked to present your boarding pass, remove your belt, "No, not your boarding pass, your passport, stupid," and so on—deeply harrowing, like being a part-time refugee, but with worse catering: the Exodus sponsored by the Tie Rack. But Haneda Airport was a revelation: clean, quiet, efficient, and full of excellent shops and restaurants representing virtually every main category of Japanese food. If I had been told our trip would end there and that I had to make do with the facilities at Haneda for the next two months, I could have survived quite happily.

But we were leaving Tokyo and wouldn't return for many weeks. I was a little reluctant to go—so many restaurants, so little time— and Lissen felt the same, but after three weeks it felt right to venture forth, particularly where the children were concerned.

We had had a few food battles with Emil and, in particular, Asger, but they were gradually becoming more open to new things, and we had successfully adhered to our strict "no pizza or burgers" principle. They had enjoyed tempura and loved the ninja restaurant in Shinjuku, which we had had to enter through a hidden door and over a glass drawbridge, and where the waiters performed magic tricks. They were also now genuine sushi enthusiasts to the extent that, left unsupervised, they could easily amass a sizable tower of plates at a conveyor-belt sushi joint.

Though thrilling for us all, I did sense that the ceaseless clamor of the Japanese capital had been difficult for Asger and Emil to adjust to. Though Tokyoites are friendly and helpful and showed great interest in our boys, theirs is not an especially child-friendly city, even compared to Paris. There were no real play parks to speak of, nowhere for them to run wild and let off steam, and the sheer number of people was, I sensed, a little unsettling from time to time.

So, after Tokyo, Sapporo's space and pace came as a breath of fresh air. As did the actual breath of fresh air that greeted us as we disembarked from the plane. Hokkaido's climate is markedly different from Japan's central island, Honshu. At its northernmost tip, Japan comes within a few miles of Russian territory, and even in the southwest of Hokkaido the winters are harsh and snowbound. At summer's wane, when we arrived, the temperature was already pleasantly cool, yet still warm enough for short sleeves.

Hokkaido is vast, accounting for roughly a fifth of Japan's land area—equivalent to the size of Austria. You would have thought that with twice as many people as the UK but only a quarter of the habitable land, the Japanese would have swarmed Hokkaido centuries ago. Yet it has historically been thought of as remote and inhospitable. It was colonized only 150 years ago, and then only following government inducements to business and industry and countless "Gosh, Look at All This Space!" billboard campaigns. Until that point, it had been the home of the Ainu, Japan's indigenous people, who had arrived there hundreds of thousands of years ago, most likely from Siberia. Despite continued government prodding, still only around one-twentieth of the population lives here—just under six million people—and it boasts large tracts of wilderness and virgin forest, neither of which are the first things that spring to mind when one thinks of Japan. But Hokkaido's geography is not its only unique selling point. The food is quite different here, too.

Japan manages to produce only 40 percent of the food it needs (compared to, say, the United States, which imports about 15 percent), and a large proportion of that comes from Hokkaido. It is the nation's larder.

The island is the center of Japan's dairy farming industry, producing excellent butter, cream, and milk, and not-so-excellent cheeses (a vaguely artificial, flavorless brie sold in most supermarkets is the most widely available). They also grow potatoes and corn and, ironically, given that this is one of the poorest parts of the country, Hokkaido is home to those $150 melons (the current record for one of these Yubari King melons is ¥2.5 million [$22,000]—although, again, the purchaser was making a political statement in support of what is actually a very poor part of the country). Hokkaido is also renowned for its varieties of crab and its wild salmon.

Sapporo, its capital, seemed like a cool, relaxed city. No one was rushing, there was plenty of space on the vast, American-sized sidewalks, and the traffic was sparse. Our hotel was an eighties throwback, but pleasant enough. (It reminded me of the Sapporo hotel the protagonist of the Murakami novel *Dance Dance Dance* checks into only to discover a mysterious extra floor: a dark, dank portal into a parallel mind-zone inhabited by a strange man dressed as a sheep. Ours didn't have this.) From our room, on the sixteenth floor, we could see mountains, the ski jump built for the 1972 Winter Olympics, and, right across the street, a Ferris wheel. The air was thick with dragonflies, many of them mating as they flew.

From the moment they clapped eyes on the Ferris wheel, Asger and Emil petitioned without pause for a turn. I had my own petition going for a visit to Ramen Yokocho (Ramen Alley), filled with nationally renowned ramen noodle shops. It was a toss-up as to which of us was the whiniest and most irritating, so we split into two groups.

Ramen Yokocho is the best place to eat Hokkaido's famed *bata-kon*—or "butter corn"—ramen made with the two eponymous local ingredients. From the street, Ramen Yokocho looked like the back entrance to an office basement, an impression that was hardly altered by its interior: a dingy corridor, lined on one side by small counter-style ramen restaurants. Unusually for Japan, the owners of the half dozen or so restaurants called out to me as I walked down the corridor, gesturing to their laminated picture menus. I chose one at random and settled down at the counter for a nuclear-hot bowl of butter-corn ramen, piled high with sliced roast pork, cubes of chilled butter, tinned sweet corn, shredded spring onion, sheets of nori, and half a boiled egg, all atop a tangle of frantic, curly noodles.

It was sensational. The best ramen I had eaten so far. The oil globules on the surface of the soup had given me cause for concern as I dipped my ceramic spoon in for the first taste, but after that, I was in ramen heaven. It was porky, mildly greasy in a satisfying way, incredibly salty and garlicky, with the chilled butter and corn a shock to the palate amid the piping-hot soup. The spring onion gave it a welcome acidity and the chili oil a lingering masochistic pleasure. I tell you, that soup had it all.

I had planned to taste the ramen in at least three different places, but my compulsion to finish every last morsel of this first one, combined with its monstrous scale, meant that any thoughts of eating further were ruled out by the disconcerting sloshing of my stomach as I rose to pay.

Ten minutes later I was sitting down to eat again. Sapporo is famous for its crabs, which grow to an enormous size in the cold waters here and are exported throughout Japan. As I left Ramen Yokocho nursing my balloon belly, my eye was caught by a giant fiberglass crab waving its claws, beckoning to me from the front of a restaurant across the street. Inside, I crossed a small crab-filled moat, removed my shoes, and settled on the tatami floor at a window to taste of one of Japan's most revered delicacies.

The menu listed a royal flush of crabs: king, queen, snow, spiny, and hairy, each, judging from the picture menu, looking like some deep-sea H. R. Giger nightmare. Traditional Japanese music played as, around me, families and couples went to work diligently dismantling these fearsome crustaceans. Mine arrived: various cuts and species arranged beautifully in pieces in a bowl made from ice, with leaves, twigs, and purple and green seaweed for decoration. The taste of the raw crab was elusive; initially my taste buds struggled to find any flavor, then slowly a faint sweetness of the sea and traces of iodine emerged from the pleasantly slimy texture. The green part of the crabmeat had more flavor and the king crab the most resistant texture, but I really couldn't see what all the fuss was about. Sitting there on the floor watching the pair of giant mechanical crab claws slowly waving back and forth outside my window, I felt quite underwhelmed.

Which made what happened over the coming weeks all the more peculiar. As we traveled on south through Japan, I began to pine for those Hokkaido crabs; in quiet moments on trains and planes, my thoughts would return to their delicate flavor, but mostly it was the texture—that intriguing half-liquid, half-solid state of raw crab-meat that gave it just enough resistance to remain on one's tongue long enough for it to tease with its taste. It was another example of the Japanese's ultrarefined sense of texture. They value the feel of food in the mouth almost as highly as its flavor and certainly employ it with greater nuance than they do temperature (scorching hot is the default setting for most hot dishes), whether it be in the unsettling chewy-crunch of jellyfish, the soft rubber of mochi (rice-flour sweets), or the sharp spikes of fried panko bread crumbs. More challengingly, the Japanese also value a mealy texture in some foods—like adzuki bean paste, which features as a filling for various sweets and desserts, and also snot-like ground yam. Texture variation and contrast was one of the most revelatory aspects of my eating odyssey through Japan. There is a tremendous amount we can learn from the Japanese about combining textures in a dish, or throughout a meal, to heighten the pleasure and to broaden the sensual experience of eating.

The Sapporo crab was sensuous to the point of perversion. I still pine for it. Indeed it is one of the abiding regrets of my eating career—and unusual for me when I find something I like—that I didn't take the opportunity to stuff myself silly with Hokkaido crab every day we were in Sapporo until I never wanted to eat it again. I have, in my life, done just this with a whole range of foodstuffs, from Milky Ways to pickled onions, yet here was something really worth getting sick of, and I let it go after one tasting. A lesson for the future there, I feel.

But it was the ramen I raved about when I met up with Lissen, Asger, and Emil half an hour later. Despite my distended belly and indigestion-induced grimaces, they insisted I take them back to Ramen Yokocho. I was glad they did, as Lissen's map-reading led us to the second, more inviting part of the alley, which I hadn't realized continued across the street from the inhospitable corridor I had dined in. Ramen Yokocho II was much more atmospheric, with tightly packed diners and a bustling Friday evening mood with crowds of locals wandering, like us, bewildered by the choice and the siren smells from the various kitchens.

We chose a shop run by an elderly husband and wife who were initially alarmed to see an entire gaijin family enter their restaurant. They soon softened, and the wife—whose only English was "I'm sorry, OK?"—caught a dragonfly by the wings and handed it to Asger with a big smile. Asger took the insect gently with his thumb and forefinger. He and Emil examined it for a while, Emil not feeling quite bold enough to hold it himself but impressed by his brother's courage.

I was served some *shochu*, a potent domestic spirit distilled from wheat, sweet potato, buckwheat, or black sugar, depending on where in Japan it comes from. Why is shochu not more popular in the West? It is strong but has a light, mild taste and is a dangerously friendly spirit to guzzle. Normally served in a tumbler with a gigantic spherical ice cube, here it came in a glass jar with a removable ring-pull top. Soon our ramen arrived, not quite as epochal as my first, but still good enough for me to drain the bowl, despite its containing substantially more chili and oil. By now I felt as if I were undergoing some kind of arcane Japanese torture, my stomach and bladder pushed to the bursting point. "I'm sorry, OK?" the wife asked, meaning, "Would you like something else?" I pointed to some *gyoza* on the menu. Well, you never know when you're going to eat again, do you?

Our introduction to Sapporo had been revelatory. What else could you ask of a city but a Ferris wheel, randy dragonflies, and great ramen? But the next day cemented its place in our hearts forever.

We began with an uninspiring morning visit to the one-room Ainu Museum. Today there are thought to be less than two hundred "pure" Ainu left—that is, people with two Ainu parents—and their language and culture are on the brink of extinction. As with the Maori, the Native Americans, the Aborigines, and the low-caste Dalits in India, the Ainu suffer from varying degrees of persecution and prejudice in their homeland. Unemployment is disproportionately high among the Ainu population, and educational standards are low. This being Japan, the establishment does a very good job of keeping quiet about the Ainu, although recent legislation has helped their cause slightly. And it has to be said there are other minorities as badly off, if not worse, in Japan—the Burakumin, for example, who are genuine outcasts, ghettoized descendants of butchers or tanners and thus thought of as unclean, or the Korean and Chinese communities in Osaka and elsewhere.

The official Ainu population, including those of mixed heritage, is said to be around twenty-five thousand, although Ainu pressure groups claim there are twice as many—they simply choose not to admit to it. Alcoholism is a major problem for the Ainu, as, prior to the arrival of the modern Japanese, they drank only occasionally during rituals and have a low tolerance even today (this is not unusual; around half the population of Japan suffers from aldehyde dehydrogenase deficiency, which means their blood pressure drops when they drink).

Now, I don't want to sound even shallower than a man who drags his family to the other side of the world for some dinners may already sound, but although I was of course touched by the Ainu's plight, I was more interested in what they ate. Back in Tokyo we had visited an Ainu restaurant, Rera Cise, or "house of wind," which opened in 1994 as a focal point for the Ainu cause and to promote awareness of their culture.

An Ainu spokesman we met there had told us a little about his people: "Our religion is quite similar to Shinto, but the bear plays a very special role," he said.

"Do you know any bears?" asked Asger.

The spokesman looked puzzled. "No, but we do have a ritual where we kill a bear."

Asger went quiet.

In fact, they don't just kill the animal they revere; they eat it, too. Nineteenth-century British anthropologist John Batchelor—who founded the Ainu Museum in Sapporo—recorded that the Ainu ate bear cooked in horse fat, concluding, "In no sense are the Ainu epicures."

The spokesman had a present for Asger and Emil, he said, and pulled from a woven wool bag what looked like two fancy chopsticks. He placed one end of one chopstick over his open mouth and began to twang the other end. It was a *mukkur*, a kind of wooden Jew's harp, which he was obviously skilled at playing.

The food began to arrive: pickled cucumber and seaweed, and what the Japanese call mountain vegetables, edible wild ferns and bulbs, although these were special Ainu mountain vegetables, called *kito piro*. "They have lots of vitamin E, D, iron, and minerals, good for colds and constipation, high blood pressure, contagious diseases, and getting rid of evil spirits," our Ainu friend said. This was followed by rather less appealing deep-fried potato and pumpkin cakes, and venison, cheese, and onion wrapped in phyllo pastry, which was delicious but rather greasy and, it turned out, not all that authentic.

As I tried some slightly bitter greens, I asked why so many Ainu left Hokkaido for Tokyo: "The discrimination is much worse for us in Hokkaido. We stand out because we have thicker hair, thicker eyebrows, darker skin—people say we are stinky or dirty. There are many more foreigners in Tokyo, so we aren't so obvious. The government says there are 2,700 of us in Tokyo, but I think there is double that. Many Ainu keep their heritage a secret. You know, if you are Ainu, you cannot join the police force, for instance, and there are many other areas where there is prejudice against us. We don't have much money, so it is difficult to get a good education. The Japanese are still in denial that there were people on these islands before they arrived from Japan. They say we were only in Hokkaido, but there were Ainu people all the way to Okinawa."

Back in Sapporo, after visiting the Ainu Museum, our spirits were lifted by some deliciously nutty black sesame ice cream, and a sighting of a Daihatsu Naked as we drove across town to the city's wonderful indoor market, Nijo. Here we saw sacks of salmon roe, taut and bursting with luminous orange-red eggs; herring being smoked on the sidewalk; and a gigantic boiled octopus, its deep red tentacles curled like the ends of a Victorian villain's mustache.

We entered one shop entirely filled with open tanks of crabs. The owner, a young woman, approached us. The hairy crab was the best to eat, she said, but also the most expensive, at ¥5,000 each (around $60). She was from the southwest of Hokkaido—konbu territory. I mentioned that Asger and I were taking a trip there the next day, and she enthused about the people and the beauty of the coast. As we were talking, before we could protest, she had removed the largest king crab, with a span of almost three feet and a body as large as Asger's head, from one of the tanks and was offering it to him to hold.

Lissen, Emil, and I took a step backward and made encouraging faces. Asger offered his arms outstretched and was soon holding an eight-legged, pinky-red, prehistoric monster, easily big enough to overpower a small dog. Asger stood rigid, proud and exhilarated but with a beseeching look best described as *Will you just take the damn photograph?* To Emil, who had already seen his elder brother defeat a sumo ten times his size, Asger now attained the stature of a hero of Greek mythology. What none of us knew was that the next day we would encounter a far more dangerous natural predator.

16. SEAWEED

There are bears in Hokkaido. Not just cuddly koala types either, but proper, big, scream-for-your-mommy grizzlies. It's hard to imagine where the *higuma* hide themselves in a nation of 135 million people sardined onto usable land the size of two football fields. Perhaps a number are passing themselves off as hairy geishas—who knows?—but there are, it is claimed, thousands of them roaming free as the breeze on Japan's northernmost island.

I know for sure there are bears in Japan, because I saw one. Vicariously, but that still counts, doesn't it? It was the day Asger and I, together with my researcher, Emi, drove to visit the konbu farms that lie southwest of Sapporo, along a coast road that sticks in my memory for two reasons, the first being its majestic, volcanic splendor, with giant birds of prey wheeling in the deep blue sky above, the second, as I said, because I *didn't* happen to look up into a forested hill above the motorway and see a large, dark, bear-shaped shadow moving through the undergrowth.

Emi did.

"I just saw a bear," she said before looking back down at the map on her lap.

"What do you mean, you saw a bear?" I said, frantically craning my neck as I drove, the car veering toward the median strip.

"A bear. Up there." She pointed to a fast-receding point behind us.

I repeated the question a few times, during which, to her credit, Emi remained patient.

"Emi just saw a bear, Asger!" I shouted above the strained din of the Daihatsu's electric-toothbrush engine, but he was as under-awed as Emi. Of course she'd just seen a bear. What was the big deal? Hadn't he just the other day watched a ninja make five red sponge balls appear in his hands from nowhere at the ninja-themed restaurant in Shinjuku?

We continued along the coast road beside Uchiura Bay, heading south to Hakodate, passing through shabby, desolate towns of low-rise, corrugated iron houses and shops. Great mounds of buoys littered the empty lots between buildings, while sixty or so feet out at sea the surface of the water was covered with hundreds more, like a giant, unfinished game of solitaire—the telltale signs of a konbu "field."

I was still glancing around nervously, on the lookout for nine-foot, hairy carnivores, when we finally arrived in Minamikayabe-cho on the Pacific coast, an area famed throughout Japan for producing some of the finest konbu (sometimes spelled "kombu") in the land. Over 15 percent of all Japan's konbu—worth ¥10 billion ($89 million) a year—comes from this part of Hokkaido; they even supply the emperor.

It is hard to overestimate the importance of this great, green, leathery sea plant to the diet of the Japanese. They eat around fifty different types of seaweed, but konbu is king. It is the one constant ingredient in dashi. In traditional Buddhist cuisine, there even is a dashi that is made simply by letting a piece of konbu sit in cold water for a few hours—it is delicious, with a barely-there hint of the sea.

Konbu isn't just used to make dashi—although given the myriad uses for dashi in soups, sauces, marinades, batters, and dips, that would be enough to warrant it podium position in Japanese cuisine. They also soak it in vinegar, dry it, and then shave it to make *tororo konbu*, which is often used in miso soup instead of nori; or cook it slowly with water, soy, mirin, and sugar, then sprinkle it with salt to make *shio konbu* (salt konbu), a popular snack. It is also used as a wrapping for *saba-zushi* (pressed mackerel sushi). And, as I learned from my chastening visit to Ajinomoto, konbu, of course, has the highest levels of glutamate of any natural substance and was the inspiration for the invention of MSG.

There is every reason to believe konbu is one of the most significant foodstuffs in terms of the Japanese's famed good health and longevity. It has more minerals than anything else they eat, including potassium, iron, iodine, magnesium, and calcium, as well as vitamins B and C, and is thought to aid in the removal of toxins from the body. Seaweed also contains lignans, believed to prevent cancer. Plus, of course, it is fat- and calorie-free. As I would discover a couple of months later, the Okinawans eat more konbu per capita than any of their compatriots. And guess who lives not only the longest in Japan but in the world? The Okinawans (although there are considerably fewer bears on Okinawa, which I can't help feel must be a factor).

It is difficult to get a sense of how konbu looks in the wild from the small, dried, black-green strips the Japanese buy prepackaged in their supermarkets. I really wanted to see where konbu grows and talk to the people who farm it. Hence the five-hour drive from Sapporo (Lissen stayed in town with Emil, who was threatening to hold his breath unless he got to go on the Ferris wheel again). But konbu farmers are a secretive and suspicious bunch, wary of outsiders, perhaps because they are rumored to earn upward of $100,000 a year for tending their small plots of ocean. It had taken weeks of e-mails and phone calls from Emi to set up a meeting, and even then I eventually had to send a copy of my passport to assure them I wasn't involved in some kind of seaweed espionage.

"It's been the worst year ever for konbu," Takahiko Sasaki, head of the Minami Kayabe Fisheries Cooperative Association, explained to us when we finally arrived. "We usually produce around 3,500 tons a year, but this year it's been less than half that. The problem is storms. The konbu is very exposed and is damaged easily by rough tides."

We were standing in a warehouse beside the harbor watching a team of robust-looking middle-aged women tying together fifteen-pound bundles of whole, dried seaweed leaves, which looked not unlike tobacco, each bundle roughly the size of a bale of hay. They quite overwhelmed the tiny pickup truck sent to transport them.

Sasaki-san, wearing a polo shirt embroidered with a small cartoon of a bear playing golf, explained that the konbu is grown just beyond the harbor walls, a few yards out at sea. Konbu leaves, which are narrow and tonguelike, with frilly edges, can grow up to six yards long (over twenty yards has been known). They are a translucent, browny green and are harvested at either one or two years of age by men with bamboo poles with hooks on the end who use them to rake the leaves aboard boats. Drying has to be done within a day or the seaweed starts to turn white and the quality suffers. When it is finished, the seaweed is very dark green, stiff, and brittle, like sheets of dried spinach lasagna. Farmers traditionally begin to harvest natural konbu on July 20 and continue until late August, with folks flocking from all over the region to help pick the leaves. It is tough work, starting at two in the morning and working through to eight in the evening.

They still dry some of the konbu the natural way in these parts, first brushing it clean on a machine that looks like a giant shoe polisher, then hanging it out in the sun in large, wooden-framed open sheds. But most is dried by machine in small warehouses at around 160°F for twelve hours or so. Should you ever need to, you can tell the difference between sun-dried and machine-dried konbu, as the former is greeny brown, while machine-dried is darker, almost black. Real konbu connoisseurs can also tell where on Hokkaido a piece comes from. For instance, in the area around Minamikayabe-cho, cut a piece of konbu and it will be white inside, hence the area's name—which translates to White Mouth Beach; elsewhere the konbu will be black inside—from Black Mouth Beach, near Hakodate. There are over ten species of konbu, and it comes in a variety of quality grades, depending on color, gloss, and thickness. The thicker, the better (an eighteen-pound bundle of prime konbu will contain eighty-four pieces; a bundle of lower-grade leaves will contain more), but of course, this being Japan, appearance is the most important factor in grading—the straight, uniformly shaped konbu is most prized of all. The ultimate piece of konbu would, then, be wild grown, naturally dried, thick as a passport, glossy, and symmetrical.

The variety of konbu can have a radical effect on the flavor of dashi, ranging from delicate and light to rich and dark, depending on the beach where the konbu grew and even the year—as with wine, climate has a large effect on the flavor of each year's konbu. The very best *rishiri konbu* is laid down for two years in a temperature- and humidity-controlled process known as *kura-gakoi*, which deepens the glutamate flavor. It is much appreciated by so-called *konbuliers*, the konbu equivalent of a sommelier.

Drying makes the konbu leaves crinkle up at the edges so they look like ventagli pasta, so the higher grades of leaves are steam softened at 212°F to enable them to be rolled flat. This is done by hand using a machine rather like a mangle. We followed Sasaki-san in his truck farther west along the coast to watch this being done by a husband-and-wife team in a ramshackle shed on the beach. The husband gently fed each piece of konbu through the machine before passing it to his wife, who would trim it by hand with a pair of shears and fold each yard-long piece into thirds for packing. She'd been doing this job for thirty years, she told me.

They also harvest "wild" konbu in these parts, which, because it grows on the ocean floor, both tastes better and has more minerals than the farmed variety, which they cultivate close to the water's surface. It is far harder to harvest, of course, which means it costs twice as much. It is also even more vulnerable to the weather.

"This year, there has been practically no natural konbu," Sasaki-san told us. "Maybe fifty or sixty kilograms [110 to 132 pounds] in all. Usually we harvest a thousand. Low pressure in October meant that the seabed was damaged by rough water."

The decimation of the konbu crop—most likely as a result of climate change—would really be something to worry about for the Japanese. Perhaps it will prompt them to rethink their carbon footprint and switch off all those electric toilets.

We wished Sasaki-san and his ladies well and thanked them for their time. Asger departed with yet another handful of sweets, Emi and I received a gift pack of konbu, I gave Sasaki-san a box of English tea, and we set off for home in our Daihatsu buzz-box.

17. KYOTO STORIES

We flew from Sapporo to Osaka the next day, passing over Mount Fuji along the way. Fuji is the perfect mountain; not even the tangle of golf links encroaching on its base can spoil the quasi-spiritual effect of seeing it for the first time from the air.

From Osaka Airport, a striking example of Japanese future-scope engineering on reclaimed land in the Seto Inland Sea, we took the train to Kyoto. It was clear from the ceaseless sprawl of urban development that the two cities are, essentially, one gigantic conurbation with precious little countryside to provide breathing space between them. And the concrete sprawl continues west, too, merging into the third major city of the region, Kobe.

The three cities and their inhabitants could not be more different. Kyoto, 280 miles west of Tokyo, is the cradle of Japanese culture and religion. It was the imperial capital of the country from 794 to 1868, home to the royal household, as well as the country's spiritual and cultural heart. The legacy of Kyoto's royal history has, it is said, bred a people who are refined and aloof, not a little standoffish and secretive. Kyotoites are famed for their obfuscation in matters of diplomacy and pride in their local cuisine. The best families in Japan still keep houses here, although they might live in Tokyo.

Kyoto is located well inland and surrounded on three sides by mountains. Because of this, it remained relatively sheltered from the otherwise pervasive cultural influence of China during the Middle Ages, allowing a distinctive Japanese culture to foment in the arts of calligraphy, poetry, theater, painting, ceramics, and, of course, food.

Kyotoites consider themselves to be the most discerning diners in Japan, if not the world. The city was the birthplace of the tea ceremony and has its own highly cultivated cuisine, *kyo ryori* (meaning Kyoto cuisine), from which evolved *kaiseki ryori*, the extravagant and costly multicourse feast usually served in private rooms in *ryotei*, or inns, overlooking Japanese gardens. It still has almost two thousand temples and gardens, famously saved from atomic attack during World War II by Henry L. Stimson, the then U.S. secretary of war, who had visited Kyoto in the 1920s. He realized its cultural importance, and the eternal bitterness there would be toward America were it to be destroyed.

The more everyday Kyoto cuisine is known as *obanzai ryori* and is centered on tofu and its by-product *yuba*, the skin that forms on the surface of simmering soy milk, which is either dried or sold as it is and has the highest protein content of any foodstuff on earth. Kyoto is also known for another intriguing substance called *fu*, a kind of dough made from wheat gluten. And as Kyotoites have never tended to eat out as much as Tokyoites, the city also has a strong market culture, centered on the famous Nishiki Ichiba, which still exists in the city center.

Obanzai ryori home cooking is remarkably healthy, largely vegetarian, very low in fat and sugar, and heavy on vegetables. Recent years have seen a revival of traditional strains of local vegetables— radish, eggplant, burdock root, pumpkin, and cucumber—known collectively as *kyo yasai* (Kyoto vegetables). These previously rare strains have been rediscovered by Tokyo food lovers, too—partly out of fad value, partly because they are full of flavor, but also as a symptom of the Japanese's inherent xenophobia, exacerbated by recent health scares regarding Chinese produce. The *senshu mizu* (Kyoto eggplant) is the height of chic on the dining tables of Tokyo.

In contrast, Osaka is a massive modern metropolis with giant office towers and endless malls, great swooping overpasses, and an industrious and fluid populace quick to react to trends and demands. It has always been a trading city, dependent on constant reinvention. Its people are supposedly down-to-earth, somewhat impatient, and hungry for innovation—there is virtually nothing in the city older than thirty years. I was perhaps more excited about eating in Osaka than in any other city in Japan, having been told by François Simon, esteemed restaurant critic of *Le Figaro* (and the inspiration for Anton Ego, the coffin-faced critic in the film *Ratatouille*), that Osaka was, in his opinion, the greatest food city in the world.

Osakan cuisine is usually characterized by one word, *kuidaore*, which literally translates as "eat till you go bust"—both physically and financially. Osakans have big appetites, they love fried fast food, and, unusually in Japan, they cook with wheat flour—most famously in the form of *takoyaki* (small savory doughnuts filled with chunks of octopus); *okonomiyaki* (a kind of thick pancake with various fillings); *kitsune udon* (soft, squidgy udon noodles served in a slightly sweet dashi with deep-fried tofu skin); and *kushikatsu* (deep-fried, breaded skewers).

Kobe-ites, meanwhile, have a more international outlook. There are said to be a hundred different nationalities living in the city, squeezed onto a slender strip of land between the mountains and the sea, including some of the country's most influential expat communities. Kobe has always had stronger links with the outside world than the rest of Japan; from 1868 to 1911, it was, in theory, the only

Japanese port open to the outside world, and ships would stop off there to stock up on the city's excellent fresh water from springs beneath the mountains. Today its residents drink more wine than other Japanese and have more European-style patisseries per capita than any other city in the country (I ticked off about twenty in one afternoon with Asger and Emil—for once eagerly—in tow). Above all, though, its great culinary gift to the world has been Kobe beef—a much misunderstood name, of which more later.

We arrived at Kyoto Station late in the morning. It was warmer here. Autumn in Kyoto is characterized by an oppressive, humid heat caused by its location, surrounded by hills and mountains, quite unlike the refreshing weather we'd experienced in Sapporo.

The station is a splendid cathedral-like place whose ten-story atrium makes those old European steam-era stations, like Saint Pancras or Leipzig, look like parish churches. As usual, even for the most densely populated parts of Japan, all was calm, quiet, and ordered, and I can't express the joyous sense of ease I felt as a neurotic father, expert at fantasizing nightmare scenarios wherever I travel, to be in a country where no one will steal your bags or try to cheat you. I know there is crime in Japan, but I suspect you'd really have to go looking for trouble to find it.

We had arranged to pick up the keys to a house Lissen had found for rent on the Internet from a woman called Junko, a friend of the owners, who worked as a lecturer at the International Center on the northeastern outskirts of the city. We took a taxi across town, passing mammoth "bird perch" gateways to temples and dark, shadowy *machiya*—Kyoto's historic wooden town houses. We found Junko in the middle of a class showing a group of foreign students how to make takoyaki.

In Osaka, takoyaki (the aforementioned "octopus balls," a kind of savory doughnut with a chunk of octopus at its core) are usually served freshly made from street stalls, where they are made to order and served in a cardboard "boat," eight at a time, and come slathered in a dark, gloopy sauce made from mirin, Worcestershire sauce, ginger, garlic, sugar, sake, and perhaps dashi. They are sometimes also topped with katsuobushi shavings, which do their customary shimmy in the heat blast from the dough beneath.

To make takoyaki, you need a special cast-iron takoyaki griddle, with ten or so inch-wide, semispherical cups (at home we have a very similar Danish griddle used for making *æbleskiver*, traditional Scandinavian doughnuts). Heat it up over a stove, oil the cups with sunflower oil or something similar (not olive oil), and pour in your batter until it fills the cups to around the three-quarters mark. This is a runny batter made from cold dashi and flour, plus eggs (1⅔ cups dashi and 1⅔ cups flour, with two beaten eggs). You don't need to mix it too thoroughly, but a little more than for a tempura batter. Then add a chunk of octopus tentacle—or, if you prefer, king prawn—and perhaps some chopped *benishoga* (pickled ginger), spring onions, or something with a bit of tang to cut through the batter and complement the seafood. As the batter sets (timing is everything here), use a toothpick to turn each ball over so that the central, uncooked batter falls down into the cup, creating the other half of the sphere.

We tried some of Junko's takoyaki. They were pretty good, a tasty, almost liquid dough with the rubbery crunch of cooked octopus inside. We all soon learned, however, that you have to treat fresh-cooked takoyaki with great caution. As with the Taiwanese soup dumplings, *xiao long bao*, you need to break them open with a toothpick to let out some of the raging steam before you gingerly nibble a little dough.

After Junko's demonstration, she introduced us to some of her students from Canada, Australia, and South America. A Serbian man, called Sasha, introduced himself and explained that he was working at a restaurant in Kyoto. We must drop by, he said.

Another taxi took us together with Junko across Kyoto. We skirted the grounds of the Kyoto Imperial Palace, obscured by trees, before the taxi dived into a warren of residential backstreets in an area called Kamigyo-ku.

Our house was located deep among tightly packed houses, some modern and functional, others, like ours, wooden and ancient. The streets had no sidewalks; only tiny front yards crammed with bicycles and potted plants—or occasionally one of those boxy little Japanese cars designed like carry-on luggage to fit an exact space—divided the front doors from the street.

The house was built in the traditional Japanese style and was over a century old, Junko told us. The sliding windows had mesh covers and heavy wooden shutters. They opened onto the neighbor's windows, which were almost close enough to touch. It was as close to authentic Kyoto as we could have hoped for, not least as the doors had no locks.

Inside, it was cool and dark and smelled of dust and jasmine. The first floor consisted of one large room, empty apart from a pretty vase in the tokonoma (the display alcove). The futons, Junko explained, were folded away in the cupboards, so we began to unpack them to see if we would have enough. "There's something funny in my pillow," said Asger. It turned out to be stuffed with buckwheat husks, a traditional pillow filling. There was a small kitchen with a two-burner cooktop but no oven—Japanese domestic kitchens rarely have ovens, but do usually have a small grill—and a tatami floor with a low-slung futon sofa. Emil had followed a trail of tiny brown pellets that led underneath the sofa to several large cockroaches, which Lissen dispatched with the heel of her shoe as I supervised from halfway up the stairs. "They look like Transformers!" said Asger as the last came to an end in a crunchy squelch.

Also in the cupboards were several lightweight patterned dressing gowns. These were *yukata*. We all decided they were the coolest thing we had ever seen and put them on, only later learning that to tie them right over left is a serious breach of yukata etiquette, as this is how they dress the dead (but it at least explained the look on the face of one of our neighbors one day when I went down to take the trash out while still wearing mine). Emil in particular hadn't been so attached to an item of clothing since his Spider-Man costume.

We ventured out into our new neighborhood for the first time shortly after Junko left and soon found ourselves lost in a maze of houses.

We knew the old royal palace and its park were nearby, but our map was useless, as there were no street signs and no obvious land-marks. It didn't matter. I could have wandered for hours peering in through front windows and savoring the details of Japanese every-day life—the unlocked bicycles, the miniature shrines on every street, and the smell of incense in the air. In one parade of shops, an elderly woman sat in the middle of an open shop front mending clothes. There was a pretty good supermarket, small but still with superb fresh fish, perfect fruits and vegetables, and astonishing cuts of heavily marbled, deep-pink beef. Just around the corner from our house was a traditional soy sauce brewery. We peered in through the doorway to see three giant, dark wood barrels, each around three or four yards high with ladders up the side. I asked the man behind the counter if I could take a look and climbed up and peered into a bottomless black hole of soy, the smell deliriously rich and yeasty. Nearby was a unicycle shop; a French patisserie run by Japanese students of my cooking alma mater, Le Cordon Bleu, serving perfect croissants just like back home; while outside on the street, we passed a woman leading a dog with two wheels where his back legs had once been. "Transformer dog!" said Emil. It seemed the kind of neighborhood where anything could happen.

A short walk away we came to a wooden workshop clearly of great age, where they made fu, or wheat-gluten cake. Fuka, as we discovered, is the supplier to the royal household and numerous top restaurants and was founded over a century and a half ago. Inside, I met Shuichiro Kobori, the son of the owner, who very generously— considering we had no appointment—showed us around and explained how this curious foodstuff is made by mixing flour with the beautifully soft water from their centuries-old well in the backyard. The resulting dough is kneaded under constantly flowing water so that the starch sinks to the bottom, leaving pure wheat gluten, which is formed into a sticky, rubbery block. The technique originated in China and came to Japan with the Zen monks as a kind of meat substitute used to bulk up hot pot dishes. You can fry fu as well as boil it, and Fuka sold theirs in a variety of colors and flavors. Kobori-san was especially proud of their new bacon and basil flavors.

On our way home, we were drenched by a thunderous downpour. We had no choice but to brave the rain, as we had no umbrellas and were, again, slightly lost. The wind was whipping up, too. Treetops were bending. A rubbish bin bounded across the road, narrowly missing us. As an old typhoon hand, I recognized the signs.

The typhoon, which we later learned was a force eleven—far stronger than the one in Tokyo—showed no signs of abating, but we had to make a move and run for it back to our house, which, fortunately, turned out to be only a few seconds away.

The next day, more tribulations: a wasp nest appeared just above the front door. I first became aware of it when I was dive-bombed by insects the size of Coke cans. Something had to be done. Preferably by someone else.

I made a dash for it, engulfed by loud buzzing, and grabbed a passing neighbor, a mother out with her two sons. She looked aghast and hurried off, returning a few minutes later with a large can of insecticide. She said something in rapid-fire Japanese and hurried off again, this time leaving her two sons standing looking at me with shy curiosity. She returned, spoke at length again, then just stood, waiting. I smiled awkwardly. Did she expect me to do something? Surely not to go and spray those monstrous zeppelins. I could see Asger and Emil peering out of the first-floor window at the two Japanese boys, who were around their age. Knowing they were playmate-hungry, I beckoned them out, somehow in that moment stupidly forgetting all about the wasps.

Emil exploded from the front door, in his customary excitable, pre-play frame of mind, and almost immediately, as if they had been waiting for just such an opportunity, one of the wasps stung him slap bang in the middle of the forehead. He screamed, which only made the other wasps even more agitated. I rushed him indoors, where Lissen applied some mom magic (from the same knowledge bank that tells her exactly what to do with red wine stains on white carpets and bubble gum on a wool sweater) in the form of a hastily assembled unguent.

By the time Emil's screaming had subsided, there was a knock at the door. A young man in a gray suit was outside with a bicycle and a clipboard. He didn't look like a pest controller, but I assumed that's what he was and followed him outside, where, from a safe distance, I watched him liberally douse the wasps with the neighbor's insect repellent.

This really annoyed them. They swarmed from their nest and flew off on various seemingly random trajectories. They didn't get far. Within about ten seconds, they began dropping from the sky like a biblical plague, landing on the ground, where they twitched and fizzed before finally conking out.

The man made a few ticks on his clipboard. I tried to offer him some money, but he looked horrified, bowed, got on his bike, and cycled off. I thanked the neighbor, and she beckoned us into her house for tea and mochi and awkward smiling silences.

That night on television, we watched Baruto, our Estonian sumo friend, win seven bouts out of seven at a tournament in Osaka, which meant that he stood a good chance of ascending to the next division. There was an unforgettable moment during the third bout. "Look," said Asger. "His nappy's coming off!" The two wrestlers had literally frozen in mid-grapple while the referee helped Baruto's opponent retie his gusset. Once he was neatly trussed once more, they resumed the bout exactly as they were, as if nothing had happened. Asger and Emil were so taken with this spectacle, they spent the rest of the evening reenacting it for us.

I know I promised not to mention anything about Japanese toilets. I am sure you have heard plenty before about how they have bracing jets of water and steam, play music or fake flushing noises, and generally make going to the lavatory a thoroughly twenty-first-century experience. But such things were all very new to Asger. Our house may have been traditional in virtually every respect, but there was one room that had more microprocessing power than *Apollo 13*: the bathroom. It contained the most sophisticated lavatory I have ever seen—it did everything short of reading the newspaper aloud for you—and it didn't take Asger, renowned in our family for his ceaselessly inquisitive fingers, long to start exploring the control panel for its blue-sky/clean-bottom capabilities. He grew rather obsessed to the extent that, throughout our three weeks in Kyoto, whenever Asger had gone missing for more than a few minutes, we always knew where he would be: sitting on the toilet with a faraway, almost transcendental smile on his face.

The evening of the wasp attack, with Emil now sporting a bindi on his forehead, we walked beside the Kamo River, which runs through the eastern side of Kyoto. Cranes and bats caught the moonlight as they skimmed the water. Courting couples sat with their legs dangling over the sloping embankments. There were distant sounds of traffic, clamorous pachinko parlors, and water rushing over a weir. The western bank of the river is overlooked, high above on stilted platforms bedecked with lanterns, by the restaurants of

Ponto-cho, the nightlife area frequented by the "practitioners of the arts," or geisha, of which there are said to be around five to ten thousand still in Japan.

A few minutes later we were sitting down to eat on one of the restaurant terraces, tucking into deliciously tender beef cheek cooked in soy sauce. Emil chomped happily on crunchy chicken-cartilage yakitori, which was becoming one of his favorite Japanese dishes. Through the bamboo fencing that divided our restaurant from a more expensive neighbor, we saw occasional flashes of butterfly-colored kimonos and glossy black hair. It was, sadly, as close as we would get to the world of the geisha.

18. THE KYOTO COOKING CIRCLE

Kyoto is a small, rather insular city in which it is impossible to pass unnoticed for too long, particularly if you are a temporarily resident foreigner with an entourage of two small children who have no qualms about going out dressed as their favorite superheroes. It is a city of whispers, rumors, secrets, and gossip, so it didn't take long for word of our arrival to get out. But Japanese whispers clearly have much in common with the Chinese kind, as, a week after arriving, I received an e-mail from something called the Kyoto Cooking Circle, the city's leading cooking club, run by a woman called Natsumi. How she got my name and e-mail address, I never really found out, but her sources were clearly a little out of the loop.

She wrote:

> Dear Mr. Michael,
> Welcome to Kyoto! We are here at the Kyoto Cooking Circle, welcome you. You are French chef? Yes. Please to come to show us French cuisine? We meet on Wednesday. Please telephone.
>
> Thank for kindly intercourse,
Natsumi

I rang the number.

"Ah, Mr. Michael, please to talk to you!" said Natsumi.

I explained that I wasn't really a chef, but had written a book about training to become a chef and had worked in a couple of Michelin-starred restaurants in Paris.

"Yes! Good! So you will make a demonstration?"

"What, you mean, come and show you how to cook? I don't thi—"

"Yes, yes, that's good, thank you. We're looking forward."

"Well, I suppose so. I mean, what kind of—"

"Good! Good! You can come Wednesday, eleven!"

And she hung up.

"I think I've just been press-ganged into giving a cooking demonstration," I announced to the rest of the family.

"That's great," said Lissen, who had often let it be known she didn't think I got out enough. "It'll be good for you to get out a bit. Think of it as 'giving something back.'"

I replied that, personally, I would have thought traveling half-way across the world might count in some quarters as "getting out a bit," but I had to agree that, having spent the last month making often unreasonable demands upon Japanese hospitality, it would be good to offer something in exchange. But what was I going to show them? What ingredients were available to work with? It was time for a trip to Nishiki Ichiba, Kyoto's famous food market.

If you are looking for ingredients for a classic French cooking demonstration, you could hardly choose a less fertile hunting ground than Nishiki Market. Aside from the fresh fish, virtually nothing is recognizable from the European larder. Even some of the fish looked like they had come from other planets, not least the dried, flattened octopuses hanging on a line like Neptune's washing. That, of course, is part of the thrill, and to me, Nishiki is as thrilling a market as they come, its 123 vendors, lined up on either side of a colored, glass-roofed corridor (a distinctive Japanese species of shopping mall called *shotengai*), sell the kind of produce you simply will not find anywhere else in the world. There were freaky things to see at every turn; even Asger and Emil were captivated.

The smells were arresting, too—dried seaweed; roasted chestnuts; funky, fruity miso; and tangy pickles all mingled in the muggy, crowded alley. The market was packed the afternoon we visited with housewives, chefs, and tourists poring over ¥50,000 ($443) matsutake mushrooms (similar to porcini, as prized in Japan as truffles); inspecting the local kyo yasai—the rare Kyoto vegetables that even other Japanese would be hard-pressed to identify; the knives at Aritsugu, knife makers to the imperial family; and vast tubs of pickles. Kyoto is the pickle capital of Japan, and there were entire shops dedicated to preserved vegetables, cured mostly in glistening, wet rice bran.

Emil's eye was caught by a packet of dried scallops that looked like Queen Elizabeth I's wooden false teeth. He had mistaken them for boiled sweets. Though usually well behaved when shopping, Emil can sometimes become intensely covetous of improbable items. He once had a screaming meltdown in a hardware store over a bulk pack of red clothespins, for instance. From experience, I could tell from the way his body had gone rigid, like a pointer on a scent, that we were in for a torrid battle. He wanted those scallops, and he wanted them bad.

> **EMIL:** I'm hungry. [*Translation: I am not remotely hungry, but I want those.*]
>
> **ME:** Well, you will have to wait for dinner now, Emil. We've had lunch. [*Translation: We both know where this is going, but we have to follow the usual procedure.*]
>
> **EMIL:** [*Pulling hard on my arm*] Can I have some of those? [*Translation: You know what's coming if you say no.*]

ME: No. You won't like them. [*Translation: We both know I
   will say yes eventually, but after that you are on your own.*]
EMIL: [*Makes noise like a car alarm*]
ME: How much are these, please?

Emil immediately spat his scallop out onto the floor and started
licking his brother's T-shirt to eradicate the taste, something I don't
think the shopkeeper had ever seen before. I apologized and started
to clear up the mess, making a big deal out of tasting the scallops
myself and showing my approval. Dried scallops are one of a range
of unique Japanese drinking snacks, most of them with a funky-salty
flavor profile (dried fugu fins are another, as are fermented sea cucumber entrails). The scallops are supposedly excellent with sake,
but I never want to see one again as long as I live. Emil made it clear
that he felt the same way. "Dad, why did you give that to me?" he
asked, bewildered by his father's cruelty.

This did little to calm my mounting sense of panic that I wasn't
going to find any ingredients that I could use in my demo. The lack
of ovens ruled out half my repertoire; there was no pork to be seen,
nor any whole chickens; the beef was all Japanese, and so suitable
really only for Japanese dishes; the only flour was rice flour; and
there were few dairy products. There was plenty of *kamaboko* (ground
white fish, steamed and formed into cakes), tofu, yuba, and fu, but
nothing I had the faintest idea how to cook.

In the end I decided on a simple fish dish—sea bream with a
sauce made from a reduced fish fumet that I would make from
its bones, with a *brunoise* of tomatoes and fine-chopped chives
for a little color. I found some fennel bulbs, which, sliced fine
and wilted in white wine and butter, would make a bed for the fillets. I also picked up some Valrhona chocolate—at a shocking
price—and, after much searching, some tiny cartons of cream,
both found in a posh supermarket food hall nearby. I figured

that if things went badly, I could also show them how to make truffles.

The Kyoto Cooking Circle met in a light, airy kitchen on the third floor of a large educational building in the center of town, just a couple of minutes' walk from Nishiki Market. Two dozen expectant faces—all but one of them female—greeted me as I entered the next morning with my produce, confident that, as I would be making a dish I had made many times, and I had the session planned, things should go well.

Kyotoites are famously inscrutable and aloof—a legacy of the city's time as a royal seat during Japan's most highfalutin cultural era—so I don't know for sure what the lunching ladies really thought of my demonstration, but I do know this: halfway through, as I was frying the bream fillets in a cast-iron pan to get their skins nice and crisp, I looked up and saw just the slightest flickers of consternation on the faces of my audience.

This unsettled me slightly, but it took a few more moments, as the smell of frying fish began to fill the air, before I realized they found the whole notion of frying a fish until cooked all the way through not a little repellent. The Japanese might sometimes grill a whole *ayu* (a river fish) or eel over white-hot coals, or at a push steam a whole fish, but the Kyoto Cooking Circle was not impressed by this self-proclaimed French chef frying up what the Japanese consider to be their "king of fish."

Finally, one of the students sheepishly raised her hand to ask a question. "Yes?" I said, thankful for the interruption.

"Why do you cook the fish?" she said. "In Japan, we do not do this."

I thanked her and tried to explain how the protein in fish changes its texture and enhances the flavor if you heat it, how nice the crisp skin is, and so on, but my heart wasn't really in it. Cooking a fish as beautiful and fresh as that sea bream was like spray painting a wild orchid a different color to match your furnishings.

I did redeem myself slightly with my fine dicing of the tomato, which prompted appreciative cooing noises, but things soon took a turn for the worse again when I moved on to the chocolate truffles, which melted almost instantaneously in the heat.

As I stood there, soft chocolate oozing through my hands, smudged on my white shirt, and dripping on the floor, I had one of life's great *What am I doing here?* moments. Not for the last time in Japan a thought struck me: *Everything I know is wrong. Everything I have been taught about food is overblown, overcomplicated, fussy, and wasteful. What am I doing showing these people what to do with bream and some tomatoes? I should be watching them cook.*

So that is what I did.

Luckily, I wasn't the only act on the bill that day, and soon we had all gathered around a new teacher, Mrs. Oka, who was going to show us how to make proper Japanese food. At least, that's what I had hoped. However, in honor of their Western visitor, the Kyoto Cooking Circle had decided to demonstrate a yoshoku dish, one of a range of Japanese-Western hybrid dishes, like "rice and curry" and tonkatsu (pork schnitzel), that the Japanese have adapted and made their own—in this case it was *omurice*, or rice-filled omelet covered with ketchup.

Mrs. Oka began by making a stock from carrot, onion, and celery, to which she added two chicken tenderloins. After they had cooked awhile, she sweated some onion while adding the stock to a roux, made from flour and butter. She cooked with the quick efficiency of an accomplished chef: no movement was extraneous; there was no stress. To the stock she added some mirin, red wine, and Worcestershire sauce—a favorite with the Japanese since the late nineteenth century, when it was introduced by the British via India. Reduced, this stock made for a lovely, dark brown demi-glace sauce.

Into the steamed rice went the tenderloins and carrots, now chopped, along with the onion she had sweated earlier, some boiled peas, and ketchup. For the omelet she gently beat milk and eggs together with chopsticks, poured the mixture into a hot pan, and, when it was cooked, used it as the wrapping for a mound of the rice mixture, molding it into the shape of a rugby ball with some grease-proof paper. An elegant drizzle of the sauce and some ketchup finished off the dish.

As I was finishing off my mouthful, the lone male of the group approached. It was Sasha the Serbian, whom we had met briefly at Junko's takoyaki demonstration a week earlier (I did say it was a small city).

"Good demonstration, but I don't think cooking the fish was such a great idea," he said, smiling warmly.

Sasha, it turned out, was training to be a chef, working by night in a restaurant in the city and attending cooking classes during the day. It takes six years to train to be a chef in Japan, and he had already completed three years of his improvised education, working in the kitchens of various Kyoto restaurants and learning Japanese. He looked washed-out, pale, and exhausted. "It is very, very tough," he said. "They shout at you a lot, and the hours are endless. The food in Kyoto is very, very beautiful. The Kyoto style is small and expensive, but the most beautiful in Japan." He paused, picking at his portion of omurice and looking at it doubtfully. "But I am not sure it is the best tasting . . ."

We talked about the Kyoto food scene. Sasha insisted that I come and eat at the restaurant he was currently working at, called, for reasons I never fully understood, the New Sapper. "The chef is old, but he is a master. He is amazing. He changes the food every night. Once a month the richest man in Japan eats there, and he cooks something very special for him."

What kind of a restaurant was it? "It is a karaoke restaurant," he said. I wrinkled my nose. "No, I know they are usually bad, but this one is very sophisticated. There are no separate rooms; you sing on a stage in front of the other guests. Very elegant."

I thanked him for the invitation, and we did later eat a memorable meal at the New Sapper. I shan't easily forget Asger's karaoke version of Aqua's "Barbie Girl"—the slow-dawning realization of just how explicit the lyrics actually are, and the open distress on the faces of the other diners at having to endure a heavily amplified six-year-old singing his heart out. But I had a proposition of my own for Sasha the Serbian. It involved hard alcohol, massage, and farm animals . . . but before that, a couple of more uniquely Kyotoite experiences awaited.

19. THE MOST BEAUTIFUL MEAL
IN THE WORLD

The most exquisite recipe book I have ever seen is called *Kaiseki*, a lavishly photographed journey through a year in the Kyoto restaurant Kikunoi, written by its head chef and owner, Yoshihiro Murata, with forewords by Ferran Adrià and Matsuhisa Nobu. The recipes are almost all dauntingly complex—some have up to fourteen separately prepared elements—staggeringly beautiful, and founded upon a devout reverence for seasonal ingredients.

The recipe for chilled tomato soup is one of the simple ones: "Push some tomatoes through a sieve. Simmer half the juice until it thickens, then add the other half, some salt, light soy sauce, and lemon juice." That's it. Of course, it relies upon the very finest fruit plucked straight from the vine at the point of optimum ripeness, but for elegant simplicity, it cannot be surpassed.

Kaiseki is the traditional meal that is, for many, the pinnacle of Japanese cuisine: an ultrarefined, multicourse piece of culinary performance art that, in its modern incarnation, has developed from the paradox of Zen-like restraint with no expense spared. Many chefs in the West are coming to appreciate that kaiseki may well represent the ultimate expression of the culinary arts.

Kyoto is the home of kaiseki. It evolved there from the fourteenth century onward, initially as an accompaniment to the tea ceremonies so beloved by the city's noblemen and royal court. From the early seventeenth century until well into the nineteenth, when Japan was virtually closed to the world during the *sakoku*, or national isolation, the tea ceremony and all those other intimidatingly rarefied pastimes, like kabuki, flower arranging, calligraphy, pottery, and Bunraku, began to mutate into their uniquely Japanese forms.

Kaiseki began rather more simply as just miso soup with three side dishes (in fact "soup and three" remains the basis of any Japanese meal, like "meat and two veg" in the West), intended to soak up all the undesirable elements—the tannins, the caffeine—in the vast quantities of tea participants had to drink. This *cha-kaiseki*, as it was called, then developed under the influence of the vegetarian cuisines of *shojin ryori* and the local Kyoto cuisine, *kyo-kaiseki*, into the classical nine-course kaiseki meal for which, today, Japanese captains of industry pay tens of thousands of yen to eat in what are often, effectively, private members' restaurants.

This ritualistic repast didn't get the name *kaiseki*—meaning "bosom" and "stone," referring to the practice of monks holding warm stones to their chests to stave off hunger during winter—until the 1850s. I read about this in *Modern Japanese Cuisine*, by Katarzyna Cwiertka, who argues that though the Japanese revere it as an ancient art, the kaiseki we know today was actually created by two twentieth-century chefs, Kitaoji Rosanjin and Yuki Teiichi, and was given economic and social impetus by the postwar economic boom and food television.

Today, Kyoto's finest kaiseki restaurants are housed in ancient wooden villas, mostly in the eastern temple district, and surrounded by precision-tended gardens of other-worldly harmony. Their tatami rooms are graced with priceless wall hangings and ceramics, and meals are served on porcelain and lacquerware that can be hundreds of years old and valued at millions of yen. The ingredients used are no less rarefied. As Shizuo Tsuji writes in *A Simple Art*, when the Japanese talk about seasonal ingredients, this can sometimes refer to a type of produce that is available for just a couple of weeks—sea-cucumber roe, for instance: the sea cucumber spawns only once a year, and its roe have to be eaten at the peak of freshness. These are some of the ingredients kaiseki chefs value most highly of all. The plates and bowls will change with, and evoke, the season, too, often obliquely. To give you some idea of what the outsider is up against in trying to decode a kaiseki meal, the bowl the soup is served in might be a copy of another, more famous bowl, the reference being the season the *original* bowl references.

To experience a kaiseki meal was one of my prime ambitions during our time in Japan, but not only are most Kyoto kaiseki restaurants fearfully expensive, many also have an unwritten "no foreigners" policy. Others are closed even to most Japanese, apart from invited guests. But Murata is unusual among the world of kaiseki masters in that he has, over the years, built a public profile in Japan and beyond, appearing on television and publishing books. He had, I also knew, trained in France in his early years, before taking over Kikunoi from his father (who had inherited it from his father), and had a more relaxed attitude toward kaiseki traditions. He was the first kaiseki chef to use a food processor, for example, which even today is felt by some to be sacrilegious—part of the essence of kaiseki being the effort that goes into its preparation. The more hard-core kaiseki chefs serve only raw or cold food, but Murata serves hot dishes and meat, including duck and foie gras. He calls his restaurant "a culinary amusement park for adults."

There are some Japanese who say that kaiseki can never be properly understood by outsiders, that the symbolism, the references within references, the "humor," the intricate appreciation of the seasons, and the tiny portions are beyond our ken, but if I wanted to learn more about kaiseki, Murata was my best chance.

Lissen and I agreed that it would be testing Asger's and Emil's patience beyond reasonable endurance to expect them to sit through a contemplative dinner lasting several hours, plus they probably wouldn't do much for the restaurant's serenity levels, so, as we had no babysitter, I would dine alone (believe me, of all my self-indulgent dinners during our time in Japan, this was the one I had to barter most heavily with Lissen for, the starting point for negotiations being that she and I would return together someday). It was a misty, steamy evening as I made my way to Higashiyama, the temple district in the eastern part of Kyoto, my taxi passing the famous 1,200-year-old Tō-ji temple, featured in many a Kurosawa film, on the way. The low clouds touched the rooftops, hugging the base of the hills that enclose the city, and with the tourist hordes gone for the day, the only sound as I walked through the flagstone-lined alleyways was the calling of crows and the chirruping of cicadas.

As I arrived at the large, ornate wooden building, an Australian woman, clearly overawed by the occasion, had misunderstood the doorman's invitation to remove her shoes, and was attempting to enter the restaurant on her knees. The restaurant staff rushed, embarrassed, to help the poor woman to her feet. *There but for the grace of God go I*, I thought to myself. Kaiseki has an intimidating reputation for elaborate ritual and etiquette, which I was almost certain to fall foul of during the course of the evening.

I was shown into a large tatami room with wooden beams, an elaborately woven wooden ceiling, and beige clay walls. There was just one low, red lacquer table at the far end of the room and a floor seat—just a back and base, no legs. I was to be the sole diner. I creaked down into place and sat, imbibing the stillness, looking out through the large plateglass window over the moonlit courtyard, the air-conditioning humming gently in the background.

I was already feeling pleasantly relaxed as a young waitress in a kimono poured me some sake. It was Kikunoi's own, delicate yet full of nuanced floral flavors, the best I had ever tasted. She returned moments later carrying a woven basket. She lifted the lid. Inside was an ayu, a small river fish, at the height of its season. It flapped around, glistening, fresh, and alive. The waitress indicated that the ayu and I would meet again during the course of the evening, put the lid back on, and left.

My next visitor was an older woman, immaculately coiffed. She introduced herself in English as the chef's wife. "This is a special room," she said, smiling calmly. "We call it the bridge, just like the bridge of a ship. You can see everything coming and going from here. In the spring, the front garden is full of cherry blossoms. You must come back then."

We chatted about children and the seasons, which she said were the beginning and end of Kikunoi's cuisine. We talked, too, about her husband, whom she clearly adored, then she bowed and left me to enjoy my meal.

The first course of a kaiseki meal, the *sakizuke*, is, according to Murata, the most important. "It must be something to put the diner at ease," he writes in his book. Mine was a walnut tofu with Delaware grapes, tiny *shiso* flowers, and a dashi en gelée, thickened with some kuzu root to a light paste. The walnuts brought a welcome crunch to the cool, fresh tofu, while a touch of raw wasabi added a playful zing. It was soothing and stimulating, and gone all too quickly.

The *hassan*, or second course, is "an overture to establish the seasonal theme"—in this case a dashi with chrysanthemum leaves floating on the surface. As I write this some weeks later, I can still conjure the aroma of the clear dashi, lightened by yuzu juice, with its spongy piece of *hamo* (pike conger, technically a fish, though closely resembling an eel, which must be sliced twenty times per inch with a special knife to render its many bones edible), a slice of the rare and expensive matsutake mushroom—rich and woody—and a golden crescent of solid egg custard within. It was autumn in a bowl, and at the bottom were pieces of toasted rice that must have been added literally as the bowl went out the kitchen door to retain their crispness. Sashimi, lightly grilled barracuda sushi, consommé, duck breast marinated in koji (the fermenting agent added to sake), chestnut rice, and pickles all followed in leisurely succession, slowly stretching my belt like the ring around a bulging barrel. Each course—and these are just some that I ate that evening—was rigorously constructed, immaculately plated, and full of compelling flavors and textures.

One course was yet more entrancing still. It came contained within a bamboo cricket cage. I lifted the cage to find a cube of hamo, alongside another cube of eel-roe cake (looking like a chunk of omelet but with a mealy texture and mildly fishy flavor), with chewy, bittersweet, sake-glazed ginkgo nuts and a grilled chestnut the size of a golf ball. On top were what looked at first glance like two pine needles but were in fact delicate, thin green tea noodles. Salted ayu entrails were stuffed into a hollowed-out *sudachi* (a type of citrus) alongside. In his book, Murata-san writes of this dish that he wanted to "evoke a little of the sad and sentimental feeling we have for departing friends," in this case the crickets leaving as autumn arrives. This kind of sentiment, inspired by the passing of the seasons, is characteristic of kaiseki and can equally apply to a new ingredient. Of another dish he writes, "I hope to evoke a feeling of picnicking under cherry trees on a regal crimson carpet, while watching the delicate pink petals fluttering elegantly to earth." Hard to imagine Gordon Ramsay writing something like that, isn't it?

The ayu fish turned up later, incidentally, salted, grilled whole, and threaded through a skewer in an S shape, as if leaping across the waves.

The next day I had arranged to meet with Murata-san himself, back at Kikunoi. I was shown into a large meeting room overlooking the front yard and decorated, somewhat incongruously, with mid-nineteenth-century French antiques. Murata entered, a stocky man with short, wavy black hair and a lived-in, walnutty face. I had been expecting a severe, humorless Zen-master type, but the chef was relaxed and welcoming. He smiled warmly and invited me to sit opposite him.

I thanked him for the meal the previous evening, and we talked a little about some of the dishes I had eaten and their ingredients. I wanted to know if he thought Kyoto was still the preeminent food city in Japan. I knew he had opened a restaurant in Tokyo, so I wondered if Kyoto wasn't perhaps rather too stuck in its past to be relevant today.

"Yes, Kyoto is still the best," he said, as if there were no question. "The level of quality is actually low in Tokyo. It is too easy to have a success there; there are too many people. We only opened there to be able to serve authentic Japanese cuisine there because they didn't have it, and it is the gateway to the world, like Paris is for France."

I knew that as a young man in the early seventies Murata had served an apprenticeship in Paris. What was that like? His smile vanished. "I soon learned that the French knew nothing about Japanese food. They laughed at me. They said Japanese food was never a proper meal, just food. Even today I sometimes can't like the French. I think they are a little crazy, but in a way everything started for me there."

I thought of my friend Toshi, who had experienced similar chauvinism some decades later. Having trained in France and Japan, how did Murata compare the two nations' cuisines? "For me, the difference between Japanese and French cooking comes down to this: In Japanese cooking we think the ingredients are a gift from God, and we try not to change them too much; we think a daikon is in its ultimate form as it is. It seems to me that often French chefs want to change the things they cook with, to put their own mark on them." In other words, in Japan the chefs work with what God provides; in France the chefs think they are God. Murata echoes this in his book: "When I was young I thought it was my job to always add another taste dimension to every ingredient. But these days I find that approach a little arrogant. The real work of the chef is to coax out the fundamental taste that is innate to any ingredient."

He continued on the subject of the differences between Japanese and Western cooking: "In haute cuisine, you cook by adding or layering flavors of different ingredients in complex ways; in Japan, and particularly in Kyoto, where we cook mostly with vegetables, the aim is to extract the essential flavor of each ingredient by removing those we don't particularly want, like bitterness. Japanese cuisine is a cuisine of subtraction."

"It must be gratifying that the world is starting to take notice of kaiseki," I said.

"Yes, indeed, very, because I hadn't expected to reach the point where the world is watching with deep interest. They are starting to realize that Japanese cooking fits well into a civilized era; it uses many ingredients in small volume, just a thousand calories for an entire meal. This has been my life's work." He sat back in his chair with a broad smile.

Right now kaiseki is the hottest restaurant trend in New York, but can it conquer the world? "I see some possibilities, but kaiseki doesn't use oil or grease, and the food is extremely lean. It will be rather complicated to bring it to a wider audience. You need to eat a certain quantity of a food to understand, to appreciate it, for your senses to adjust. As when you eat truffle for the first time, you don't really understand the flavors. The first time people eat kaiseki food, they do not notice the tastiness. It took some years for uncooked fish to be eaten in the West, for you to discover how tasty it can be. Right now kaiseki is too subtle, I think, for Western palates. Think about wasabi. That was a taste that you had to acquire. In Japan, we had to learn to like bread. At the start, we used to sweeten it with bean paste. We thought French bread was too crisp, so we made it softer to suit our palates.

"And then there are the cultural differences," Murata continued. "Once in America I was invited to a Japanese meal. I was served yakitori, sushi, teriyaki, and they said that was kaiseki! No, I said, that is not kaiseki. For kaiseki, you must have two elements: nourishment for body and mind and the seasonal element."

At times, the meal I had enjoyed the night before had veered close to the transformative theatricality of molecular cuisine. I knew that kaiseki had directly influenced the multicourse style of meal pioneered in the West by French chefs like Joël Robuchon, which the molecular chefs have in turn taken to an extreme, but I wondered if Murata-san saw any parallels.

"Ferran Adrià is a good friend. He has been here, of course. He is a genius. But for me, food is either delicious or not, interesting or not. My philosophy is to do anything I can to bring pleasure to my guests, regardless of whatever category of cooking other people call it, and I think Adrià is the same. If he thinks it will delight his guests to use liquid nitrogen, then I cannot argue. If I have to stand upside down, then so be it. Although, obviously, I can't." He laughed. "I have to say, he makes tempura at 450°F, but I still think authentic tempura tastes better, and for me, taste comes before surprise. Saying that, in order to pass down traditions, you need to protect some things, but to break from traditions, too. I am cooking for my guests, not for me or for posterity. I am not interested in acclaim."

As we talked, behind him, in the courtyard below, I could see his many chefs scampering to and fro carrying pots and plates. No one walked; everyone trotted. Later, after proudly showing me his

new, state-of-the-art kitchen ("all Japanese"), Murata-san introduced me to Derek Wilcox, a young American intern who had
been working at Kikunoi for six months. "It has been tougher than
I ever imagined," he told me, looking a little shell-shocked. "I work
from six in the morning to midnight every day without a break." I
half expected him to slip me a note saying, "Please help me. They
are holding me hostage!" What kept him going? "Sometimes I really
don't know. I think it's about how deep the education is—you learn
everything here from simple home cooking to the most sophisticated
exotic ingredients. Murata-san is so open to young chefs. It can take
decades to learn this stuff. For the first year, all I do is clean up, wash
dishes, wash towels, scrub the bathroom in the dorm, prepare vegetables, gut and scale fish—some days I do over a hundred fish. But
I decided Kyoto was the best place to come to learn to cook."

The night before, I had left Kikunoi in the late evening. The air
was humid. I took a deep draft of the smell of fresh rainfall and
damp pine. The alleys of Higashiyama were deserted and dark. If it
hadn't been for the glow of the soft yellow streetlights, I might have
been walking through the city in the fifteenth century on my way
to an assignation with an obliging geisha or to disembowel myself
according to the samurai code for some breach of chopstick etiquette. I turned a corner and arrived at a great, four-story pagoda
lit only by lanterns and candles. I stood still for a moment, holding
my breath, reluctant to break the spell.

20. FIRST TAKE YOUR CRYSTAL-CLEAR, FREE-FLOWING MOUNTAIN STREAM . . .

agashi-somen is a unique and improbable dish that few people even in Japan have tried, though most have heard of it: a meal—more a way of eating, really—that is symbolic of the purity, simplicity, and natural harmony that Japanese cuisine so often strives for.

Here is how it works (because nagashi-somen is very much a "how it works" dish, as opposed to a "how to make it" dish): The chef boils some *somen* noodles, ultrathin (less than 1/16 of an inch uncooked) wheat noodles made with a little sesame oil and dried in long, thin bunches like rope. When they are cooked and drained, he drops them, in small servings, into a nearby fast-flowing mountain river. The noodles travel downstream, becoming chilled by the glacial water along the way, and as they pass by, diners, sitting on wooden platforms called *yuka* over the water, pluck them from the stream with their chopsticks, dip them into a sauce, and eat. It sounded like an improbable fast-food delivery system, and not without its health and safety issues.

The fresh, clear, clean, soft water that flows from the mountains that surround Kyoto is an essential ingredient in its renowned and mineral-rich tofu, as well as its excellent sake, the tea ceremonies, and the dashi that is the foundation of kaiseki. It is also ideal for nagashi-somen, and I had heard there was a nagashi-somen restaurant close to the city—the only thing was, I didn't know exactly where. I spent some fruitless days asking everyone who ought to know where it might be until, in the end, I did begin to wonder if the whole concept wasn't just a myth propagated by the city's tourist and water boards. But then came a chance meeting with an elderly kimono dealer in one of the city's atmospheric old machiya, wooden houses built narrow but deep to circumvent the sixteenth-century shop-frontage tax. We'd gone to browse for vintage kimonos, a project that I naïvely thought might take an hour or so, but which ended up lasting the best part of a morning. As you can imagine, there are an awful lot of vintage kimonos in Kyoto, and I think I must have offered my considered opinion on a good number of them, while Asger and Emil slowly imploded with boredom.

But there was one silver lining: one of the kimono vendors managed to interpret my drawings of how I imagined a nagashi-somen restaurant might look. It turned out that one of only two nagashi-somen restaurants that she knew of in Japan was in the twin onsen towns of Kurama and Kibune, in the hills outside of Kyoto. She wrote the restaurant's name—Hirobun—in both kanji characters and English and gave me detailed directions. We had to catch a train from the northeastern part of the city, get off at a station close to the end of the line, and walk uphill. There was only one road, which ran alongside a river toward the Kifune Shrine (dedicated to the god of water), she said. It wasn't far from the station.

This was late September, the very end of the nagashi-somen season, she warned. She gave Hirobun a call just to check if they would be open and discovered that they were due to close for the winter the next day. This was our last chance to taste nagashi-somen.

We hurried straight from the kimono store to the nearest metro for the ride across Kyoto to take the local train up into the deep green, pine-covered mountains to the north. After an hour or so, we got off where the kimono seller had told us to, at the station by the Kibune River. The stationmaster there told us it was just a five-minute walk to the nagashi-somen restaurant. "Keep to the road beside the river," he said, somewhat unnecessarily, as there was only one road, lined on the other side with impenetrable jungle.

This is where things started to go awry. "Five minutes! We can walk that, no problem," I said gamely.

"Are you sure, Michael? It is quite a steep hill, and there's no sidewalk," said Lissen. Asger and Emil, playing with a large, now-dead hairy caterpillar they had found on the road, were too preoccupied to argue, and so we started walking, me a few yards ahead whistling a cheery hiking tune.

What was supposed to be a recreational family lunch outing soon turned into something rather more challenging, up a steep incline on a forest road strewn with the corpses of poisonous snakes and overhung with branches woven with the webs of spiders of a size I had never previously seen beyond the confines of a zoo.

We walked for over an hour—the shallow, sparkling river taunting our thirst—pausing every few minutes, initially to let Emil and Asger catch up, but then, after a while, to let me catch up. It had been some years since I'd tried to walk up a hill, particularly in humidity such as this. From time to time we were forced to jump into the undergrowth by rampaging buses whose timetables and stops remained a taunting enigma. I started to whimper, and I could sense Lissen's mounting irritation at yet another arduous lunch pilgrimage, but Asger and Emil were happy enough poking the dead snakes.

We spotted civilization amid the pine trees ahead. We climbed farther until we eventually came to an onsen hotel and restaurant complex. But it was not our restaurant. Naturally, Hirobun would turn out to be the very last in the village, a further twenty minutes' hike uphill. Along the way we passed about a dozen seductive wooden restaurants and hotels, many with wooden platforms over the river, decorated with softly glowing red lanterns and peopled by happy, relaxed diners and waitresses in lavish kimonos.

Finally, we came to Hirobun. I looked down to the platform over the river in the valley below. It was empty, but the waitress still sucked her teeth doubtfully, as they are taught to do at waitress school. She wasn't sure whether she could fit us in. She disappeared into the kitchen to ask the owner, reappearing a while after to show us, grudgingly, to our table. At last, we were going to try nagashi-somen—to commune with the mighty spirit of the mountain river.

We descended a steep flight of wooden steps down the riverbank, passing a small bamboo hut, like an outhouse, and sat on the tatami platform suspended a foot or so over the shallow riverbed, beside the mossy rocks of the bank. In front of us was an open zinc gutter. It led from the wooden hut down to the platform, where it continued along a narrow counter in a loop in front of the diners' seats.

As it turned out, rather than being dropped by the chef directly into the river for us to pluck as they flowed by, as if we were blessed visitors in some sylvan Arcadia, our noodles would be dumped into the gutter by the waitress just a couple of yards away, hiding out of sight in the hut.

It was a bit of an anticlimax. The waitress stuck her head around the corner of the hut to tell us to prepare for noodle launch. It was at that point, just as the first noodles rushed down-gutter toward us, catching us all by surprise, that I realized that I was sitting farthest downstream from the source of the noodles, with three other very hungry people, none of them renowned for their restraint at mealtimes, ahead of me. Needless to say, I spent most of lunch scrambling for leftovers. It soon became apparent that nagashi-somen has another flaw: the more wet noodles come your way, and the more you dip into your sauce, the more the sauce becomes diluted, so that, after a few mouthfuls, you end up dipping watery noodles in even more watery sauce. But by that stage we all just wanted to fill our groaning stomachs, and it was at least a quick way to do that.

The last bundle of noodles was pink and ume-, or pickled plum–, flavored, which our waitress had said would indicate our meal was over. "That was great!" said Asger. "Why can't every dinner be like that!"

21. THE SAKE CRISIS

The Japanese sake industry is in crisis. Consumption of what was for centuries the country's most popular alcoholic drink— so integral to the economy that it was used as a tax substitute—and its industry, run by the government, is in decline and has been for years. The Japanese now drink just over a third the amount of sake they did forty years ago—185 million gallons per year compared to 449 million in 1975. Instead, beer has been the drink of choice for the majority of Japanese since 1965, with wine rapidly on the rise, too—both are now produced with varying degrees of success domestically. (Japanese beer: terrific. Japanese wine: I've tasted it, so you don't have to.)

Sake breweries are closing throughout Japan (down from 30,000 a century ago to just 1,450 today), with many more facing bankruptcy. Making sake is a tough, labor-intensive, low-profit business, and young members of the Japanese workforce would rather work in offices and shops than slave in uncomfortable conditions making a drink no one wants anymore. The skills of the master sake brewer are in danger of disappearing forever. The world of the sake brewery is one of the most traditional, hierarchical, and chauvinistic in this most traditional, hierarchical, and chauvinistic country. Until very recently—and still to this day in some cases—sake breweries were run more along the lines of monasteries than businesses, closed to the outside world and suspicious of innovation.

Which makes it all the more improbable that my two sake contacts turned out to be an Englishman and a woman. We'll meet the Englishman first, because he gave me my introduction to the world of sake, a baptism by firewater.

Philip Harper and I had arranged to meet in a vast sports hall an hour or so outside of Hiroshima. I could already smell the sake in the parking lot, the sweet, yeasty aromas of rice wine wafting gently on the breeze. Inside, the fumes were almost overpowering, as Japan's best sake producers displayed their wares and tasted each other's products. The hall was filled with ten rows of trestle tables sporting serried ranks of green sake bottles; each table had a long, winding queue of patient sake enthusiasts—around five hundred in all—brandishing plastic tasting cups. This was the largest and most prestigious sake-tasting event of the year, the National Assessment for New Sake, founded by the National Research Institute of Brewing, itself founded by the tax department of the Ministry of Finance in 1904.

It was clearly a serious-minded occasion. The hall was virtually silent but for the odd clink of glass and porcelain and a symphony of staccato slurps and exaggerated sniffs. The floor, covered with plastic sheeting, was sticky with spilled sake. I joined a queue with my own plastic beaker, having spotted the only other Westerner— presumably Philip—in the room, a little ahead.

I began tasting my way up the tables. Each bottle had a small porcelain dish in front of it, like an ashtray but decorated with a blue spiral and traditionally used to judge the clarity of sake. Tasters used small plastic pipettes to pipe sake into the dish to observe its color and into their cups for tasting.

I tasted my first, from a bottle with a promising gold medal hanging around its neck. It was flowery and fruity with a milk-like viscosity. The second was a little sour and yeasty, not so nice. By the third sake, and from that point onward, my only real tasting note was "petroleum." Apparently, my palate was not all that well equipped to appreciate the nuances of sake.

"There's no cheap stuff here!" said Philip, finally spotting me. "We're all checking up on each other, the competition. Everyone wants to win a medal here; it is about the only acknowledgment you can get in the sake world. I have had a silver medal in the past, but nothing this year."

I asked Philip, age forty-two, with curly red hair and a plump, expressive face, to explain a little about what was going on. "This is the higher echelon of sakes. The rice used to make them will have been polished to 35 percent." I must have looked a little befuddled at this point, as Philip stopped suddenly.

"Do you know anything about sake?"

"I, erm, uh . . ."

"OK," he said, mentally rolling up his sleeves. "Sake is graded according to how much of the rice used to make it has been polished away before fermentation. They take the rice, put it in large revolving tanks, and spin it until the outer husk of the grains is worn away. It is the single most important element of sake making. The rice used to make the sakes here will have been polished to 35 percent, which is used to make the most refined type of sake. The less they polish the rice, the less refined the sake will be."

Why was sake in such decline in Japan? I asked. "Consumers in Japan perceive it as old-fashioned. Also there is a lovely convention with sake that you never pour for yourself—the person you are dining with should pour for you. But I think part of the problem is that in the corporate world this has been abused so that the new guy always has to drink until he pukes, because the bosses keep pouring.

It has that association for some." Apparently, a few years ago rumors also spread—I'd guess from the beer industry—that sake gave you bad breath and was acidic in the stomach, which can't have helped.

We were tasting as we talked and, though we were spitting into aluminum buckets, I was beginning to feel a little swimmy. My mouth had gone slightly numb, too. Philip was encouraging me to note the "melon, honey, and yeast" flavors of the sakes, but all I was getting was "white spirit."

"Luckily, it is picking up in the States. Sake has kind of followed in the wake of sushi over there, and they take it very seriously," he said. "Wine people are discovering sake and realizing you can do things with it that you can't with wine, because it isn't as acidic as wine. It doesn't mess with your stomach so much."

As well as the degree to which the rice used to make it is polished, sake is graded on a sweetness-to-dryness scale, ranging from +15 for the driest to −15 for the sweetest. It is slightly stronger than wine, typically 14 to 16 percent alcohol, although *genshu* sake, which isn't diluted prior to sale, as other types are, has an alcohol content of 20 percent. I assumed that, as with wine, there are sake snobs, and that they would prefer the dry stuff. Philip shook his head. "There are good sakes throughout the range. Actually, I don't think there is enough snobbery about sake. It is really underappreciated in Japan." The Japanese are famous for paying massively over the odds for French wines and Scottish whiskeys, but when it comes to sake, they will rarely spend more than ¥10,000 ($83) on a bottle, and even the most expensive bottle of high-grade *dai gingo* sake, the type being tasted here, won't cost more than ¥30,000 ($240). "The gold medal winners here won't sell for more than ¥10,000," Philip added. That said, true sake obsessives take their passion to extraordinary lengths: there are sake fans who devote themselves not just to one type of sake or rice but to one producer of the koji culture used to ferment the rice, for example. And they are not averse to using the wine snob's florid similes; comparing one sake to "the smell of slate when it's split" is one of Philip's, for instance.

Philip first came to Japan as an English teacher twenty years ago but only gradually grew to appreciate Japan's national drink. "When I first came, I would often drink the cheap stuff, but then met some friends who were into good sake." There was no looking back from that point; the drink became his life as he went to work at a brewery in 1991, after almost a decade becoming a *toji*, master brewer— the first foreigner ever to achieve this ranking. It wasn't an easy journey: "They all pretty much ignored me to start with; it was like joining a monastery. Early on, I had one Japanese person tell me that I would never be able to taste things the way a Japanese person could. There's no point in talking to those people."

By now my mouth was in a state of near paralysis. "Here, taste this. It's from Tokyo. Tokyo's known for its rather rough sake," he said.

I tasted. It was aggressively floral, cloying, acidic, with more of a petroleum aftertaste.

"Now try this one."

"Ugh, that's not much better," I said.

"Oh," said Philip. "That's mine."

I blustered about no longer being able to taste anything, but Philip was very understanding. "Don't worry, it's not one of my best. And, you should know, this event is designed to show the sakes at their very worst—room temperature really shows their faults. If a sake tastes good at this temperature, then it is really good." This explained a lot.

I asked Philip, who has written an excellent guide to sake called *The Book of Sake*, about the myths surrounding sake. What were the most misleading? "Some people still think it is a spirit [sake is brewed and has more in common with beer]. Then there are some that say only the best ones should be drunk cold and otherwise it should be drunk warm. Actually, that's complete bollocks. There are good sakes at every temperature, but even the Japanese are quite ignorant about sake. Another is that they shouldn't be aged, at least not beyond two years, but some can be, and I think aged sake will be the next big thing. Aged sake tastes a little like sherry; it's great. Unpasteurized sakes are also getting more popular—although they have to be kept refrigerated and drunk young."

The Japanese have never really paired sakes with food in the same way that we do with wine in the West. With wine, it is often the case that local food goes well with local wine, or the wine becomes an ingredient in a dish, but in Japan, though you can sometimes note regional consistencies in sake, sakes from the same town are just as likely to be similar as they are to be different from one another, depending on the type of rice used and, of course, the degree to which the rice has been polished. Shizuo Tsuji writes, firmly, that sake should never be drunk with any dishes containing rice, basing this on the flimsy logic that, as it is also made with rice, these two like poles will repel. Philip disagrees. "Most sake goes with most food because of its umami content [it has high levels of amino acids]. People also say sake doesn't go well with Western food, but it does. Sake is packed with umami flavors—it goes particularly well with Italian food, for instance. And, you know, all those people you see drinking beer with sushi are making such a mistake. Beer goes horribly with the vinegar and sugar in sushi, but sake is brilliant with all fish. It is also nonsense that sake gives you bad hangovers."

That was good news as, by now, having tasted over forty different sakes, I was well and truly in my cups. I bade a slurred farewell to Philip, who, as we parted, gave me a contact for a brewery in Kyoto that he said might be of interest.

———

Sake brewing has much in common with soy and miso production: you take a crop—in this case, rice—steam it, add a bacterial fermenting agent, or koji, and leave it for between a fortnight and a couple of months. Thus, you can make sake wherever there is a good supply of water (an average brewery might use up to 2,500 gallons in a day during the busy season, preferably with a low iron content). The Fushimi quarter of Kyoto, on the banks of the Uji River, is especially renowned for producing quality, refined sakes, largely because of its good supply of soft springwater. We happened to be staying in the city just as the brewing season started (sake is brewed in winter because it is easier to control fermentation and discourage bacteria in cool weather), so I went along to the Tama no Hikari brewery, one of seventeen breweries in this part of town, where I was met by Akira Toko, Philip's contact.

Tama no Hikari is a small, high-quality producer of a *junmai ginjo* sake (made with rice polished down to 60 percent or less), founded in 1673 by the Ukita family, who still run it to this day. Akira-san, a petite, friendly woman in her early thirties, took me on a tour of the brewing plant. The rice harvest had recently finished, and they had begun the polishing, the first stage of sake production. All rice starts off brown, of course. To make sake, this brown husk is removed, layer by layer (and, unfortunately for the Japanese, who prefer the appearance of white rice, nearly all the vitamins and nutrients are contained in the brown husk), depending, as Philip had said, on the quality of the sake that will result: the best sake is made with rice stripped down to a small, pearl-like nugget.

The noise from the five polishing machines was deafening as they churned the rice to remove, in this particular case today, 40 percent of each grain. The polishing causes the rice to heat up and so, afterward, it is left for a month to cool down naturally.

"Good fermentation means slow fermentation!" Akira-san shouted.

"No sugar or alcohol added. But the real secret is really good rice. We use *omachi* rice, which is an old type of rice that our company revived. It is difficult to grow because it grows very high, and that makes it vulnerable, and the yield is low. You know, even some sake experts don't know that omachi rice was the original sake rice."

I asked Akira-san if she agreed with Philip that there was a crisis in the sake industry. "It's true, it is very bad economically. It's since we started getting so many more different wines to choose from about twenty years ago. Chinese sake has given it a bad name as well, and sake is not cool among the young. But they are starting to appreciate it in America. If we could just get a small portion of the premium wine market over there." With this in mind, the company president was leaving for the States the next day, where the world's second-largest sake tasting is held.

We passed through the bottling plant. It was run by a man wearing a T-shirt with a slogan that said: "I am getting in touch with my inner bitch." Next, we washed our hands and donned white hats to enter the brewing house and temperature-controlled seed-mash rooms, with walls eight inches thick.

The smell inside was wonderful: heavily sweet, sweaty, and yeasty. It was the smell of fecund decay, noble rot Japanese-style—in this case prompted by the addition to the steamed rice of a yellow powder, a koji, or *Aspergillus oryzae*. This produces enzymes that turn the starch into sugar and kick off the fermentation. "I think making sake in the traditional way like this makes for very different flavors," Akira-san said. "High-quality sake needs human senses: touch, taste, smell."

Akira-san introduced me to the toji, the man responsible for the fermentation of the rice, Masuo Kobayashi, a squat, stern man with forty years' experience tending moldy rice. I asked him the secret of good sake: "Lactic acid is the key to good flavor," he said enigmatically (Akira-san translating), then walked off to attend to his rice. He showed me a rice mash that had been fermenting for just one day—it looked like rice that had been boiled, then left to dry. But the two-day mash was already liquefying thanks to those powerful enzymes, and it was beginning to smell a little funkier, too. He told me that over the next two weeks it would warm to almost 105°F. Apparently, after a while, the mash begins to move in waves, all by itself, caused by the fermentation; it looks as if a sea snake were hunting beneath its surface and produces a good deal of carbon dioxide, too.

I left Tama no Hikari with a generous gift of a large bottle of their finest-grade sake. It was a revelation after my tasting trauma in Hiroshima. Philip was right; it was full-bodied with a satisfyingly rich umami depth and a lovely, fresh fruitiness. Perhaps I could become a sake fan after all.

22. BEYOND SUSHI

It is virtually unheard of for a Japanese taxi driver to give up on a destination, but that day mine finally had to admit defeat after twenty minutes' fruitless circling, his honor in tatters. He let me out and waved away the fare with a dejected shake of his head. I was on foot from here, with not much to go on.

We had been in Kyoto for over a week, and I was on the trail of a culinary missing link that I had heard could be found in Higashi-yama, the eastern quarter of Old Kyoto. The trouble was, no one seemed to know where, or for that matter what, Izuu was.

I'd been reading about the history of sushi. Some believe it came to Japan from Thailand, from the Mekong Delta, where locals have, for more centuries than anyone knows, used cooked rice to pack and preserve fish. The alcohol and acids created when the rice starts to go moldy kill off any bacteria in the fish, which means it can be kept for months. The fish itself is rendered a stinking mush, but at least it won't kill you, and besides, decomposing fish is not to be sniffed at: from the Roman sauce garum, made from rotting anchovies, to modern-day Vietnamese *muoc mam* and other related fish sauces from Southeast Asia, fermented fish create what we now recognize as powerfully umami-packed flavors. From

Thailand, the practice of preserving fish in rice spread to China, where it appears ultimately not to have caught on, but then, in the eighth century, it traveled to Japan.

Here, possibly around Lake Biwa, close to Kyoto, locals discovered that the lactic fermentation of the rice added a pleasantly acidic touch to their muddy-flavored freshwater fish. The dish was called *nare-zushi* (the *z* and *s* in *sushi* seem to be interchangeable) and can still be enjoyed in the villages close to the lake, where these days it is called *funa-zushi*. *Funa* are carp, which in this case are pickled with rice during spawning time, their eggs still in situ, and left for six months before the rice is discarded. The dish is sometimes referred to as "Japanese fish cheese" and, I'd guess, is one of those acquired tastes few rush to acquire. After some years enjoying nare-zushi, the Japanese decided that they couldn't wait for the lactic process to run its course, and at some point in the fifteenth century, they started to eat the fish earlier, discovering that the rice— previously too rotten to eat—tasted rather good.

The next step in sushi's development came with the discovery of rice vinegar, in the seventeenth century. Rice vinegar allowed cooks to add tanginess to the rice without having to wait for it to ferment. This they called *haya-zushi*, or "quick sushi," which they made using stones to press the fish on top of rice in a large box, before cutting the resulting "cake" into smaller rectangular pieces.

By the late eighteenth and early nineteenth centuries, Tokyo, then called Edo, had usurped Kyoto as the capital of Japan, becoming the largest, most populous city on earth in the process. A series of fires, however, threatened the future of the world's first conurbation, and so open flames were banned in restaurants, and the city's burgeoning fast-food industry was virtually wiped out overnight. To the rescue came sushi, which could be assembled without need of a flame. Of course, the fish served with sushi in those days was unlikely to have been raw—there being no refrigeration—but it was a simple matter for sushi chefs to lightly poach, pickle, or grill their fish before bringing it into the city to add to the vinegared rice.

Tokyo's nineteenth-century workers, much like their descendants today, were time-poor. *Noren*, the curtains that traditionally hang at the entrance to sushi restaurants, date from this time, for example, and were originally there for customers to wipe their hands on as they hurried in and out, an especially filthy noren being a sign of a good restaurant. Even back then, customers demanded to be fed in double-quick time, and so, in the late nineteenth century, a local Edo chef called Yohei Hanaya came up with the idea of squeezing the rice into blocks by hand and topping them with fish as the orders came in. *Nigiri* means "to squeeze"; *sushi* refers to the vinegared rice—it has, as I'm sure you know, nothing to do with raw fish; and thus nigiri sushi, sometimes still referred to as "Edomae sushi," after its home city, was born.

Meanwhile, back in Kyoto, one of the great schisms of Japanese cuisine was unfolding. As well as deciding to put more sugar in the sushi rice than Tokyo chefs do—as we also tend to do in the West— Kyotoites had developed their own type of "pressed" sushi, not unlike the original haya-zushi. When making this so-called saba- zushi—or pressed mackerel sushi—they took this usually highly per- ishable fish and first briefly salt-cured it, then lightly pickled it in sugared vinegar, placed it on top of some rice, and wrapped the lot in simmered konbu before packing it in foot-long bamboo logs. As with ceviche, the acid in the vinegar slightly "cooked" the mack- erel, which was useful in a landlocked city half a day's journey from the sea.

But while nigiri and maki conquered the world, saba-zushi, and its Osakan cousin, *oshi-zushi*—a similar kind of pressed sushi made in cedar boxes—remained local delicacies only, slowly declining in popularity even in their home cities as the invention of refrigeration negated the need to pickle fish to preserve it.

It was this pressed, heavily vinegared saba-zushi I was in search of—the historic, hard-core übersushi, if you like. The most famous saba-zushi restaurant in Kyoto is Izuu, which opened in 1781. It's still there: a small wooden-beamed building, both windowless and nameless. Having finally found it, I parted the clean, white noren and effectively time-traveled two centuries.

Inside, the restaurant looked like something from feudal-era Kyoto with rough wooden furniture, paper screens, and a slate floor. A heavily made-up lady in a kimono sat in a booth on the left and gestured that I should take a table. The only other diners were an aged Japanese couple, who stopped eating and eyed me suspiciously as I bowed and smiled my way to my table.

My saba-zushi arrived on a blue-patterned porcelain plate. It was a sizable cross-sliced log, almost a foot long, of densely packed rice topped with mackerel and wrapped in glistening, dark green konbu. There was no soy or wasabi. Saba-zushi is eaten unadorned, all the better to appreciate the acidic rice and delicate, oily fish. This makes sense. Soy would be too heavy a flavor to compete; wasabi too much of a challenge to a palate already coping with the vinegar. The rice was the star of the dish—it was the finest-quality short-grain rice, each grain as wide as it was long, probably koshihikari, soft on the outside with a slightly resistant core to give bite, glinting and lucent. The fish was excellent, too, a muted rainbow ranging from pale rose to deep purple to light brown.

I had a misunderstanding with the elderly waitress/cashier at this point. At first, I thought she was gesturing at me from her kiosk *not* to eat the soft konbu the sushi had been wrapped in. Then, when she saw I was leaving it on the side of my plate, she seemed to be encouraging me to eat it. I looked over to the elderly couple, who instantly averted what had until that moment been a fixed gaze in my direction. By now they were sipping their tea, and I noticed all their konbu was gone. I ate some of mine. It was leathery and sticky, a bit like eating flypaper, although I am sure very healthy.

I have to say, saba-zushi was pretty fantastic—sweeter, more vinegary, and more fishy in a nice way than conventional nigiri. It had been a fairly filling lunch, but I was still hungry and, not for the first time in Japan (or elsewhere, come to that), alone and without Lissen to rein in my gluttony, I had thought I might try to squeeze in a second lunch that day. I had something in mind, just a little snack, really.

Kyoto is the undisputed tofu capital of Japan, and Toshi had warned me that I would regret it for the rest of my life if I didn't eat in a local tofu restaurant.

Until the seventeenth century, tofu was a luxury dish enjoyed mainly by noblemen, which is odd, as it is a relatively simple food, made from cheap ingredients. You soak soybeans overnight, then boil them and press their milk out. To the milk a coagulant of some kind is added—magnesium chloride, which the Japanese call *nigari*; or magnesium sulfate, better known as Epsom salts; or calcium sulphate, also known as gypsum, and particularly rich in calcium. The liquid is then poured into cheesecloth-lined molds to set.

Tofu is rich, not just in protein from the soybeans (pound for pound it has more protein than meat, in fact) but also iron, vitamins B1 and E, zinc, potassium, magnesium, and calcium. It is said to lower blood pressure, slow the aging process, and be good for one's bones. It also contains oligosaccharides, a type of simple sugar that is excellent for promoting healthy bacteria in the gut, preventing constipation, and lowering blood pressure.

Depending on how finely the tofu is strained, and whether or not it is pressed, the result is either *momen-dofu*, or "cotton tofu," which is firm and stands up better to cooking, or the finer, lighter *kinugoshi-dofu*, or "silk tofu"—a slight misnomer, as it isn't actually strained through silk. According to Shizuo Tsuji, if you can't get hold of tofu, then "calves' brains are remarkably similar." He's right, in a way, at least in terms of texture; good-quality sweetbreads have something of the same loose jelly density, and melt-in-the-mouth texture, but the flavors are hardly comparable.

As with the sake, the tofu is especially good in Kyoto thanks to the city's endless supply of fresh, soft mountain water—the quality of the water used in its making being the most important determinant of good tofu. Close to the famous Nanzen-ji shrine, on the very eastern edge of the city, where majestic, swoopy-roofed temples emerge from the forested hills, is one of the city's most famous tofu restaurants, Okutan, housed in a large, wooden thatched hall, dating back over three and a half centuries and surrounded by customarily serene gardens. I left my shoes in the rack outside and was shown to a place on the tatami floor by a low table. The restaurant, which was full even this late in the lunch service, serves only tofu dishes, so I ordered their classic tofu hot pot and some *dengaku*. The hot pot arrived within a couple of minutes, piping hot and featuring luscious cubes of tofu, the texture of crème caramel and served with small side dishes of spring onion, ginger, and soy. Picking ectoplasmic tofu from a cauldron of hot water is surely the ultimate test of chopstick technique, and I must say, as I glanced in embarrassment around the room, I could see a number of Japanese people were struggling, too.

The dengaku was easier to handle. In this dish, tofu is skewered on double-pronged wooden skewers—the name comes from the Japanese for "stilt-walker," whose legs the skewers evoke—coated with white miso and grilled. The fresh, clean tofu is the perfect foil for the fruity, nutty, salty miso. Actually, tofu is the perfect foil for all sorts of assertive flavors, although a little fine-grated ginger, spring onion, or katsuobushi is all the dressing you need for really good, fresh tofu, served chilled in summer.

The golden rule with tofu is that it must be eaten the day it is made; otherwise, the flavor turns stale. This, I think, explains the bad rap tofu has in the West, where it is often a cheap punch line for hippie jokes: flavorless piety food for sanctimonious vegans. It perhaps also explains tofu's declining popularity in Japan, where small, local tofu makers have been going out of business over the last few years. Tofu used to be delivered to households daily, as milk once was in the U.S. and the UK, but that tradition has been lost in most cities. If I had my way, and if we could guarantee it always tasted as good as Kyoto tofu, fresh deliveries of soybean curd would be introduced to every street in every town.

23. THE FASTEST FOOD IN THE WORLD

Which of these useful Osakan-themed trivia facts are true and which are false?

1. In Osaka the conveyor belts in sushi restaurants move 14 percent faster than they do in Tokyo.
2. Osakans walk faster than anyone else in the world, at 1.74 yards per second, compared to 1.7 yards per second in Tokyo.
3. The coin slots on public transport ticket machines are wider than anywhere else in Japan so that customers can get the coins in faster.
4. A customary greeting is "Are you making any money?"
5. It is the convention to stand on the right while riding on escalators; everywhere else in Japan, you stand on the left.
6. The fastest fast food in the world was invented in Osaka.
7. Osaka has a GDP equivalent to Switzerland's.

Answer: all of the above are true. (Even the escalator thing: which means, presumably, that there is some point between Osaka and Kyoto where people switch sides, which in turn begs the question, how do they know where it is? Is there an official dividing line? Or is there some kind of razor-wired escalator no-man's-land?)

Osakans are the most impatient, contrary, mercantile people in Japan. They make Tokyoites look like slackers and, perhaps as a result, their city rarely features on tourists' itineraries—the city has virtually no historic sights and few museums and consists almost entirely of featureless high-rises, endless shotengai—corridor malls—and densely packed side streets. Nevertheless, I had been looking forward to coming to Osaka perhaps more than to any other city in Japan, and I could hardly contain my excitement as we took the short train ride there after our three weeks in Kyoto.

Asger, Lissen, and Emil were ready for something a little more twentieth century, too. The royal palace and gardens had afforded some space for Asger and Emil to hare about burning off excess energy, but Kyoto is even less child friendly than Tokyo, like a giant library in which one sometimes feels metaphorically shushed by the locals.

But still, it was a genuine shock arriving in Osaka, looking out from the taxi as we drove past the numerous mega-malls and skyscrapers between Osaka Station and our hotel.

Shortly after checking in, Lissen announced, "Right. Shopping!" while rubbing her hands together briskly, and left. Which left the day free for me, Asger, and Emil to explore the city. I knew exactly where we would head first: Dotombori, the fast-food heartland of Japan's fast-food capital.

Dotombori is a brash Vegas-style food street—about the only place in the country where it is acceptable to walk and eat. It is famous throughout Japan as the spiritual home of two Osakan fast-food specialties, takoyaki—the octopus dumplings we first encountered in Kyoto—and okonomiyaki.

I've heard okonomiyaki described as everything from "Japanese pizza" to "Osakan omelet," but its only real resemblance to either is that it is round. It's more a pancake-tortilla hybrid made with a flour-and-egg batter with cabbage mixed in, and it can come with a variety of fillings and/or toppings. As one would expect from a dish whose name translates as "cooked to taste" or "as you like it," finding an exact recipe is like asking a Frenchman to make the definitive cassoulet. One of the secrets seems to be the use of ground yam, and others add dashi to the batter instead of water, ideally freshly made rather than the powdered instant variety. Disagreements focus on the toppings. In Hiroshima, the toppings—typically pork, seafood, perhaps kimchi, but really anything does go (I've had okonomiyaki with cheese and mochi on top, for instance)—are blended in with the batter. Here in Osaka, they go on top with, usually, some *aonori* seasoning, perhaps some Japanese mayonnaise, and katsuobushi flakes. Others add yakisoba (fried ramen noodles) and *tenkasu*, crispy, fried tempura batter. Techniques for making okonomiyaki also differ. Usually you are given a bowl of batter and ingredients that you mix yourself, then pour onto a hot plate built into your table, flipping the resulting inch-thick disk with a metal spatula when one side is cooked, and serving it divided into pizza-style slices with the same spatula. But there are other restaurants where they compress and steam the okonomiyaki before serving, and in Tokyo they serve it as *monjayaki*, using a sloppier batter that never really sets in the familiar okonomiyaki disk (which was frankly just annoying). The sweet, brown teppanyaki-style savory sauce (the familiar mix of ketchup, soy, Worcestershire sauce, perhaps dashi, mustard, sugar, mirin, and sake) that is slathered on the top with a shaving-type brush is an essential ingredient, too, although, of course, pinning down a chef's secret recipe for this sauce is impossible, and most buy ready-made sauces when they make okonomiyaki at home.

I knew it was too late to convince Asger and Emil of the pleasures of takoyaki—they were already wise to the lurking octopus body parts—but I felt I had a chance with okonomiyaki, as long as I could shield from them the fact that it contained vegetables and seafood. But which restaurant should we try first? There are said to be over four thousand okonomiyaki joints in Osaka, a good number of them located on Dotombori. The first we came to had over ten different types of plastic okonomiyaki models in the window, and we agreed we simply couldn't deal with that level of choice at this early stage in our okonomiyaki education.

We walked on a little farther, taking in the cartoonish extravagance of Dotombori's restaurant fronts—a chaotic jumble of animatronic clowns and giant crabs, lanterns, liquid crystal, and inflatable fugu fish. Yet amid this visual cacophony, Asger and Emil zoned in on one establishment in particular.

They were initially drawn to the Bow Wow Relaxation of Dogs Gallery by the two small dogs tethered outside, tended by a uniformed member of the staff. "Look, Daddy!" said Emil. "He's licking my hand!"

"Yes, but we were looking for okonomiyaki, remember?" I said.

Asger, meanwhile, had his face pressed against the glass window behind which were more small dogs, lounging listlessly. They were for sale, for telephone number prices, but this wasn't just a pet shop. The staff member beckoned us inside. I tried to resist politely, but Asger and Emil were already halfway up the stairs to the first floor before I could grab their hands. I followed them into what turned out to be a kind of canine harem where guests came to enjoy the company of small dogs while sipping coffee. There was no way I was going to persuade Asger and Emil to leave without risking a conniption fit on an enormous scale from one or both of them, so I paid the entrance fee, and we removed our shoes and entered through a small gate to the dog-frolicking zone.

The admission included a drink each and a bag of doggy treats. The dogs, of which there were about twenty, none larger than a

handbag, roamed freely among the tables. They were clearly familiar with the drill, and we were soon engulfed by the pack.

Soon, Asger and Emil were roaming the tables on all fours with
the rest of the dogs, something I don't believe the waiting staff had
ever seen before. I pretended they were nothing to do with me and
sat back with my Coke to take in the scene.

The guests ranged from mothers with their daughters to lone
middle-aged females and even businessmen, which was weird. I
guessed that Bow Wow catered to residents of high-rise apartment
blocks with no room for pets, or people who worked standard Japanese hours and so had to make do with these prostitute Pekingese.
It was all a bit tragic really. Lonely people seeking the company of
greedy animals. The smell was appalling, too. Several of the dogs
were wearing diapers. One of them stopped its scrounging for treats
and became engrossed in its own genitals for a while, before jump-
ing up onto the lap of a morose young girl and giving her a good
slurp in the face.

Finally, I managed to isolate Asger and Emil from the pack by
scattering some doggie snacks in the opposite direction, and attempted to bundle them out of the shop. But their new gang were
having none of it, and soon our ankles were surrounded by fur-balls
again. Asger and Emil could quite happily have made their home
here indefinitely, but my stomach was rumbling, and the knowledge
that some of the world's greatest fast food was still within my grasp
spurred me on through the canine melee. I grabbed Asger's wrist
and scooped Emil up under my arm, to barks and yelps from both.
The dogs, sensing their new leaders were under attack, lunged properly for my ankles. It took three waiters to hold them off as I forced
my way through the gate to where our shoes were waiting.

(Needless to say, the pressure to return to Bow Wow was ceaseless for the rest of our stay in Osaka, and we did return twice. Asger and Emil still talk about it as their undisputed highlight of the

entire trip to Japan, ahead of lunch with sumos, meeting ninja warriors at Himeji Castle, and even finding a real, live dead turtle on the beach in Okinawa.)

Clearly, as a moneymaking idea, a dog café was right up there with phone companies charging for their complaint lines: people pay to play with your dogs and are emotionally blackmailed into either buying them by their children or at the very least footing their food bill. I made a mental note to add it to the list of brilliant Japanese business ideas that were going to make my fortune once we returned, along with the soft-closing toilet seat.

We wandered on for about half an hour, inadvertently straying into the love hotel quarter, where sheepish couples loitered hesitantly beneath signs for the Hyper Sexy Club and Happy Love Make Joy Hotel. We ended up back in the center of Dotombori outside Sammy's Ebisu Plaza, an exact re-creation of 1950s Osaka with authentic-looking restaurants and shops from the period. It was one of the several food theme parks that have sprung up in various cities in Japan in recent years, which typically contain groups of restaurants arranged in indoor malls decorated to a particular theme, usually jazzed up with vintage shop fronts and period advertising (and all set in the immediate postwar era for some reason).

In the first restaurant we came to I ordered one okonomiyaki and one *modanyaki*—an okonomiyaki with yakisoba mixed into the batter. Both were slathered in the sweet brown sauce that I felt sure would guarantee their appeal to a six- and four-year-old, but Asger and Emil toyed with them briefly before rejecting them on the grounds that they had "too much stuff inside."

Oddly, given that his book generally takes an Osakan- or Kansai-oriented slant on Japanese cuisine, Shizuo Tsuji makes reference neither to takoyaki nor to okonomiyaki in *A Simple Art*. It is true that the popularity of these so-called B-grade indigenous fast foods—to which list you can add ramen and yakitori—has increased exponentially in the years since the book was published, but there is still a snobbery about them in the higher echelons of the Japanese food world. Perhaps Tsuji felt street food was beneath his remit. I do still think, though, that okonomiyaki could be the next global Japanese food trend: it's quick, cheap, simple, relatively healthy (it is around 50 percent cabbage, after all), theatrical, and utterly, compulsively delicious. If I were younger, more foolish, and had some venture capital behind me, I'd be looking to roll out a chain before Christmas.

As it is, the world has instead embraced two other Osakan fast-food innovations: kaiten sushi (conveyor-belt sushi) and instant noodles, both invented in the same year: 1958.

The idea for kaiten sushi came to restaurateur Yoshiaki Shiraishi during a visit to a bottling plant, but it took him a while to perfect. The speed of the conveyor was the trickiest part: too fast and people grew anxious (I call this "uni angst" and suffer from it terribly when I eat at conveyor-belt places: *What if someone takes the sea urchin before it reaches me?*); too slow and they were bored. Eventually, he found three inches per second to be the optimum rate. His Genroku chain was wildly successful, as the so-called dwell time of diners was reduced to around twelve minutes, which meant he could pack as many as four sittings into one hour, instead of two over an entire evening. The original restaurant is still going in the east of the city, but Shiraishi died in relative poverty after he tried to take the staffless restaurant concept too far and plowed all his money into developing robot waiters.

Instant ramen noodles were the invention of Momofuku Ando, who died in 2007, a revered Japanese national hero and multibillionaire. Inspired by seeing how air and water instantly evaporated from tempura, leaving tiny holes in their wake, he reasoned that the same could be done with noodles, which could then be rehydrated via the holes with hot water. Today, over eighty-five *billion* servings of instant ramen are consumed in the world each year.

That afternoon, with Lissen maintaining radio silence somewhere in a distant Uniqlo changing room, we took a quick trip to the north of the city to the Momofuku Ando Instant Ramen Museum. In a swish, modern building that looked more like a contemporary art museum than a memorial to a noodle magnate, we learned of the early days of Ando's invention, which he refined in his garden shed, and marveled at a vast wall covered with different plastic noodle pots through the ages. Upstairs, we could create our own recipe and then sit down to eat it.

We finished the day at Osaka's one true, original tourist attraction: the aquarium. It is the world's largest, its main tank several stories high. The star is a captive whale shark, the largest fish in the world, and a staggering sight to see behind glass.

Big fish, dog cafés, and fat pancakes: we couldn't have asked anything more of a day's sightseeing.

24. MIRACULOUS MISO

This is what U.S. food writer Harold McGee has to say about miso soup in his seminal work on kitchen science, history, and culture, *On Food and Cooking*:

Miso soup is a delight to the eye as well as the palate. When the soup is made and poured into the bowl, the miso particles disperse throughout in an even haze. But left undisturbed for a few minutes, the particles gather around the centre of the bowl in discrete little clouds that slowly change shape. The clouds mark convection cells, columns in the broth where hot liquid from the bowl bottom rises, is made cooler and so more dense by evaporation at the surface, falls again; is reheated and becomes less dense, rises, and so on. Miso soup enacts at the table the same process that produces towering thunderhead clouds in the summer sky.

Isn't that fantastic?

Shizuo Tsuji writes that "in many ways miso is to Japanese cooking what butter is to French cooking and olive oil to the Italian way." From what I already knew about miso, this didn't sound quite right. Miso isn't used for frying, for instance, or to add gloss to sauces, but he was right about its ubiquity. Over half of Japanese still wake up to the smell of miso soup for breakfast—to them it is like toast and coffee.

Most people have tasted miso paste in miso soup, of course, and possibly in that ubiquitous modern fusion dish cod with miso, and I'd recently tried it in the Kyoto tofu restaurant, grilled on tofu as dengaku. That last had been wonderful, with a meaty, peanut flavor and a complex acidity. But there was also a whiff of something ripe and funky about miso, which—as with so many of the tastiest foodstuffs (truffles, well-aged game, Roquefort)—both repelled and intrigued me in equal measure.

All of this and worse was confirmed before I had even entered Tony Flenley's miso factory in the shadow of the spaceship-style Osaka Dome stadium. What *was* that appalling smell of backed-up toilets?

"Ah yes, that's the drains. Sorry about that," said Tony, a tall, cheerful Englishman in his early fifties, sighing, as he welcomed me to his Portakabin office.

"Phew, thank goodness for that. I thought it was the miso." I laughed.

"Oh yes, it *is* the miso," Tony said. "It's just that we have to hold on to our waste to let the sediment settle before we can release the water into the sewer. The local council doesn't really understand what we do here. Because we use bacteria, they don't want us to pump waste directly into the sewer. I try to tell them it's good bacteria, but they don't listen."

There are, Tony explained, three basic types of miso—one made with soybeans, salt, and rice; one made with soybeans, salt, and barley; and one made with just soybeans and salt. They range in color from deep reddish brown to light sandy beige. Light-colored miso tends to be slightly sweet, while the red has a richer, more powerful flavor. "Red's got more amino acids, so it is better for you. They say one bowl a day keeps cancer away. You know, in Japan we don't say that you 'drink' miso soup; you 'eat' it—because it is usually full of vegetables, tofu, and fish."

With over two thousand miso producers in Japan, there is a huge number of regional variations. Around 80 percent is *kome miso*, made with soybeans and rice; on Kyushu they often use barley and beans—this is *mugi miso*, while miso from Nagoya is made with beans only—*mame miso*. Tokyo miso is traditionally dark, rust-colored, sweet, and powerful, while *sendai miso*, from Miyagi Prefecture, is salty. Predictably, Kyoto miso is refined and subtle, and a pale cream color. Tony, meanwhile, also produces Osaka's unique sweet, white miso. The ingredients, whether or not they are steamed or boiled, fermenting time (some stand for two to three years)—all of these can affect the color and flavor of miso, he said.

Of course, making top-quality miso requires experience and an empathy with moldy rice and beans—you need to judge the amount of salt to add, the proportion of beans to rice or barley, and at what point optimum fermentation has been achieved. Above all, you need to know how to work with koji, rice inoculated with that magical fungus *Aspergillus oryzae*. When the koji starts devouring the beans, it heats up but must be kept below 105°F, as the koji's enzymes first turn the starch into sugar and then break the beans down into amino acids. The sugar is important for white miso, and the amino acids give flavor to red miso.

Tony showed me around the factory, a fairly basic warehouse with various pipes and valves, tanks, and dials about the place. It all looked rather rudimentary: to make miso you basically need a big barrel, a grinder, a rice steamer, a bean cooker, and a koji room. As with sake and soy sauce (which was originally a by-product of miso manufacture), the koji, specially manufactured for use in miso-making, is added to the steamed beans and acts as a starting agent to get them fermenting. Salt is added, and the mix is left with a heavy weight on top and minimum contact with air for two to three weeks for white miso or one to two years for red. "You can speed the process up," Tony told me. "But it doesn't taste so good. We do it the proper way. Natural fermentation." After fermentation, the beans are usually ground to a paste (although in some parts of Japan they are used as is or minced) and steamed to stop them from fermenting further. I can testify that miso can be left in the fridge for many, many months (frankly, years, although that's probably not advisable).

For all its simplicity, the resulting product—a solid brown paste not unlike peanut butter—is a complex substance. Along with amino acids, it contains lactic acid, which helps balance the glutamate flavor and works as a preservative. As well as being a good source of protein and minerals, it also contains cholesterol-lowering compounds, while the fermentation process appears to boost the antioxidant levels already present in the soybeans. There has long been an association between miso consumption and reduced rates of cancer, in particular breast cancer, due, it is believed, to the presence of isoflavones, antioxidants unique to beans. When news came to Japan of the Chernobyl nuclear disaster, their response was to send miso, for instance. A survey of 270,000 people also indicated an association between miso soup and reduced gastric cancers—thought to be because miso purges the gut of various toxins—and some scientists believe that it slows aging by suppressing the oxidization of cellular lipids.

Ironically, just as the rest of the world is waking up to the miracle powers of this remarkable paste—exports have doubled over recent years—Japan is turning against it. Like that of sake, fresh dashi, and tofu, miso's appeal appears to be waning with the Japanese, who are increasingly adopting Western-style diets and finding they have less time to cook from scratch. Consumption has dropped to less than 500,000 tons a year, compared to 580,000 tons in the eighties.

I asked Tony about natto, another fermented soybean product. Natto is a healthy traditional breakfast dish in Japan. It is made from only partially fermented soybeans, which turns them into a—to my eyes—deeply unappetizing, stringy, lumpy, vomit-like substance, with a taste that subtly blends soil and old cheese. I'd had my first taste of natto at the hotel breakfast buffet in our hotel in Sapporo. For me, perhaps the most off-putting thing about it was the determined, mucus-like strands that clung to the beans as I tried to pick them up. Along with the foul-smelling durian fruit and truffles, it has to be one of the most polarizing foodstuffs on the planet. "That's made with a different fermenting bacteria," Tony said. "We don't make it. Actually, they say that you should never make miso and natto in the same premises because the natto bacteria is stronger and can affect the miso koji."

What were his tips for cooking with miso? "Oh, loads. You can mix it with mirin and mustard and use it as a dip. With dengaku, you mix red and white miso and put it on tofu, then grill it. I use it in chili con carne instead of chocolate. It is great as a seasoning, instead of salt in a Western-style stew. You get a real, natural MSG boost—just remember that white miso has 5 to 6 percent salt and red has 10 to 12, so you need to adjust the salt accordingly. Red miso apple cake is nice, and a gratin with white miso works well. I've heard some London restaurants are serving pork with miso, which is a classic combo. We even made a miso ice cream once."

Later, experimenting back home, I found a dessert spoon or so of miso works really well in tomato sauces. You can use it instead of a stock cube to enrich the flavor of a dish, and miso mixed with vinegar, water, sugar, garlic, and a neutral oil makes a great salad dressing.

I asked Tony how he ended up in this warehouse in the wilds of Osaka. He had lived in Japan for twenty years, having moved there originally as a TEFL teacher. He speaks the language fluently and is married to a Japanese woman; it was her family who founded the Osaka Miso Jyozo company a hundred years ago. The miso industry is very traditional, and originally his in-laws were against even the idea of their daughter marrying a foreigner. How did he win them over? "I guess when they realized I wasn't going to run away with her there was a slow thaw. Anyway, her dad's a boozer like me. We got on. In Japan, before the son takes over a company, he is sent off to another company to get some training, so I did that. After ten years, the old man grew weaker, and I started taking on visiting clients. He died three years ago, and I took over fully.

"Actually, I was always interested in fermentation. I made ginger ale when I was twelve—I found out if I put lots of sugar in I could make it more alcoholic! I taught English in Kuwait for a couple of years and used to make wine in my basement, then made yogurt; now I make bread."

How did the company's clients react to him? "Well, I suppose the people who were offended were too polite to say anything, but it still causes a stir. It is seen as a very tough profession. It didn't help that we got hit by the Kobe earthquake [in 1995]. Even though it was across the bay, there was a lot of damage here. We lost the original factory, which was where the car park is now. I was on the thirteenth floor at home at the time, and all the crockery was smashed." Apparently, the ground where the factory stands is still rather unstable. "Every time there is a concert in the Osaka Dome over the way there, it is equivalent to a force-three earthquake!"

Tony brought out a plate with some different misos for me to taste. The white was yeasty and sweet; the one-year-fermented red paste saltier, with a slight Marmite flavor. "Yes! You're right. You know, I have thought about making a miso spread for bread. That'd be good, don't you think?"

We tried a two-year-old red miso. It had an astringent, burning flavor. "It goes very well in a broth. It clears the palate well, which is what miso soup is supposed to do, of course. You should only have it after a meal. Often it is served with the other dishes but meant to be left until the end." A white barley miso was next—it was sweet, with a hint of pineapple. "That's very popular in Osaka. They have a real sweet tooth here."

Tony and I chatted more generally about Osaka and life in Japan. He generously offered to introduce me to his contacts at the fish market—the second largest in the country—so that I could get to see the predawn tuna auction. "Let's go right now; I can show you around," he said.

The market was on the other side of town, so Tony drove me there in his Toyota station wagon. After making the introductions, he invited me for lunch at his favorite market restaurant, a dingy place on the first floor filled with stevedores and traders. They greeted him as an old friend, and we sat at the counter in front of a large, square steel vat filled with a murky brown liquid in which floated several unidentifiable foodstuffs.

"What do you mean you haven't tried *oden*!" Tony said, seeing my grimace. "It is delicious; you have to try it." Oden is the Japanese equivalent of a good stew, a winter warmer in which you can find bricks of tofu, various meats, burdock root, daikon, potatoes, fish cakes, seaweed, and boiled eggs. You might also chance upon the curious konnyaku. Pretty much anything the chef has on hand goes in, and it is said that a really great oden is eternal—the vat literally never stops simmering, with each day's serving merely a top-up of the previous day's.

The chef fished out a few choice morsels—some deep-fried tofu, spoon-tender pork, daikon, and a hard-boiled egg. It was delicious; I can imagine it being quite comforting during a tough winter.

Osakans are a hospitable and generous people, even adopted sons (Tony had insisted on paying for the oden). This was underlined the next evening when I hooked up with a couple of friends of friends, local food lovers who had promised to show me some of the addresses from their little black gourmet books.

We met outside the National Bunraku Theatre. Hiroshi, in his late forties, was wearing a Kangol flat cap and surfer shirt. With him was Chiaki, a woman around the same age. They introduced themselves with customary Japanese diffidence, but as we began to talk food, the shyness soon disappeared. "Osakans like to eat at lots of different places in one night," Hiroshi said with the hint of a wicked grin. He wasn't kidding.

There was a stunning okonomiyaki, cooked in front of us in a grimy old-school joint, on a hot plate caked in black grease. Hiroshi said it was the very best in the city, and I didn't doubt it. "Osakans eat it straight from the spatula," said Chiaki as she divided it up with her metal spatula. "We are always in a hurry, you know." The waiter was keen to engage me in rugby talk, as England was playing Japan in the World Cup that night, but I was more interested in the sauce he brushed over the okonomiyaki. "Secret recipe," he whispered, laughing.

Next stop was Daruma, the most famous kushikatsu restaurant in Japan. Daruma has been serving these moreish breaded, deep-fried skewers of meat, fish, and vegetables for over eighty years, which makes it positively ancient in Japanese fast-food terms. We took our place at the counter, feet splashing down in water spilled by the kitchen staff as they ducked and swooped around the tiny open working kitchen. These may have been shabby environs, but I couldn't have wished for a finer introduction to the art of kushikatsu. The quails' eggs and tomatoes were standouts, the thin, crunchy batter with its fine sandpaper finish cracking to unleash its meltingly delicious interior. The skewers cost less than a dollar each.

As with okonomiyaki, it is inexplicable to me why kushikatsu has not taken the world by storm by now. This is another of the great Osakan fast foods and deserves to be right up there with tempura and yakitori—to which it is related—as a globally known Japanese style of cooking.

The secret is in the batter, which in Daruma's case is made with puréed yams, flour, eggs, water, and a unique blend of eleven spices. It forms a thin, crisp crust around whatever is being deep-fried, the true mastery of which lies in making sure the former adheres to the latter—we also had beef, shrimp, asparagus, chicken, and scallops. The skewers are cooked in beef oil at 375°F. The special meaty-sugary, ebony-colored dip is served in a communal pot on the counter bearing a "No double dipping" warning in English.

"Are we planning on going anywhere else? Because if we are, I had better stop," I said to Hiroshi at one point. We were, but I couldn't. The skewers and the beer kept on coming. By the time we left, a long queue was already forming outside. "They queue here for miles every night," Hiroshi said. Ferran Adrià—whom, by now, I felt I was stalking through Japan—had eaten there recently, the chef told us.

The evening started to blur after the fifth or sixth beer, but I do remember going to Shinsekai, the city's main food market, and then on to a standing bar, a current Osakan trend. Here we chatted a little more about the character of Osakans. "Osakans are friendly; they have a sense of humor; they like cheap, good food," said Chiaki. "You can see the history of the city in their character. We are a mercantile people, outward looking, tough at business, but fair and adventurous. We are down-to-earth, not pretentious like the Kyoto people. We are blunt and to the point."

In Osaka, everyone from heads of corporations to the men that mend the roads eat side by side, standing up in this kind of bar. We ordered hamo, fluffy and mealy, and then garlic miso with sea bream. Then came a sizable triangle of deep-fried tofu with ginger and spring onion.

The drinks took a more serious turn at this point. A large tumbler of sweet potato shochu appeared first, which made everything go that much blurrier than before, but then came a milky sake full of sediment—this was *nama-sake*, or unpasteurized sake, something of an acquired taste.

Hiroshi had written an article for a local newspaper on this particular bar, which was almost a hundred years old and run by the third generation of the same family. The article was framed on the wall behind us and included a photograph of the chef's father. He had died the week before, the chef told us. His mother emerged from the kitchen, tiny and sad but with a brave face that said, *Life continues. People must eat.* His ten-year-old daughter pulled a beer for another customer, while the chef peeled a huge daikon in front of us, gently teasing off its outer skin with an equally gigantic but obviously razor-sharp knife. The technique is known as *katsuramuki*, meaning "column peel," and is considered a basic test of a good Japanese chef, in the same way that a perfect quenelle is for a French chef.

Next up was an udon noodle place chosen by Chiaki. I had tried to protest this last addition to our itinerary. I really was stuffed, and more than a little drunk, but I am glad she persuaded me, for at Chiaki's favorite udon restaurant I tasted heaven.

It was just a simple dashi broth with small, crisp, deep-fried gyozas floating on its surface. The discussion had taken a more personal slant. "Michael-san," Hiroshi asked me. "Your favorite food? What would your last meal be?"

I paused. Would it be elaborate tasting menus at Ducasse and Robuchon, or a great British roast? I did consider fresh oysters, lobster, pan-fried foie gras, and I had already eaten so many memorable meals in Japan that several of them would suffice. But the truth was, right at that moment, I had eaten nothing more delicious than that dashi. It was as sweet as spring peas fresh from the pod, yet complex, with the tang of ocean, and when you bit into the gyoza, a satisfying porky punch with a zing of spring onion and herbs. I may have been dribblingly drunk, but I remember it as being as good as anything I had tasted up until that point and said so. Chiaki and Hiroshi beamed.

I had to know how they made it. To alarmed looks from my dining companions, I stood up from the table and tottered into the open kitchen. This absolutely is not done in Japan, but as is often the case, being foreign can provide a passport to all sorts of forbidden territories. I eventually managed to communicate my inquiry and was shown the blend of three dried fish they used to steep in the konbu broth: katsuobushi, sardine, and mackerel.

It had been the food crawl to end all food crawls. I had eaten more in ten or so hours than I would usually consume in a couple of days. I don't know how I got back to the hotel that night, and I certainly don't remember the journey, but I do remember that, true Osakans that they are, Chiaki and Hiroshi never let me pay for a thing.

25. THE FOREST OF LOST SOULS

This has to be the most unsettling place I have ever visited, but I am having to put on a cheery face, as the children are beginning to sense something isn't quite right. As we walk farther into the heart of the forest, I glance across at Lissen. She has the same brave face, but in the flicker of the candles that light our way I can see her eyes darting into the pitch-black undergrowth. The stony, blank faces of dead children peer back at us, bathed in the dancing lights.

It is at this moment that I realize Emil is no longer with us.

There is a place at the foot of Mount Fuji where a number of Japan's thirty-four thousand annual suicides go to die. It is called Aokigahara forest, and the very air itself there is said to be congested with the spirits of the tormented. Twice a year a squad of cleanup guys fan out through the forest and harvest the corpses, usually finding well over seventy in various states of decay.

We are not there—what, do you think I am *insane?*—but Aokigahara is on my mind as we take what was supposed to be a pleasant early-evening stroll into the cemetery amid the forest of lost souls on the top of Mount Koya.

We had arrived earlier in the day on the sacred mountain plateau, encircled by cedar and cryptomeria conifer forests one and a half miles above sea level. Koya-san, as the Japanese call the mountain, is the spiritual heart of Japan. It is also as good as the geographical center of the country, located a three-hour train ride south of Osaka followed by a short, vertical ride up the mountain in a clunking old funicular. The journey is grindingly slow—deliberately so, I suspect—to allow decompression from modern Japan, for Koya-san is most assuredly not modern Japan.

This is the resting place of the great spiritual leader, scholar, and polymath Kobo Daishi. In A.D. 804, aged thirty-one, Daishi—then named Kukai—traveled to China, where he studied esoteric Buddhism, known in Japan as Shingon, or "True Word" Buddhism. Shingon is a kind of fast-track Buddhism. It teaches that one can attain enlightenment during a single lifetime, which has the obvious appeal of allowing you to circumvent all those tiresome stages of reincarnation as bugs and cattle and so forth. Daishi founded the head temple of the Shingon order on Koya-san on his return from China in A.D. 816; legend has it that he threw his trident to determine where to build the temple, went looking for it, and met a hunter with a two-headed dog who told him it had landed on Koya. The mountain's popularity as a pilgrimage destination for the upper classes of Kyoto and Osaka grew from the eleventh century, surviving anti-Buddhist movements and, eventually, the admission of women in the late nineteenth century. It remains an important religious site to this day.

Prior to the arrival of Buddhism in Japan, the country's main religion was Shintoism, which, despite its drastic subsequent decline, remained the official state religion until World War II. Shintoism is a complex yet in a way quite primitive belief system based on the worship of gods (*kami-sama*) believed to be present throughout the natural world. Shinto's equivalent of Genesis tells us that the sibling gods Izanagi and Izanami made love and created humans, which explains those giant penis shrines the TV travel shows always visit when they come to Japan. Today, fewer than 2 percent of Japanese practice Shintoism, but Japanese Buddhism incorporates many elements of Shintoism to the extent that, for many, the two still blur somewhat.

There were once around 1,500 temples on Koya-san. Today there are a little over a hundred, but the town, which has a permanent population of just seven thousand people, is busy year-round receiving over a million pilgrims.

We had come to Koya-san for a different reason. I wanted to try the local vegetarian cuisine, a highly refined multicourse meal called shojin ryori, featuring, among other things, a special way of preparing tofu, called *koya-dofu*—freeze-dried, legend has it, after a monk left some tofu out during a cold night and observed how it turned interestingly spongy when reconstituted (and apparently it's even more nutritious than regular tofu). Over the centuries, shojin ryori has developed into a sophisticated, refined form of dining in which great effort is made to make the most out of relatively humble ingredients in order to express three Shingon key tenets of sincerity, cleanliness, and presentation. Kaiseki ryori evolved in part from shojin ryori, which is almost entirely fat-free.

As does the Franciscan brotherhood, Shingon Buddhism has a tradition of hospitality, and around half of the temples on Koya-san have guest rooms, some of them boasting flat-screen TVs, private baths, and minibars. Judging by the signs at the gates, most take MasterCard, too. Though charming, our *shukubo*, as these religious hostels are called, wasn't one of the luxurious ones, and the traditional tatami room we had been shown on arrival was virtually empty apart from a low table, some cushions, and an electric heater, as, even in summer, it can get chilly at night.

"Where's the TV?" Emil asked after a few frantic minutes of searching.

"I'm afraid there isn't one," said Lissen. Asger frowned, then laughed, thinking we were joking.

Time to explore. The town is divided into the Garan, or Sacred Precinct—the main temple district centered on a short high street with a few restaurants and tourist shops—and the Okuno-in, the forest cemetery where Kobo Daishi is interred, supposedly not actually deceased but merely sleeping. Apparently, local monks bring him lavish dinners every night.

Even in the bright afternoon sun there was a strange, weighty atmosphere about the town, enhanced by the smell of incense, the occasional maudlin ring of a gong, and the glimpse of black-robed monks clip-clopping down the street in their wooden sandals.

The monasteries were extraordinarily graceful, though, their gardens dotted with moss-covered boulders ringed by precision-raked gray gravel and ancient pines whose boughs were propped up by wooden posts like elderly pilgrims. We turned back at the entrance to the forest, as we had to return for dinner.

Back at our monastery, we left our shoes at the door and transferred to complimentary red vinyl slippers. As usual, these were about five sizes too small for me and made me totter like a low-rent tranny. At 5:30 on the dot, our paper door slid open, and a monk silently placed a lacquered tray filled with an array of colorful dishes on the low table. We knelt around the table and began tucking in to lovely, light vegetable tempura; kamaboko (ground fish, pressed into colorful cakes, steamed and served in slices), udon noodles, salad, fresh tofu, crunchy pickles, miso soup, and fresh fruit.

Afterward, I wandered down to the kitchen to say thank you. I met a shaven-headed Mexican woman, a nun, called Veronica. She told me she had lived in the monastery for eight years, making dinner for around fifty people every night. Did they ever eat meat? I asked. "Not really, but if we are given meat we have to eat it," she told me, before hurrying off with more trays for other guests.

We decided to go out for an evening stroll, this time to the forest itself. It soon became clear that this was not a Koya-san convention. The main street was now deserted, and I later found out that the Japanese rarely if ever venture into the Okuno-in after dark. At the entrance to the forest, we passed the only people still out and about, two elderly ladies selling pine sprigs and satsumas as offerings. They seemed alarmed to see us and looked away when we smiled. I wanted to see Kobo Daishi's tomb, which lay at the far end of a stony path deep in the forest, so onward we went.

The atmosphere amid the tall pines was airless and still. Koya-san's thousand-year-old forest is said to be full of the kami-sama, the Shinto gods who inhabit everything that is natural, from animals to trees and rocks, and, after dark, with only lanterns to light our way, it was all too easy to imagine this was true.

Entering the forest, we came upon an astonishing sight: row after row of stone shrines, stupas, and pagodas nestled among the trunks of the pines. In between them were eerie little statues of figures, like children, each with a small red cotton bib hung around its neck, some with knitted hats. Many had offerings of sweets or coins placed before them; others sat leaning, as if they were dozing, in their own wooden huts, like lazy parking-lot attendants. Some of their faces had been worn away by the weather, and the rain had made the dye in some of their bibs run pale pink. The statues are called *jizo* and are, among other things, memorials to children and infants who have died. We didn't tell Asger and Emil this, for obvious reasons, but they had sensed a mood change regardless. Deeper into the forest we came across a giant ziggurat made up of even more jizo, perhaps sixteen feet high, standing sentinel, waiting.

Koya-san has been the burial place of many of Japan's notables over the centuries, and in recent years there has been a trend of Japanese corporations building small memorials to deceased employees here. Living employees visit these memorials—many designed to represent the companies' products (one is shaped like a coffee cup; another is like a space rocket)—and leave their business cards.

It was while we were photographing the rocket that we realized Emil was no longer with us. We started to retrace our steps, calling out—more "whispering out": there was something about this place that inhibited shouting. I was growing anxious. Emil often goes missing—that wasn't unusual—but he had never done so in a haunted forest cemetery, at night.

Eventually, we found him. It seemed an age, but was probably less than five minutes. He hadn't gone far. He was crouching beside a jizo, his hand on its head, talking.

Lissen picked him up and told him softly that if he wanted to wander off, he should always tell us.

"What were you saying to the statue, Emil?" I asked, trying to sound cheerful.

"We were just talking," he said. "She said she was lonely."

Finally, we crossed the Mimyo-no-hashi Bridge, where pilgrims ladle water over a statue in memory of babies who drowned or were aborted, and then came to the Toro-do, or lantern hall, where Kobo Daishi still awaits the next Buddha. The hall was lit by ten thousand oil lamps, two of which, it is claimed, have burned since the eleventh century—one of them originally lit by the then emperor. The only sound was of the stream outside. We took a quick glance and hurried back, trying hard not to run.

Back at the monastery I met up with a Swiss monk called Kurt, who I had been told acted as a kind of unofficial ambassador for

Koya-san, giving talks around the world on Shintoism and the mountain.

"I came here for enlightenment," Kurt told me as we sat in his office drinking rough Italian wine. "I came to Japan for the first time twenty-seven years ago to research spiritual design. I was an artist—performance, installation—I took a kind of holistic approach, anything to express my thoughts: speech, writing . . ."

I asked him about shojin ryori. What does it mean? "It means 'pure food.' A Buddhist monk must eat what is given to him; he must not order the killing of another animal, but if someone gives him meat, he must eat it. Here at the monastery, of course, we only do vegetables. And no onions or garlic because they stimulate sexual desire. Some foreign guests don't like the tofu, but I have noticed they are neurotic."

But wine is OK? "In Buddhist terms, no drugs are allowed, because they take away consciousness. You must be conscious and present in what you are doing; that is why Buddha suggested meditation, because that way you can understand your own mind. I drink it to boost blood pressure and because you are here. Actually, many years ago, I was a specialist dealer in beer, spirits, and wine. But luckily Buddhists don't judge people. We are not missionaries. While Christians say, 'This is right and this is wrong,' Buddhists are tolerant; they don't judge one way or the other. There are as many ways to reach liberation as there are sentient beings. We respect them for who they are. We know people are not perfect."

It sounded like an appealing approach to life. He explained to me that he rose each morning at four for prayers and offerings. Would I like to join them the next day?

"Maybe," I said.

I asked about his beliefs. "No, I am not a believer. I doubt. Everything is energy. This gives you a liberalistic outlook because attachment causes misery—to ideas, to concepts, to notions of perfection. You know suffering comes from attachment. Buddhism requires that you look within your own mind as it really is. Once you discover the mechanics of your own mind, you can reach a liberation and just be present. Happiness is in the moment. The moment you lose your ego, you are free."

26. THE BEEF DELUSION

After the dainty, health-giving, vegetarian cuisine of Koya-san, I had a yearning for some meat, lots of it, preferably rich, red, bloody beef. If the stories are to be believed, the Japanese accord their cattle a greater reverence than the Hindus do theirs—at least up until the point of slaughter. They are pampered to a degree that Paris Hilton's Chihuahua might find excessive, enjoying beers and massage, sake rubs, and relaxing piped music. This, we are told, is why their beef—which we in the West know, variously, as Kobe or Wagyu beef—is so extraordinarily tender, its flesh patterned with river deltas of creamy white fat, and, of course, why it is so costly and desired. But, unicorns aside, there can be few more heavily mythologized beasts than the Japanese cow.

Cows have also played an improbable but important role in defining the Japanese's self-image as devout, self-controlled, and abstemious vegetarians. It is said that when Buddhism came to these shores, around A.D. 730, the consumption of meat was outlawed. Not another shred of beef passed Japanese lips until, one morning in 1872, the emperor woke up and decided he fancied a little beef for his dinner and made a public pronouncement to that effect, and the Japanese became meat-eaters overnight. Even then, the historical blame for the Japanese's loss of carnivorous innocence is typically placed at the feet of the mercantile barbarians from the West. As Shizuo Tsuji writes in *A Simple Art*: "The first cows slaughtered in Japan were for the tables of Western residents."

Unusually, Tsuji is quite wrong. Let's get this straight: the Japanese have always eaten meat. The A.D. 730 decree, which is generally held to be the vegetarian watershed, was in reality as much a pragmatic solution to the problem of overconsumption of animals that were needed for farmwork; it was intended to stop everyone from eating the cows and horses that pulled the plows.

As I have mentioned before, being partial to wild boar, the Japanese promptly renamed them "mountain whale" to circumvent the no-meat edict. Samurai in particular remained especially keen carnivores. As noted historian Naomichi Ishige writes in *The History and Culture of Japanese Food*: "The main purpose of the ban was to prohibit the eating of beef and horse meat and protect the livestock population as well as to prevent drought, insect damage, and famine. Moreover, it was limited to the spring and summer months which constitute the paddy farming season."

The truth is, the Japanese kept on eating meat using the same excuse that my grandmother employed for her nightly whiskey: that it was for "medicinal purposes." They realized the health values of meat and cloaked their love of game with the term *yakuro*, or "medicinal hunting."

Increasing contact with Westerners in the sixteenth and seventeenth centuries also alerted the Japanese to the fact that they were physically smaller, a situation they attributed to the Western traders' meat-eating habit. Around this time, according to historian Katarzyna Cwiertka, so-called beast restaurants, serving horse, wild boar, and venison, became popular.

By the second half of the nineteenth century, as the trading ports of Nagasaki, Hakodate, Yokohama, and Kobe opened up to the

West, eating meat became yet more popular—even the emperor was at it, and it is true that the floodgates opened with his 1872 announcement (followed by a public meal of beef on January 24, 1873) that meat was permitted. Within five years, Tokyo was consuming twenty-five cows a day, and within ten years, hundreds of restaurants serving meat sprang up across the country.

Beef consumption increased dramatically in the postwar period for much the same reason as in the latter part of the nineteenth century: the Japanese saw that their American conquerors were bigger and stronger and attributed this to their meat intake. In 1955, the Japanese ate an average of six to seven pounds of meat per year per capita. Today, according to some estimates, they eat over sixty pounds.

Those open ports were also the starting points of a more general craze for Western food and dining practices, such as the use of tables and chairs. Improbable as it may sound, initially at least, the Japanese adopted British cuisine as their favorite foreign food, because it was simpler and cheaper to produce than French cuisine—hence the otherwise perplexing rise of Worcestershire sauce and curry rice, both still popular in Japan today. The Japanese had seen how the British suppressed India, and they didn't want it happening to them. The solution? Get with the meat program!

And this is where the misnomer "Kobe beef" stems from. Of all the nineteenth-century international trading ports, Kobe was the most cosmopolitan. These days there are still said to be over a hundred different nationalities living in the city, and visiting seamen always knew they could rely on finding a good steak on arrival. Much later, Kobe was the birthplace of one of the most popular ways of eating beef in Japan, which helped cement its position as a recognizable global brand. The dish was teppanyaki—in which cubes of beef are briefly seared on a hot plate—invented in the 1950s by an okonomiyaki chef who wanted to offer American diners a dish they might recognize.

But not all Japanese beef is Kobe beef; in fact, since most countries had until recently banned beef exports from Japan after the BSE ("mad cow disease") crisis of 2001, anything purporting to be Kobe beef that you might have encountered in, say, one of those outlandish burgers with foie gras and truffles in New York or London has probably come from the American Midwest, Australia, or China. Even in Japan, Kobe accounts for only a small percentage of beef production. It is, after all, a city crammed onto a small stretch of land between the mountains and the sea. There ain't much room for grazing.

A better name might be Wagyu beef, but that too is a little broad (it means simply "Japanese beef"). The main cattle-raising districts of Japan are Maesawa, Yonezawa, Yamagata, Kobe, and Matsusaka (not to be confused with matsutake, the posh mushrooms). Over 80 percent of cattle raised in these areas today is black-haired, short-horn Tajima-gyu cows, or "Japanese Blacks," many of which start their life on the southern islands of Okinawa before coming to mainland Japan to be reared. The consensus among the chefs and foodies I had spoken to so far was that, of these, the best beef comes from those raised in Matsusaka, between the Kumozu River in the north and the Miya River to the south. The beef from here is said to be more tender, tasty, and beautiful than any other.

We'd seen this extraordinary meat, like inverse raspberry ripple ice cream, with the branches of fat—called *sashi*—lacing extravagantly through the red flesh, on sale in supermarkets everywhere, but our first chance to taste it came in Kyoto, in a shabu-shabu restaurant in the city's famous Ponto-cho nightlife district.

Shabu-shabu is half dinner, half performance art in which bacon-thin escalopes of beef are wafted in a small charcoal-heated samovar—a *hoko nabe*—full of a very light, simmering konbu dashi. Shizuo Tsuji says that the name *shabu-shabu* comes from the supposed sound this wafting of the beef makes in the water, but it is not a traditional Japanese dish at all; it arrived in Japan only in the early twentieth century and is generally considered Mongolian in origin. The meat is wafted for mere seconds and then dipped either in ponzu or a sesame-based sauce, or sometimes raw egg.

After the precious meat had been eaten—with great enthusiasm from Asger and Emil; these kind of theatrical cooking techniques might well have been invented for small boys—mushrooms, onions, cabbage, and tofu went into the pot. As with the chanko nabe experience in Tokyo, just as we thought we'd conquered the whole lot, the waiter brought us noodles to add to the broth, which had by now become lightly flavored by the ingredients.

We tried another way of eating Japanese beef, *sukiyaki*, the next day. Sukiyaki uses slightly thicker escalopes of beef fried in beef tallow on a hot skillet, then dipped in a sugary soy-mirin sauce. (Japanese Food Schism No. 286: in the east, they cook the meat in the sauce; in the west, they use it as a dip.) It was a little too sugary for my taste, although the children devoured it like wolves: but then again, it is no great leap from sugary beef to a Big Mac, is it?

On both occasions the beef itself was a vivid pinky red and webbed with veins of fat to the extent that it was a split decision as to whether we were eating fatty meat or meaty fat. Its texture was akin to the tenderest milk-fed veal, as unctuous as Brylcreem, and it lingered on the tongue for just a few moments before melting away like butter in a hot pan. Alone it had a creamy, indefinably savory flavor, like uncommonly tasty fat.

I wanted to get to the bottom—the rump, if you like—of this extraordinary meat. How could they breed beef that was so rich and fatty without the cows keeling over from heart attacks? Could all the rumors concerning the beer, the music, and the sake rubs be true?

The rumors are to be found in the most reliable of sources: Japanese food writer Kimiko Barber says, for instance: "The beef is marbled because the cattle are massaged with beer to distribute the fat throughout the meat." I had seen this claim made for Japanese cattle-rearing in newspapers and books countless times. But could massage actually *move* fat around in this way? And did beer really add to the fattiness of the meat, as others claimed? Could there be farmers on earth who played music to their animals?

If all the rumors were true, I had a very clear vision of what I wanted to achieve with my research. Since I'd started reading about Japanese beef, I had formed a childish ambition. I hadn't mentioned it to anyone, not even Lissen, for fear that she would dismiss this entire Japan project as the self-indulgent folly of a crazed and immature man.

I wanted to give a massage to a cow.

It was partly the absurdity of it that appealed, but also, I'll admit, the cheap kudos of participating in the production of one of the world's greatest gourmet products. I became fixated on capturing the money shot of me standing next to a cow, giving it a meaningful rub. And if Matsusaka was where the best beef was raised, this was where my cow groping would have to take place.

Matsusaka is a historic castle town in central Mie Prefecture, about three hours by local train southeast of Osaka. Figuring that out had been the easy part. The rest—finding people from the cattle industry in Matsusaka who were willing to talk to me—was less straightforward.

Initial confusion on the part of the various local authorities I contacted—"Sorry, we don't export"—was soon replaced by mistrustful suspicion, then stalling, with endless e-mails bounced back and forth. Could you send copies of articles you have written about beef before? Tell us again, what was your interest in Japanese beef? What did you say your name was? And so on, round and round in an endless, polite holding pattern. And I hadn't even dared mention the real reason I wanted to visit a Matsusaka cattle farm.

Eventually, through sheer persistence, some dates and meetings were set up at the renowned Wadakin ranch, but I was not allowed to bring anyone apart from a translator. I set off from Osaka station for Matsusaka with my new friend Sasha, the ponytailed Serbian (who spoke Japanese) from my cooking demonstration in Kyoto.

The three-hour train ride gave us a chance to get to know each other. Sasha's dream, he told me, was to return to Serbia to open an authentic Japanese restaurant. "It will be over many floors of the same building," he told me. "The ground floor will be common people's food like ramen and curry rice, then the higher you get, the more refined the food will be until, right at the top, you will have kaiseki."

When you arrive by train in Matsusaka, the nature of the town's main industry is immediately obvious. Advertising billboards promote beef restaurants, butchers' shops, and ranches wherever you look. As we arrived at the Wadakin ranch—which looked more like a well-manicured country club than a place for raising cattle—I had my strategy all planned out. I would listen attentively as the farmers explained their methods, taking assiduous notes and asking serious questions in order to appear a proper cow enthusiast for as long as was necessary. At no point would I be so crass as to ask outright whether or not they massaged the cows or, heaven forbid, if I might give one "a bit of a rub." I would bide my time until I judged the moment was right, then I would ask, casually, if I might, you know, perhaps just take a quick peek at some actual cows, for "research purposes." Then, lingering by the stalls, I hoped to catch a glimpse of their secret husbandry techniques, to try to see any massage-and-beer action going down, and perhaps even to get Sasha to distract the farmers while I nipped under the fence and, under the pretense of just, you know, patting a cow, give it a surreptitious knead. At least then I could honestly say that I had massaged a cow.

What was the worst that could happen if they caught me? Sure, I would have to leave in ignominy, but if I got to rub a cow it would be worth it.

Imagine my surprise, then, upon arriving at the farm to find a field with four horned, black-haired Tajima-gyu cows with rings through their noses loitering in it, and two cow hands standing by with giant gallon-size bottles of shochu, a crate of beer, and two woven straw rubbing mats.

I was barely out of the car and shaking hands with my hosts before one of them was showing me how to spray a mouthful of the shochu over the flank of the cow before rubbing it into his hide with a bundle of woven straw, and then egging me on to try it for myself.

I heaved the huge shochu bottle up to my lips and took a mouthful of the burning liquor. I summoned all my lung power, puckered, and pointed at the side of the cow, and let rip with a messy, dribbling spurt, much of which ended up down my shirtfront. The Wadakin ranch hands looked on with broad grins. I half expected a hidden TV crew to emerge, perhaps from the back end of the cow, but the handler urged me on with the straw, showing me how to rub vertically to ensure the shochu permeated the animal's coarse black hair. He then offered me a large brown bottle of beer. The cow, seeing this, started swinging its head around excitedly. I plunged the bottle into its mouth, although in the gnashing of teeth and flailing of cow lips, much of its contents spilled to the floor as the animal desperately tried to suck the bottle dry.

The farm hands looked on approvingly, and I felt a chapter of my life had drawn to a close. I had done it. I had massaged a cow. I felt empty, shallow, and not a little foolish, but somewhere there was also a perverse sense of achievement.

Not having had much practice at spitting at cows, I had managed to swallow a good portion of the spirit, so the interview with

Kinbe Matsuda, the founder of Wadakin and one of the most respected cattle breeders in Japan, was not as coherent as I would have
wished. Here is what I could decipher from my notes.

The cows are raised to the age of ten months in Hyogo Prefecture,
another of the main cattle-breeding areas of Japan, before being
brought to the Wadakin ranch. They are bred only for meat, never
to produce milk, and not for breeding, and are slaughtered, virgins,
at three years and ten months. By this stage a diet of mostly rice
stems, with some corn, soybeans, and grain, will have brought
them to a weight of thirteen to fifteen hundred pounds. After slaughter, three-and-half ounces of their meat will sell for ¥4,800 ($40) in
Wadakin's restaurant, the only outlet for its beef in the world.

"Why the beer?" I asked.

"If one of them isn't eating as much as they should, it helps give
them an appetite," Matsuda, who is the fourth generation of his
family to run the farm, told me. "We don't do it every day." And
why shochu? "Because it is cheap and high in alcohol, which is good
against insects." And did they really play the cows music?

"No, that's ridiculous."

On the subject of exactly why Wadakin massages their cows,
Matsuda-san was a little vaguer. "We massage to stop the fat building up," he said, or at least that's how Sasha translated it. "The fat is
very important for the flavor," he added. "It is very healthy. Not
much cholesterol, like olive oil."

We got to taste some Wadakin beef at the farm's lavish five-story
restaurant and hotel complex back in central Matsusaka. The restaurant's specialty is sukiyaki, but I wanted to try Wadakin beef in
its purest state, as sashimi. It was served with just a dipping sauce
of ginger and soy, and was sweet and creamy and lacking in that
metallic, bloody flavor that rare beef has back home. It was also actually a little tougher than the other Japanese beef I had eaten,
which was no bad thing.

So, all in all, a triumphant day. But on the train home something was still nagging me: I didn't really feel I had the definitive answers I had been looking for. So, a couple of days later, following more delicately negotiated phone calls, I headed back to Matsusaka, this time alone.

I was met by the manager of the local beef research center. We drove in his none-too-fragrant Honda to a group of cowsheds, which were home to a couple hundred Herefords and black Tajimas.

Along the way I bombarded him with questions. Why was Japanese beef so expensive? And why was it so tender? What did they feed the cows? Was it true about the massage and the beer? Was Wadakin for real, or is that just something they lay on for tourists?

"Raising cows here is a very labor-intensive process," he explained. "It takes so long. We don't slaughter them until forty-six months, and they don't produce milk during that time. Look." He pointed to a concave indentation in the back of one of the cows we encountered as we arrived at the sheds. "That's how we judge when to slaughter—when that indent reaches about the size of an egg, they are ready."

Wadakin was for real, he continued. The beer does stimulate appetite, but he didn't really agree with its use. The real secret to Japanese beef, he told me, is the breed and the feed, that and the fact that most of their herd are females, which are tender more than the males. "The black Japanese cows are the only ones that you can get this marbling with. We feed them only grass to start with." He gestured to a couple of big-eyed black cows munching lazily in their stalls. "Then they get rice straw, which is one of the most important factors in creating the marbling. After ten months we only feed them rice straw with a little green straw or grass because this helps to create the fat cells. Green grass stops the production of fat cells because it is rich in Vitamin A. They still need a little Vitamin A, though; otherwise, their legs get swollen and they go blind, so they get some green stuff." He claimed that the Japanese prefer these kinds of ultra-tender meats because their "jaw muscles are not so strong because we are used to eating a traditional diet of rice."

He led one cow out of its stable and offered me a metal-toothed brush. "You can have a go if you want." Being by now an old hand at Japanese cow husbandry techniques, I began giving the animal a vigorous brushing.

And the massage? How did that affect the marbling? "It doesn't have any direct effect on the fat, but the cows like it; it keeps them relaxed, which might mean they eat more. But we usually only do it before they are slaughtered, to calm them."

I stopped brushing. So *that* was the secret. Massaging was essentially a relaxation regime—happy cows make for good meat.

27. AMA DIVERS

On the train back from Matsusaka, I browsed through some brochures from the local tourist office. In one, on the history of Mie Prefecture, my eye was caught by a strangely haunting sepia photograph of two women dressed from head to foot in white-hooded jumpsuits and wearing goggles. They looked like uncommonly stylish welders, but according to the brief paragraph underneath, these were the fabled female divers, or *ama*, who have swum in the waters off the easterly Pacific coast of Mie for almost two thousand years.

The next page was about Mikimoto, the first company to cultivate pearls, founded by Kokichi Mikimoto, the son of a noodle maker, in 1899. Mikimoto was based in the city of Toba. Looking at the map on the back of the brochure, I saw that Toba and Sugajima, two of the main areas for ama divers, were about an hour's drive from each other.

Drawing on a decade of professional experience, I did what all journalists do when presented with two small snippets of possibly related information: I fashioned them into a dramatic story. By the time I arrived back at the house in Kyoto, I was able to tell Lissen and the boys heroic tales of female divers who dressed in white to scare killer sharks and could hold their breath for half an hour while diving for pearls worth as much as a house.

The next day, I contacted the Mie tourist board to find out more. Were any of the lady pearl divers still alive? Yes, absolutely, but they didn't dive for pearls, the tourist board official told me. All the pearls produced in the region were farmed. Of course, if I had thought about it for a moment, I would have realized that you don't need to dive for cultivated pearls—that's the whole point of cultivating them. The ama divers dive instead for abalone, scallops, sea cucumbers, seaweed, and sea urchins. Was there any chance I could meet them? I asked. No problem, she said. How about tomorrow?

So the day after that—by now, we were into early October—we caught the train to Toba. We were met at the station by two representatives of the tourist board, who whisked us off on a spectacularly scenic minibus ride around Ago Bay to the village of Osatsu, where most of the ama divers live.

We drove along precipitous roads through forested hills high above a cobalt sea dotted with rocky islets. In the West, the only images we tend to get of Japan are overwhelmingly urban, but this was a potent reminder that once you break free of the concrete and the malls, Japan has natural beauty to match anywhere in the world.

We came to a ramshackle fishing village on a horseshoe bay and parked on the beach. A narrow path hugging the side of the cliffs led, above crashing waves below, to a small hut a couple of hundred yards away at the mouth of the bay. Here, we were told, our lunch would be prepared. As we walked farther out toward the ocean, we started to hear an eerie whistling noise. Then, as we arrived at a wooden hut at the end of the path, two figures emerged up a ladder from the sea to meet us.

And there they were, the sepia-toned ladies brought to life: two real-life ama divers, Tamie Kosaki and Kayo Kosaki, sisters in their early forties. They were carrying wooden tubs in which were a hand-ful of intriguing shellfish.

They showed us into the wooden shack where an open fire—or *robata*—had already burned down to hot ash in the middle of the floor. We sat around it as the women grilled their catch—sea snails and scallops, as well as some pre-bought squid and clams—and began to unravel the story of the ama divers.

Thirty years ago there were four hundred divers living in Osatsu alone, they said, but the numbers were declining everywhere, and now there were only three thousand in the entire region. There were two types of ama divers: those who swam out from the shore and fished around thirty feet from the beach, and those—usually husband-and-wife couples—who sailed farther out, around a hun-dred feet, to dive. Both types of divers are highly respected in the community, like village elders.

The women dive almost every day for about an hour at a time, while their husbands stay on the boat. I made some lame joke about marital relations at this point, but apparently women have always been the divers in these parts because the locals believe their extra body fat means they are better insulated to dive into deeper, colder waters, and—slightly less plausibly—that they have larger lungs and so can hold their breath longer.

"We use about ten kilos [twenty-two pounds] of weights to go down, and as we are pulled back up, we whistle to control our breath-ing. If we breathe too fast, it is dangerous," said Tamie. They dem-onstrated. It was the eerie, breathy whistling sound we had heard as we arrived, deeply evocative for the Japanese, apparently.

"We start usually at around twenty years old, but the oldest ama is eighty-one, and she is still diving. We dive for shellfish but also seaweed; it depends on the time of year. In March we dive for sea-weed; now the number one thing is sea cucumber."

What was their most prized catch? "Abalone, but it is so difficult," said her sister. "They stick to the rocks very firmly, and it takes time to get them off. We don't have much time because we hold our breath."

"How long can you hold your breath?" asked Asger, who had been practicing his own breath-holding on the train ride there. "I can do it this long." He puffed out his cheeks and began to turn pink, exhaling dramatically after about ten seconds.

"About a minute and a half," Tamie said, laughing. "Of course, if we are still, we can hold it much longer, but we have to use a lot of energy swimming around on the seabed looking for the shells."

I could understand why ama divers hadn't used oxygen in the past, when the technology hadn't existed, but why didn't they use it now? "Today, we have to be careful about overfishing," said Kayo. "Without oxygen, it limits how long we can search for the shellfish, so we don't catch so much. We have to check their size with this [she held up a forceps-style measure] so that we don't catch the young ones."

Lissen asked about the white suits. Were they really originally worn to frighten off sharks? "No, it is more to protect against jellyfish and sunburn. We do see sharks, though, about one meter [three feet] long, but they are not dangerous. What we do is dangerous, though. Last year one diver was hospitalized when she got trapped in the rope. We wear this symbol." She pointed at a star-shaped badge. "It is our lucky charm."

As Kayo spoke, she turned one of the *sazae,* sea snail, on the grill. Its juices spat across the hut. Asger and Emil looked on with horror and fascination, recoiling with wide eyes when offered one on the end of a fork.

As the guest of honor, I didn't have the privilege of refusal, even though my experience of snails is of a great deal of chewing with not much flavor by way of reward. I once visited a snail farm on a Finnish island. The woman running it explained that before you eat snails you have to starve them so they—and there is no delicate way of putting this—expel all their waste matter. These snails, though not the same species, had clearly not undergone this purging, having just been wrenched from the sea, which probably explained the bitter aftertaste from their dark green intestine.

Was this one of their favorite dishes? "Oh no." They both shook their heads. "Uni [sea urchin] with rice. Very simple: rice with lots of rice vinegar and seaweed and vegetables with uni on top."

Back in Toba, we had some time to kill before catching our train to Kyoto. As the home of Mikimoto, Toba is famous for its pearls. The surface of its beautiful rocky bay is covered with the wooden rafts used to suspend the oysters that grow the pearls. In the middle of it all is Pearl Island, a theme park built by the mighty Mikimoto company. Inside, lavish exhibits explain how pearls are cultivated within the shells of Akoya oysters: "A portion of the internal organs is parted with a spatula, and a small incision is made in the surface of the body of the oyster with a scalpel. Then, very gently, a path is made through the incisors into the gonads." Something to think about the next time you reach for something to accessorize that twinset.

28. THE GREATEST SOY SAUCE IN THE WORLD

The next day, I traveled by bus across the Akashi Kaikyo suspension bridge to Shikoku, in the inland sea, an island so beautiful I regarded it from the window in a kind of blissful trance. There were gentle mountains and gorges packed tight with tombstones; distant glinting seas; giant wheeling *tombi* hawks silhouetted against a crisp, blue sky; rice-straw wigwams drying in the sun; and ceramic-tiled wooden houses, as seen in dozens of samurai movies.

I was traveling to Shikoku Island to taste the world's greatest soy sauce, the soy equivalent of cold-pressed, extra-virgin, single-estate olive oil or fifty-year-old Modena balsamic vinegar, a true gourmet rarity produced in the traditional method by the descendant of a samurai family.

But first, the supermarket stuff.

The single most important ingredient in Japanese food is not rice—which is more than a mere ingredient; it is virtually a spiritual element to a meal—but soy sauce. Though the Japanese do use salt in their cooking—and, as I was to discover on Okinawa, they produce some of the greatest salts in the world—the majority of their seasoning comes from this fabulously savory, ebony brown, viscous liquid.

They consume on average over two gallons per capita per year of various types: light and salty *usukuchi*, traditionally associated with the west of Japan; less salty, dark *koikuchi*, traditionally favored in the east of Japan and accounting for 80 percent of the market; another soy made with equal parts wheat and soybeans; one made with added *amazake*, a fermented rice drink; as well as *saishikomi*, *shiro*, and tamari soy, the latter thicker and richer and made using little if no wheat.

One soy company dominates both the domestic and global soy markets. Kikkoman's distinctive little squat-bottomed bottles with the double-spouted, brittle, red plastic screw tops are ubiquitous the world over, found on every table of every Chinese and Japanese restaurant from Washington to Wolverhampton, and in most domestic kitchens, too. The company has plants in Holland, China, and the United States, producing over a hundred million gallons per year. It is the Coca-Cola of the soy sauce world. And the Pepsi, as well. Well, can you name another soy brand?

Japanese soy has traditionally been made in Chiba Prefecture, in either Choshi or Noda, and sailed down the river to Tokyo. It has been exported farther afield since the seventeenth century—Louis XIV was said to have been a fan. Kikkoman started in Noda three hundred years ago, and it still has its base there. Back when we were still in Tokyo, at the beginning of our journey, almost two months earlier, I took a train there, twenty miles north across the endless expanse of Tokyo's suburbs.

Noda is very clearly a one-company town. The air was thick with the meaty smell of soy sauce—a kind of sweet, beefy, wheaty aroma—but Kikkoman didn't appear to have brought great wealth to Noda, which was a rather bleak, ramshackle, low-rise place, dominated by the giant, rusting hulks of wheat storage tanks.

I had hoped to visit Goyogura, the brewery dedicated solely to making soy sauce for the imperial household, but it was undergoing renovation. Instead, Hiroyuki Yano, a nice man from the PR department, showed me around the visitors' center, starting with the dreaded corporate video ("Defying the passing of time and national boundaries, since times of old, that's Kikkoman!"), before we followed the process of turning soybeans into soy sauce, or shoyu, via windows into the factory itself.

It is a surprisingly straightforward process, which probably explains why home brewing of soy was commonplace in Japan until World War II. The main ingredients are steamed soybeans and roasted, crushed wheat—in Kikkoman's case, non-GMO and grown in the United States and Canada (the emperor's soy sauce is made exclusively with domestic ingredients, of course). These are fermented using the Kikkoman *Aspergillus oryzae* bacteria, a type of koji, which is mixed with brine to make a mash called *moromi* and left to develop for six months. Sugar and amino acids combine to create that deep caramel color while yeasts and lactic acid create the aromas—there are three hundred different aromas in soy, apparently, a figure comparable to wine. The moromi, an unpleasant-looking orangey-brown mash, is churned and then pressed in 2,800-yard-long nylon sacks before being pasteurized.

What was the difference between this and how the Chinese make their soy? I asked Yano-san. "The fermentation process is different. Some of the Chinese ones are made by a chemical process." He sniffed. "They can use acid to take the protein from the beans, for instance." Some companies also add corn syrup and artificial caramel, or even hydrolyzed vegetable protein and hydrochloric acid, but not Kikkoman.

Until thirty years ago, Kikkoman made its soy sauce by fermenting the moromi in traditional wooden trays, a method originally devised because it allowed the temperature to be easily regulated by lifting the trays to control the circulation of air. These days they use giant, glass-lined, temperature-controlled stainless steel tanks. There are two thousand of them in the Noda plant alone, although this isn't the biggest Kikkoman factory—that is in Wisconsin. This vast scale of production enables the company to sell its soy sauce for less than the cost of bottled water in some territories.

I was impressed by the straightforward, relatively "slow food" brewing process at Kikkoman, but a chance tasting of another, far subtler, richer, and softer artisanal soy in a restaurant in Kyoto sent me off on the trail of a rather more refined soy sauce, made at the Kamebishi brewery, on the island of Shikoku.

Kamebishi is the only soy company in Japan still making soy sauce the old-fashioned way, using the *mushiro* method, in which the fermenting beans are spread out on woven straw mats placed on top of bamboo trays. The resulting mash is left to mature for a minimum of two years.

Kamebishi was founded over two hundred years ago and is still run by the seventeenth generation of the Okada family, originally of samurai stock. The factory remains in the small rural town of Higashikagawa, in the original samurai house, a sprawling, single-story red stucco farmhouse with a heavy ceramic-tiled roof.

In charge when I visited was Kanae Okada, who returned from a high-flying career in the travel industry in Tokyo to rescue the family firm some years ago. "When I was growing up, I never wanted to be a part of it, and my father didn't force me," Kanae told me. "I went off to work in the U.S., worked in Tokyo, and had a child. I worked at the Japan Cultural Center, and many of my colleagues there had a cultural specialty, like kabuki or sumo, and I felt so ashamed that I had neglected this part of my heritage. In the States it was the same. Everyone was so interested in my family, but I couldn't answer any of their questions. So I returned fifteen years ago to start running the company."

Kanae recognized the cultural and commercial importance of her family's product and was determined to save the company from the brink of bankruptcy. This she has done with a mix of shrewd business sense, a respect for traditional methods, and some remarkable new product innovations, including freeze-dried soy for use as a seasoning, and a soy sauce that she has aged for—so far—twenty-seven years.

"We are very different from Kikkoman," Kanae told me as she showed me around. "We roast our wheat on hot sand to 400°F. We use whole soybeans; they use dried beans with the oil removed. We ferment the moromi on straw mats on top of bamboo slats at between 82°F and 86°F. We age it for a minimum of three years in cedar barrels. It is very intensive, very intuitive."

Kanae is the first woman in Japan to run a soy company. What about her sixteen-year-old daughter? I asked. Will she take over the company one day? "Actually, she isn't like I was when I was growing up. She is really proud of what we do. She comes with me on business trips and explains things to clients. Many young Japanese are fed up with being white-collar; they want to make things. We used to have a real problem getting workers—you know, we are quite a way from anywhere here—but we get many young people coming to work here now. Only a few can cope with the hard work, but I think they will come back to the old ways. Ten years ago we were having a real crisis. Sales were dead, but now they have doubled." Perhaps the traditional sectors of the tofu and sake industries could benefit from a similarly dynamic, innovative approach.

We clambered up into the dark, cobwebbed loft where the hundred-year-old cedar barrels containing the slowly fermenting soy are kept—all the better to control the flow of air and, thus, the temperature. Every surface—walls, floor, old pipes, ceilings—was caked with a thick, tar-like crust. We gingerly tiptoed across the tops of the barrels—essentially large wooden tanks set into the floor. It reminded me of Fagin's London, and I must have pulled a bit of a face, as Kanae said, "You know, it isn't dirty. It is decades of fungal growth, but actually, the whole process is extremely hygienic even though we never clean it. Someone from the government's hazard analysis department came and said we had to clean everything, but I had to explain that this environment is exactly what makes our soy taste so special. The mold here is more than two hundred years old! We did tests and found 230 different types of bacteria, yeast fungus, and microbes—all of them are part of our fermentation process. These microfungi produce lots of alcohol, so in the summer it gets above 104°F and really smells of booze." In other words, the entire building was alive with fertile microorganisms, a giant fermentation chamber.

The floor was slippery, and the barrels about seven feet deep. Had anyone ever fallen in? I asked. "Yes, I did once, when I was four. It was full of soy, too. Luckily there was someone to fish me out, or I would probably have died."

For the first two nights of fermentation, someone has to babysit the mash, stirring it and maintaining the right temperature, but the result of this incredible attention to detail is a soy that is richer and smoother tasting than supermarket soy. It sells for roughly twice the price, but that is still, to me, cheap for an artisanal product.

We retired to Kanae's office to talk about the future of soy. "I started to make soy salt for the French and Italian chefs because they couldn't season their food with soy sauce because of the color. Now lots of Italian chefs are using it. It is packed with umami. You can think of it as natural MSG. Pascal Barbot and Alain Ducasse are very interested in using it."

Then she brought out the "special stuff." "And this," she said, proudly brandishing a bottle whose contents were pitch-black and syrupy, "is the twenty-seven-year-old aged soy. The only aged soy in the world. I got the idea when I visited a balsamic vinegar producer in Modena who had a hundred-year-old balsamic, which tasted incredible. We are not going to sell this until it is fifty years old, but you can taste it now if you like." It was rich and deep, with a powerfully lactic taste, hints of sherry, cedarwood, and grilled steak, like a refined, complex Marmite but without the afterburn.

They also sell a ten-year-old soy for around $150 a bottle—presumably the most expensive soy sauce in the world—which, though not quite as intense, is wonderful drizzled over carpaccio, just like balsamic. Even more exciting were Kanae's plans for the future, which include soy maple syrup for ice cream, chocolate soy flakes, caramel soy, and balsamic soy salt. "The chocolate isn't quite ready—it needs more of an umami boost." (Since my visit, the chocolate has been perfected and is now on sale.)

Wandering around after our meeting, while waiting for my bus, I chanced upon another ancient, artisanal food producer, making *wasanbonto* sugar. This is the "king of sugars"—primarily sold as ultrafine sugar bonbons, little balls the size of peas wrapped in tissue paper and made by hand from sugarcane for over two centuries. Legend has it that a pilgrim from southern Kyushu, at that time the only place allowed to grow sugarcane in Japan, walked all the way to Shikoku smuggling a *chikuto* sugarcane plant and, upon arrival, collapsed and died. They planted the sugarcane, and as it turned out, the soil and water here were perfect for its cultivation. The cane flourished, and when processed, by squeezing, then boiling the juice, and then stone-pressing the syrup to refine it, it produced much smaller, powder-sized crystals than the same plants grown in Kyushu. At ¥3,000 (around $40) per 2.2 pounds, it is today the most expensive sugar in Japan. I just had time, as my bus came into view, to buy some of the company's bonbons, which were extraordinarily fine. They dissolved quickly on my tongue, leaving a faintly flowery, sweet aftertaste.

29. A TALE OF TWO COOKING SCHOOLS: PART 2

We had been settled in Osaka for over a week. It was time to meet the other contestant vying for the culinary papacy of Japan, the man hoping to replace Shizuo Tsuji as the leading authority on Japanese cuisine. You'll remember that in Tokyo I had met Yukio Hattori, famous for inventing the TV cook-off show *Iron Chef* and head of the Hattori Nutrition College. He had staked his claim with his in-depth knowledge of the health issues involved in Japanese food, his involvement with the Japanese government's Shokuiku program, and the fact that he had promised to take me to dinner at the best restaurant in Japan.

Now I was to meet his chief rival, Yoshiki Tsuji, the son of Shizuo and, since his father's death, in 1993, the president of Japan's largest cooking school, the Osaka-based Tsuji Culinary Institute (TCI), bastion of the Kansai method of cooking.

I had e-mailed the school before we left for Japan and had been surprised to receive a reply from Tsuji himself, inviting me to visit, which is how I found myself waiting in the TCI's grand conference room, surrounded by French antiques at a vast oval oak table beside a bust of Shizuo Tsuji. I awaited the arrival of his son.

Assistants entered first, offering tea and informing me of Tsuji's imminent arrival. Soon after, their boss arrived. With a smooth, handsome face and dressed in a sleek gray sports jacket and dark trousers, Yoshiki Tsuji, forty-three, looked like a Japanese Richard Gere. He later told me he was an enthusiastic triathlete, which explained his trim physique and perhaps, too, the sense of coiled, latent energy. He spoke softly, with a minimum of projection, as if used to people hanging on his every word.

We moved into a lounge area, part of his private office, where he explained a little about the school. There were over five thousand students in various buildings here in Osaka, he said, as well as in two châteaus the school owns in southern France—Château de l'Eclair (found for Tsuji senior by his good friend Paul Bocuse) and Château Escoffier—and a smaller school in Tokyo. There was, he said, a roughly equal male/female split among the students, who come mostly from Japan but also from South Korea and Taiwan and are aged from graduate level to over sixty. They are taught Japanese, French, and Italian cooking, as well as patisserie and baking.

I asked if Tsuji-san felt he had taken over his father's papal role in Japanese cuisine. "No, no, but I do feel extremely responsible," he said. "We are creating craftsmen here. We do have fewer and fewer students wanting to learn Japanese cuisine because it is so demanding, but we are one of the first schools to realize the danger of this."

Can he cook himself? "Only breakfast. I have had training since the age of twelve but stopped cooking once I turned eighteen." His father wrote over thirty books—not just on food but on various other passions, including music, and Yoshiki has so far written two of his own—*The Theory of Evolution of Epicurism* and *An Introduction to the Food Industry*. But his business training in the United States has helped him find new ways to develop and expand the school, taking advantage of the economic slowdown in Japan to take over a neighboring bank, for example. The TCI is now a mini-town in its own right, having spread through several neighboring tower blocks in this part of Osaka.

"Would you like to see them?" Tsuji asked. I would, I said, expecting a PR flunky to take me on a brief tour. "Then let's go," he said. Tsuji was clearly proud of his school and wanted to show it to me personally. It soon became apparent why. It was not merely the most impressive culinary school I had ever seen—making my alma mater, Le Cordon Bleu, in Paris, look like a provincial primary school in comparison—but one of the most impressive educational establishments one could imagine.

The first room we visited was a state-of-the-art kitchen / TV studio built specially for filming and photography. It bustled with students working beneath arc lights, prepping dishes for the cameras. Next was the main lecture auditorium, twice as large as the one at Hattori's school, Tsuji pointed out, with highly polished mahogany writing desks and a gigantic stainless steel workstation decorated with twelve copper pots hanging from the front, each sparkling beneath spotlights. It was designed by John Morford, the man behind the Park Hyatt hotel in Tokyo (the *Lost in Translation* hotel), and, as with the rest of the school, it was clear that no expense had been spared on materials. Throughout, the decor was elegant and expensive, like a posh health spa, with gray slate and sophisticated beige, and wherever we went, all the students were in crisp white uniforms with blue aprons and gray trousers. The chefs, meanwhile, wore single-breasted white jackets, ties, and tall toques.

All of the 490 teaching staff are Japanese, Tsuji explained, and most of them are specialists, including one who has spent over thirty years perfecting the art of the *tamago*, or Japanese rolled omelet. "We have the highest quality of teaching. There is huge competition to become a teacher here, and many can't keep up with the standard once they come." I had heard various stories about the brutality of Japanese chefs. How did they prepare students for the punishing regime of working in a real kitchen? "The teachers aren't allowed to hit with their hands or with utensils or use psychological bullying, but within those limits, they are extremely tough. They have to be," said Tsuji.

Students pay upward of $25,000 a year to attend. "It is the most expensive cooking school in the world," he told me proudly. "Even though Dorothy Cann Hamilton still insists that is the International Culinary Center in New York. I argue a little with her about that!" (Tsuji now has a foot in New York himself as the co-owner, with David Bouley, of a double-Michelin-starred Japanese restaurant, called Brushstroke, in Tribeca.)

There was an entire building dedicated to French and Italian cooking, as well as another for advanced patisserie. In the administration block, Tsuji pointed out the offices of the school psychologists, employed to help students assimilate into school life and solve personal problems, something they consider extremely important.

We sat in on a demonstration in a large, sparklingly clean kitchen. The chef was running through a sun-themed menu, showing students how to tackle an entire sack of salmon roe, followed by a salmon fillet dish in soy and yuzu. The chef pin-boned the salmon, deftly sliding the bones between his index and middle finger as he went, like an expert seamstress. Then he marinated some salmon strips in soy, mirin, onion, and vinegar together with a little dried chili. The students sat in attentive silence.

In Europe and America, the restaurant industry still relies on apprenticeships whereby keen youngsters work, often for nothing, in professional kitchens, starting on the lowest tier. The system is often abused to the extent that you might as well call it slavery, but in Japan, things are even more extreme. "It used to be that young chefs would literally have to sit outside in front of the restaurant they wanted to work in for a week, hoping to be allowed to join the kitchen—I am talking about the really famous restaurants—but that system has pretty much collapsed now. We don't have the culture of *stages* in Japan. We do have apprenticeships, which start at sixteen; instead of getting paid, they get accommodations, food, and travel costs, but that is also declining now."

In contrast, TCI graduates are eagerly sought by the top restaurants in the country—fifteen thousand restaurants send requests to the school for one of their three thousand graduates each year, Tsuji claimed.

When the demo was finished, he invited me to lunch. I followed him to one of the canteens, whose kitchen is run entirely by the students. At Le Cordon Bleu, we would watch the chef demonstrate three courses, then adjourn to the practical kitchens to make the main course. Here, though, students were making ten courses for a dining room that would soon be filled by fifty or so very picky guests.

We were early, so Tsuji invited me to spend some time watching in the kitchen. I was astounded by the students' skill and organization and the complexity of the dishes they were preparing. In one corner, one male and one female student were putting the finishing touches on some exemplary sashimi plates; elsewhere, another was deep-frying somen noodles to use as decoration for—and to add bite to—tempura batter.

The meal was superb—elegant, colorful, fresh, and inventive; I would have been hard-pressed to distinguish it from a meal in a good local restaurant. We sat with some students. I asked one—with Tsuji translating—why he had come to the school: "Because I love Japan and want to learn about Japanese culture" was his Miss World–ish reply. "Japanese cuisine is the coolest and most beautiful in the world," said another.

Over lunch, I mentioned that I was looking forward to eating in one of Osaka's best restaurants, Kahala, that evening.

"Oh yes. It's wonderful," said Tsuji. "How did you find out about it? Who are you going with?"

"Kadokami-san [Takeshi Kadokami, one of Kansai's leading food writers, whom I had met the previous day] recommended it. I am going alone. He says it's not really a place to take kids."

Tsuji looked pained. "You're going alone, but . . . no, no, we can't have that." He reached inside his jacket and took out his diary. "Let me see, well, would you mind if I accompanied you?"

"That would be great, yes, but I doubt you could get a table now, could you?" (The restaurant seats only eight and is booked up weeks in advance.)

"Oh, don't worry about that," said Tsuji, beckoning a minion and speaking to him in Japanese.

A few moments later, the assistant returned and nodded once to indicate that it was all taken care of.

So that evening Tsuji and I met at Kahala, the celebrated *kappo* ("counter" restaurant) run by Yoshifumi Mori, a short, stout, gray-haired chef in his early sixties.

Tsuji-san told me that Mori-san had run this chic, low-lit restaurant in the Kita Shinchi nightlife district of Osaka for thirty-five years. He is self-taught, and his often wildly imaginative cooking blends the most exquisite Japanese seasonal produce with French and contemporary molecular techniques. Some have called him Japan's Ferran Adrià, which seemed appropriate as far as our first "dish," a sparkling sake with wasabi, was concerned. His signature beef mille-feuille followed—five ultrathin, exceptionally tender layers of beef briefly seared on the hot plate in front of us by Mori-san—along with a glutinous shark's fin with matsutake mushroom, and hamo served with gigantic mustard seeds on a bed of soft konbu.

There were over ten courses in all, and I later discovered that the meal must have run to over ¥100,000 ($800) with the serious bottle of vintage Bordeaux that Tsuji ordered to go with it. He insisted on paying and had in fact done so before I even realized the bill had been presented, but that was not the end of his hospitality.

"Do you have time for a drink perhaps?" he asked as we left.

A couple of doors farther down the street, he turned, smiled, and led me into a basement entrance, his members-only club, he explained. We were met by a heavily made-up middle-aged woman in a glamorous frock and shown through to a long, narrow, brightly lit, windowless lounge.

My first thought—and this is honestly true—was *Ah, isn't it nice that all these men have brought their wives out for the evening.* It was only when one of the "wives" slunk over to our table and proceeded to sit next to me, so close that our thighs met, that reality dawned.

Before we had even sat down, Tsuji's personal bottle of single-malt whiskey had been retrieved from the club's storage and was waiting at our table. He poured glasses for me and the two women who had by now joined us. They were good friends, he said. "I often come here when I am alone in Osaka. My family lives in Tokyo, you see. They really are friends of mine. Sometimes I'll take one of them out to lunch or something."

I smiled at the girls, not a little bashfully. The idea of paying for female company, even platonic, has always seemed self-defeating to me. If you are paying someone for his or her company, then that person's interest in you is not far off that of the dogs in the Bow Wow café. But within seconds, I had completely fallen for the hostesses' charms. I was putty in their hands.

They were exceedingly good at their job and spoke a charming, broken English, and all too soon, I grew utterly convinced that they genuinely *were* interested in me, that I had somehow seduced them: they were that good—no matter that one looked like a young, Japanese Ava Gardner and the other had Renée Zellweger dimples, while I am heading rapidly into Homer Simpson territory.

As the evening wore on, the conversation became more personal. I asked Tsuji where he had learned his impeccable English. His father had sent him at the age of twelve to Fettes Prep School, Tony Blair's alma mater. That must have been tough. "Well, put it this way: I was the only Asian boy at boarding school." It struck me as curious that a man with such a finely honed sensitivity to food as Shizuo Tsuji would send his son to live in Scotland. "I tell you," said Tsuji, laughing, "it took ten years for my palate to recover!"

I mentioned that I had discussed Tsuji's and Hattori's rivalries with chef Murata in Kyoto. When I'd asked Murata about Tsuji, he had sniffed. "Tsuji flies first-class between Japan and Europe, and stays at the Ritz." I mentioned this to Tsuji. Curiously, he took issue with Murata's choice of hotel. "Pfft. I would never stay at the Ritz," Tsuji said, affronted. "I always stay at the George V!"

30. FUKUOKA

And so onward the Booth family caravan rumbled, south the next morning by Shinkansen, the bullet train, to the island of Kyushu and its capital, Fukuoka.

An efficient train system is often cited as a symbol of a well-functioning society, but the Japanese rail network is the paragon of paragons of efficiency. Not only are trains punctual to within seconds (and are judged late if they arrive more than a minute after their scheduled time), but when they arrive, their doors line up exactly with corresponding markings on the platform so that, if you have an allocated seat, you know precisely where to wait. There are even queue lines painted on the platform to guide you into the precise position for your quasi-reverential attendance.

The arrival of a Shinkansen is a showstopping moment, its great white snout slowly gliding to a perfectly damped halt accompanied by various satisfied exhalations.

Fukuoka is the end of the line for the Shinkansen, 730 miles from Tokyo. The line actually terminates in two cities: the smart castle town of Fukuoka, and the more mercantile Hakata. The two merged in 1889 and are now home to 1.3 million people. Fukuokans and Hakata-ites like to think of themselves as cultured and cosmopolitan—the city has high-speed ferry links to South Korea, and it takes around the same time to fly to Shanghai as it does to Tokyo. Perhaps because of this, the city has a unique food culture centered on its *yatai*, or street-cart food stalls, which we found by chance while wandering through the city center that evening.

We felt at ease in Fukuoka immediately. Of all the places we visited in Japan, this was the one we could most see ourselves returning to to live. Small enough to be manageable but large enough to be interesting, Fukuoka also has a special atmosphere—relaxed, welcoming, fun loving, and unpretentious. Throw in a great climate, excellent shops, museums, music venues, and a buzzing nightlife district, and you have everything you could ever wish for in a city.

The yatai contribute their own casual-festive ambience to the city. On our first evening wandering in the city center, we turned a corner to see the Naka River lined with these chaotic food stalls, many of them on wheels, some of them swathed in plastic sheeting and looking like the camps I used to build with my brother in the woods, with bare lightbulbs, steaming pots, and crowds of diners queuing for a place at their trestle tables. Some were open; others were curtained. We were turned away from one of the latter as soon as the cook spotted the children, deducing, probably correctly, that his food wouldn't meet with Asger's and Emil's approval. Others were more welcoming, and soon we were all seated overlooking the river in the balmy evening air on small folding stools at a communal table, each with a bowl of ramen before us.

Hakata ramen is based on a white-ish broth made from long-boiled pork bones. It's often a little spicier than other ramens, but thoroughly delicious. The next day we went in search of more and found a famous ramen shop, Ichiran, where diners eat in individual, curtained-off booths, as if at a peep show. Diners get a small questionnaire-type form to fill in where they can customize virtually every aspect of their bowl of noodle soup—the firmness of the noodles (extra-firm, firm, medium, tender, extra-tender), the strength of the onion, the fattiness of the broth, and so on. The "No Mobile Phones" and, next to it, "No Talking to Your Neighbor" signs served notice that this was a place for the serious ramen aficionado, which brought to mind an extraordinary man I had met back in Tokyo.

I had been to visit the Shin-Yokohama Raumen Museum, in Yokohama, to meet the world ramen champion, Mr. Takamitsu Kobayashi, but before we enter his esoteric but fascinating world, I should take a second to clarify the bewildering array of noodles available in Japan.

The traditional noodle division in Japan is that between soba and udon, buckwheat and wheat. Soba—thin, mottled noodles made from buckwheat flour (or more often a blend of buckwheat and wheat)—are supposedly preferred in eastern Japan, while udon— thick, soft, slippery, white flour–based noodles—are eaten in the west. This was originally because buckwheat grew well in the meager soil around Tokyo; now, of course, you can eat all kinds of noodles throughout Japan, but still the gourmands of Kanto and Kansai cherish their differences. Toshi had made clear to me that there is a certain snobbery associated with eating *zaru-soba*: cold, cooked soba, served on a bamboo draining mat with a little dipping sauce. Eating warm soba in a large bowl of soup—a dish called *kake-soba*—is thought common (although he did admit to doing this in the privacy of his own home). Soba has an earthy, almost metallic grain flavor like a French galette—both are made with buckwheat flour. If you can find the 100 percent buckwheat variety, you can be confident you are doing your body a world of good, as they are packed with vitamins B1 and B2 and have more protein than rice. Buckwheat is also rich in bioflavonoids, which are good for blood pressure, and antioxidants, thought to help ward against cancer. As buckwheat is a slow-release carbohydrate, you don't end up feeling zonked out half an hour after eating soba noodles, as one might after a big bowl of pasta. Udon, meanwhile, is largely empty calories, and probably the best thing to be said for it is that it fills you up and has a pleasing soft/firm texture. It is eaten mostly in a warm, dashi-based soup, although it can also be served with a cold dipping sauce as *kama-age-udon*.

Udon and soba are purely Japanese, while ramen is a Chinese import (the word comes from the Cantonese word *raomin*). Despite this, the Japanese eat far more ramen than soba and udon combined, mostly because of the extraordinary popularity of instant ramen noodles. Ramen came to Japan only in the early twentieth century, but its relatively high levels of fat appealed in a similar way as meat to a postwar populace looking to bulk up, and it was a useful rice substitute during times of shortage. Shizuo Tsuji dismisses ramen noodles altogether as being Chinese, and they are not included in *A Simple Art*, although he grudgingly concedes that yakisoba, which despite the name are fried ramen noodles, "are part of the ambience of every Japanese festival (as is cotton candy)."

Somen noodles, meanwhile, are thin and fine—the imperial noodle. Made with wheat flour and sesame oil, they are essentially just thin udon noodles, as are the marginally thicker *hiyamugi*. *Harusame* noodles are made from potato flour or mung bran flour and are similar to *shirataki* noodles, the clear "glass" noodles made from the same root as konnyaku (these are the noodles that turn pleasingly frazzled when added to tempura batter). And then you have the unfortunately named *wanko-soba*, served in Iwate Prefecture in mouthful-sized portions—wanko waitresses fill your bowl the minute you empty it, and you are expected to consume around 50 bowls. These are the noodles most commonly served in eating competitions (the record is 350 in one sitting).

But of them all, it is ramen that fuels this nation. Forget sushi and tempura, which are largely special-treat foods. When they are short on time, when they need a meal-in-a-bowl, when they want an umami hit, crave carbohydrates and porky protein, when they want warming and filling and to lose themselves in slurping contemplation of a bottomless bowl of sustenance, it is to ramen that the Japanese turn, whether it is instantly rehydrated in a polystyrene bowl, guzzled standing up at a bar on the way to catch a train, or lovingly served by a conscientious ramen master.

Today, a whole industry has grown up in appreciation of ramen noodles, with specialist ramen magazines and countless websites and blogs dedicated to detailed discussion of specific restaurants. In terms of chefs, you have your ramen purists, and the innovators desperate to create the hot new ramen style. Japan, and more recently the United States and the UK, are in the midst of a ramen boom that does not appear to be slowing. There are said to be over two hundred thousand ramen restaurants in Japan.

Essentially, ramen is a dish of yellow, chewy, curly Chinese wheat noodles served in deep bowl of soup with toppings—usually including a slice of roast pork. But as anyone who has seen the cult Japanese film *Tampopo*, about a young female ramen chef shown the ways of the noodle by a mysterious outsider, will know, there is a whole lot more to it than that. The potential for variety—in terms of the recipe for the noodles, the soup, and the extras—is limitless, as the Ramen World Champion, Takamitsu Kobayashi, explained:

"There are four basic types: soy ramen from Tokyo; *shio ramen*, seasoned with salt, and miso ramen, which are both from Sapporo; and tonkotsu or Hakata ramen, which is served with a white pork broth and comes from Hakata and Kyushu, generally. I fell in love with ramen at this museum, actually," he continued wistfully. "It was a pork-bone soup ramen. I never thought anything could taste so good."

I had assumed Kobayashi, thirty-two, was the world champion in *making* ramen, or perhaps the winner of a speed-eating competition (which used to be popular in Japan until the economic bubble burst in 1991 and such conspicuous consumption came to be considered a little unseemly), but he won the competition through his arcane knowledge of the techniques, chefs, restaurants, regional varieties, and sheer, endless trivia that has grown up around this dish. He had gone head-to-head against twenty-four other ramen connoisseurs for a prize of ¥500,000 ($4,500), identifying different types of ramen and individual restaurants from photographs, and even identifying a restaurant just by listening to a recording of its ambient noise.

What did he do with the prize money? I wondered. "I ate it all. Actually, I spend more than three times that on my ramen obsession in a year. I have to visit over a thousand ramen restaurants a year." Did he ever get sick of ramen? "Never, because every ramen is so different. The soups are different—there can be pork bone, chicken bones, katsuobushi, konbu, other dried fish; it is limitless. You know, I once ate eleven bowls in one day. Come, I'll show you."

We had met in the lobby of the ramen museum in Yokohama, the city with the largest Chinese population in Japan. Beyond the entrance was a small display on the history of ramen noodles featuring three hundred different ramen bowls and a shop selling various ramen-themed souvenirs. There was another display showing twelve different types of noodle, each, to me, identical, but the real draw, the reason the museum has been packing them in since it opened in 1994 (a million and a half visitors come each year) and has spawned several imitators elsewhere in the country, awaited us downstairs.

Here, in a perfect re-creation of 1950s Yokohama, permanently lit as if at dusk with old streetlamps, dark alleyways, peeling period advertising, rusty drains, and old-fashioned shop fronts, were ten or so ramen restaurants, each run by tough-looking chefs serving a different type of regional ramen.

The first we tried was the Tokyo ramen, with a dashi-based soup.

It was stunning, with a deep umami richness and sharp dashi tang. I meant only to taste it, but in what was now a familiar pattern, I simply could not stop slurping until the entire bowl was sloshing around inside me. The white miso Hakata ramen from the Fuku-oan shop was a little thin by comparison, but lighter in color and with a long-roasted pork flavor. We tried a Sapporo miso ramen next. As we entered the shop the chef was examining his ramen broth with a microscope.

"What on earth is he doing?" I asked.

"Oh, that's quite normal. He is assessing the density of the soup. Many do this."

To me, the Sapporo ramen tasted a little "high," a result of the noodles, which, in this case, were fermented and unusually chewy. It was also too salty by far. Kobayashi agreed, and I felt a small swell of pride. Might I, too, have the right stuff to become a ramen cham-pion? I doubted it, seeing as, after just three bowls, I felt like a ramen-filled balloon.

But Kobayashi continued eating noisily. He explained why the Japanese slurp their ramen so loudly: it helps cool the noodles and brings out the flavor and aroma better. And boy, did he slurp; he might as well have been tasting a great burgundy.

How could he tell a good ramen from an also-ran? "The al dente texture of the noodles is an essential way to judge a good ramen. The Japanese emphasize texture in their food; in China, they don't care so much, but we add carbohydrated sodium and natural water to make the noodles chewy and sticky. Also the Japanese love the taste of umami, so we use dashi in the soup—the Chinese do not. And of course our soy sauce is different."

I wondered if there was such a thing as a gourmet ramen restau-rant, a poshed-up version. "No, ramen is common food for the people. The most you will pay is ¥1,000 ($9). But you know the real craftsmanship of the ramen cook is that he creates this meal, his best meal, always within this limited space. I call it "the art of ramen." It is practical food. This is what I really love about ramen!" In a country where space is at a premium and everything from cars to mobile phones is designed to fit in the smallest space possible, I could see the appeal of an entire meal in one bowl. "Yes, exactly! You've got it!" Kobayashi said.

I asked what kind of physical effect eating so much ramen has on him. He was large by Japanese standards but didn't look too chubby. Were there consequences to a life of ramen dedication? "I am OK. Ramen is not as bad as McDonald's. It has vegetables, you know." And his wife, what did she think of him traveling (for two hours that evening, it turned out) at least once a week to the museum and throughout Japan in pursuit of the perfect noodle soup? "She shows some understanding. But then, I did meet her through a ramen website, and she was working in a ramen shop."

We parted with an exchange of business cards, Kobayashi's proudly proclaiming him a ramen champion. "I am glad you are going to introduce ramen to the world!" he said, waving good-bye from the entrance of the Yokohama museum.

31. ONCE UPON A TIME
IN SHIMONOSEKI

'll admit I was a little nervous when I left Fukuoka that fateful morning. For all the absurd misinformation bandied about, people have died, and still do, from eating the object of my quest that day, fugu, and there genuinely was a slight chance that I might never return from my trip to taste the world's most notorious fish dish (although, admittedly, my inability to decode a Japanese bus timetable would be a more likely hindrance).

The fugu is a type of puffer fish, or blowfish; actually, several types of similar-looking blowfish are served as fugu in Japan, but all contain varying levels of poison. Their ovaries, liver, and the layer of fat beneath their skin hold a deadly neurotoxin called tetrodotoxin, which is thirteen times more poisonous than arsenic. Each fish contains enough to kill thirty people, particularly in the summer, when they are at their most potent. If you are unlucky enough to ingest too much fugu liver (*kimo*), the first sign will be a dry mouth. Difficulty breathing might follow, then you will start to lose focus. There is no antidote, although some people do survive. Others have died painful and horrible, paralyzed deaths, eventually through asphyxiation. Captain James Cook, discoverer of Australia, once had a lucky escape from eating fugu, but the famous kabuki actor

Mitsugoro Bando was not so lucky. In 1975, he unwisely requested several servings of kimo and died as a result; the chef who served him went on to serve an eight-year prison sentence. The emperor of Japan is forbidden to ever eat fugu.

Though they are starting to breed nonpoisonous fugu, most are still toxic, and I had read that around six or seven people die from eating wrongly prepared fugu in Japan each year. Many dozens more have lucky escapes and pull through after intensive care (if you make it through the first twenty-four hours on life support, you ought to be in the clear), and all this despite tight regulations concerning who can prepare the fish. You need a special fugu license, which takes two or three years to earn, to serve it in a restaurant. These days, following some unfortunate incidents with restaurant-bin foragers, chefs must store all the poisonous parts in a locked box. Civilians can buy a fugu to cook at home only if it has been prepared properly, with the risky bits removed; the majority of the deaths are of people who catch the fish themselves and try to prepare them at home, or from thrill seekers who want to feel their tongues go numb or even experience a temporary coma. But still, some deaths are genuine accidents from fish prepared by professionals in restaurants. In January 2009, seven diners in a restaurant in Yamagata Prefecture fell ill after eating fugu sashimi and testes prepared by an unlicensed chef. One of them, a sixty-eight-year-old man, died almost immediately; the rest experienced numbness and tingling in their hands and legs for some days afterward.

(I think it is worth pausing here to revisit the famous *Simpsons* episode in which Homer eats some fugu prepared by an apprentice chef at the new local Japanese restaurant, the Happy Sumo, and is told by Dr. Hibbert that he has twenty-four hours to live. In fact, he survives. Marge realizes he is alive the next morning because his drool is still warm. Homer vows to cherish life in the future by eating diet pork rinds instead of full-fat and then watches some bowling on television.)

The acknowledged fugu capital of Japan is the harbor town of Shimonoseki, two hours north of Fukuoka, beside the Kanmon Straits, a narrow stretch of turbulent water that separates Kyushu from the next island to the east, Honshu. I could have eaten fugu virtually anywhere in Japan—you see the fish swimming in tanks in the windows of specialist restaurants in most Japanese cities—but I had heard that the best fugu chefs and the freshest fish were to be found here. More fugu are caught and processed in this small city than anywhere else in Japan, a total of three thousand tons a year, over half the annual haul. Some come from fugu farms; some are caught wild. I figured that if anyone was likely to be a safe bet to prepare me a safe piece of fugu sashimi, it was the fugumongers of Shimonoseki.

Fukuoka's bus terminal is on the third floor of a gargantuan shopping mall, which caught me out. In the end, to catch my bus I had to run for a prolonged period, something I hadn't done for some years, including up two flights of steps. Remarkably, there was none of the usual lung burn or dizziness I usually experience on the rare occasion I have to run for something. It did sap my energy for the next couple of hours, but at least I wasn't the hospital case I might have been some months earlier. Could my Japanese diet of the last two months really be making me healthier?

The bus terminal was clean, quiet, and ordered. Each bus stop was attended by a conductor in a gray polyester uniform who went out of his way to tour the hall rounding up passengers so that they didn't miss their ride. Several conductors politely rebuffed my insistent advances to board what I thought were the buses to Shimonoseki, but weren't. Eventually, like a fly repeatedly battering a windowpane, I gave up and sat down. Some minutes later, one of the conductors came and found me and helped me onto the correct bus, his white gloves gently shepherding me on board without ever actually making contact.

Its fugu riches do not appear to have bestowed great prosperity on the town of Shimonoseki, that much was apparent within moments of arriving. It has a weary, run-down look with rusty prefabricated buildings, stained concrete walls, overgrown vegetation, and a general air of neglect. But Shimonoseki is still proud of its claim to fame, which it pronounces "foo-koo." The manhole covers are embossed with a cartoon fugu fish, I noticed, and the seats in the local buses had been upholstered with fugu-print cloth. The shops were full of cuddly fugu, fugu key rings, mugs, and the fugu-themed mobile phone chains. Down by the harbor, in a prominent place where you might have expected to see a statue of a local dignitary or literary hero, I passed a large bronze fugu, instantly recognizable by its pursed lips and rounded boxy shape. I noticed a crowd of people. Getting closer, I realized they were gathered around a giant inflatable fugu. It turned out that, by serendipitous coincidence, I had chosen to visit the town on the day of its annual fugu festival.

As kids bounced happily outside, inside the market a large crowd had gathered around a fish tank. I squeezed my way to the front to find several children dangling fishing lines trying to catch one of about two dozen fugu swimming despondently around the tank. Anyone could have a go for ¥2,000 ($16). The unfortunate fish, about the size of a house brick, were being pulled from the water with hooks through their skins or eyes or tails—any method seemed fair game for the young crowd, egged on by their parents.

I noticed that the fish, once caught, were being whisked away, still alive, somewhere backstage by the market staff. After looking around to make sure no one was watching, I followed one of them. Here, in scenes that would make Sweeney Todd's head swim, they were being dispatched and prepared to be sent back out to the customers in plastic bags. I watched, mesmerized by the slaughter unfolding before me as four men stood around their metal workstation in blood-and-guts-spattered aprons and white gloves. I had wondered whether fugu had spines like other types of puffer fish, but as this would probably have been as appropriate a time as any to deploy them—what with their faces being sliced off and their innards being ripped out and everything—I concluded that they have none.

I am not especially squeamish when it comes to working with whole animal or fish carcasses, but I must admit to some queasiness as I watched the fishermen hold each wriggling fish on the chopping board in front of them, before stunning them with a swift blow of the knife handle to the back of the head. Next they chopped off their faces and fins—the latter set aside to be fried and served in warm sake as a snack—and pulled off their skin in one swift movement. The fish were still gasping for oxygen at this point, their tongues bulging from the newly created orifice in the front of their head, their gills ballooning. And they were still moving as the fishermen plunged their fingers inside them and pulled out their toxic guts, tossing them into a bucket on the floor. Finally, the eyes were gouged out and the rest of the fish chopped into large pieces, its hollow carcass included, before being bagged and sent back out to the customer. I timed it: the whole thing took just thirty seconds—not quite the level of meticulous care one might wish for in the preparation of a deadly fish, but I am sure they knew what they were doing.

I stepped closer, smiling at the men. They smiled back, apparently untroubled by having a witness to all this. I pointed at the bucket of innards. I wanted to make sure it was the poisonous stuff. I had an idea, a really, *really* stupid thought that had popped into my head just at that moment, circumventing all common sense: I was going to try to taste the liver. There was no risk, surely, from the merest fingertip touch. After all, until it became illegal, people did actually used to eat small amounts. It is said to induce a pleasurably tingling, numb sensation on the tongue.

I pointed at the bucket; I mimed choking to death with my hands around my neck, my tongue sticking out, and my eyes rolling; and finished with questioning upturned palms. They nodded. It was indeed a bucket of fugu toxin.

I loitered for a few moments more as the filleters returned to their work, then knelt down next to the bucket to tie my shoelace. But just as I was stretching out toward the bucket, one of the filleters spotted me and waggled his finger. I pulled my hand back and smiled sheepishly; he returned to his fish, and I immediately shot my hand back out, touched a piece of liver, and quickly licked my finger.

I stood up, feigning innocence. Almost immediately, the room began to go all swimmy. My vision went slightly foggy and speckled. I started to panic. What had I done? How stupid can one man be? Was my tongue that dry before? This was it: the cramps would be next, and soon I would be a writhing, frothing heap on the floor, one more notch on the fugu's kill chart. But the sensation stopped almost as quickly as it had started. I was fine. Panic over. It was getting up so quickly that had made me dizzy, not the liver. I neither felt nor tasted anything on my tongue. Maybe it wasn't even the liver I had touched. I'll never know.

Back in the market, I began my search for breakfast. A drum troupe was entertaining the crowds. Plates of fugu sashimi—each wafer-thin, transparent slice arranged in a petal around the plate in a style called *fugusashi*—were fetching from ¥1,000 to ¥20,000 ($9 to $18) depending on size. I bought a small plate and took it outside onto the boardwalk, where more crowds were gathering for their own al fresco breakfast, taking in the views across the roiling currents in the harbor and to the mighty suspension bridge above.

Fugu was never really going to be able to live up to its reputation, and I have to say it was an anticlimax—chewy with a watery flavor, a little bit squid-y, a little bit bream-y. No wonder they slather it with chili sauce and ponzu.

Deep-fried cubes of fugu were a different matter altogether—crisp, meaty, moist, and delicious. I used to think that halibut was the perfect fish for battering and deep-frying, but fugu is the best. Its robust texture and meaty flavor hold up especially well to the batter, keeping its shape but turning tender in the heat of the oil.

Still famished, I started a tour of the astonishing sushi stalls, about a dozen in all, each selling a fantastic array of sushi, all super fresh, expertly made, and, in some cases, of varieties I had never seen before. Most was about ¥100 (under a dollar) per piece. It was among the best sushi I would eat in Japan—the scallops fat, fresh, and creamy sweet, the tuna nigiri topped with huge tongues of red flesh. I ate so many pieces I began to get stomach pains. In the end, my own greed had succeeded where the deadly fugu had not.

32. OKINAWA

Urban Japan offers enough outlandish distractions to occupy even the most demanding visitors, but after more than two months of traveling, with only glimpses of countryside from fast-moving trains and planes, we were yearning for the beach and some subtropical sea.

Okinawa is an archipelago of 159 islands, historically known as the Kingdom of the Ryukyus. It lies midway between Japan and Taiwan, 425 miles from the southern tip of Japan proper. Thirty-seven of the islands are inhabited, but the majority of its 1.31 million people live on the main island, Okinawa Honto, which is also the home of the largest U.S. Air Force base in the western Pacific, with twenty thousand military personnel. These days, this is a largely unwelcome legacy of some of the most devastating battles of World War II, which left a third of this hitherto peaceful people dead. More died in Okinawa than in Nagasaki and Hiroshima combined, and much of the main island was leveled by bombing.

We rolled up—with our by now rather disheveled luggage—at a pleasant, vaguely Hawaiian-themed beach hotel. Even though it was October, the water was still just about warm enough to swim in, although the various signs on the beach warning of the myriad creatures that might cause us injury if we went into the water diminished our enthusiasm somewhat. We made do with burying each other in the sand and building castles.

As usual, I soon grew restless with sitting on a beach and managed to drum up some enthusiasm for a day trip to Naha, the capital. I had heard there was an excellent market on Heiwa Street and wanted to take a look.

On our way the next day, we stopped off in an *awamori* shop. Awamori is the local distilled liquor, similar to shochu, but made from rice. Okinawa is infested with *habu* snakes, and one use they find for them is to drown them in the liquor and leave the corpses to infuse—the 190-proof alcohol neutralizes the venom, apparently. You can't really taste the snake, by the way; actually, you can't taste much apart from the alcohol.

The market itself, though smaller than ones we had seen elsewhere in Japan, was fascinating, its produce totally different from anything I'd seen in mainland Japan. As with Tsukiji, a fish market lay at its heart, but there was plenty to divert our interest on the way in—more snakes, for starters, some six feet long, dried, coiled, and hanging from the ceiling like Gothic Catherine wheels; a preserved shark's head for ¥135,000 ($1,200); sturdy-looking Okinawan doughnuts; vacuum-packed pigs' heads (pork is very popular on the islands, a legacy of uninterrupted trading with China over many millennia); a large konbu and katsuobushi shop, an indication of the central role dashi plays in Okinawan food (they eat more konbu per capita than anyone else in Japan); and intriguing, lilac-colored sweet-potato cakes. The fishmongers' stalls were filled with the most extraordinary tropical fish, some orange and yellow striped, others blue as a David Hockney swimming pool—and not just fish, but crustaceans: monster crabs, strange clawless lobsters, smaller purple crabs, massive conches, and sea snails.

One of the vendors explained that we could order anything we liked, and it would be sent upstairs to a restaurant to be cooked for us. I had to be physically restrained by Lissen from ordering a giant conch, but not before I had ordered numerous other, smaller fish, along with a serving of *irabu-jiru*, or snake stew, for us all.

Upstairs, in an enjoyably chaotic bus station–style atmosphere, at a ramshackle restaurant (one of several in an informal food court there) with mismatched chairs and paper napkins, we awaited our snake. We were slightly taken aback to see that it still looked very much like snake, black skin and all, but, to their credit, both Asger and Emil tucked in, picking the flesh from the hundreds of small bones. I could hardly balk at it myself now, so I took a deep breath and a small nibble. It was a little like a slow-braised oxtail, tender and gamy and full of bones, but I couldn't see past the fact that I was eating a serpent and quietly moved the bowl aside to attack the whole grilled fish and astonishingly good sea urchin. The latter was locally caught and ferociously expensive, but simply one of the most sensuous and transcendent foodstuffs I have ever tasted. If mermaids were to open a small, artisanal ice cream parlor, this is how their vanilla ice cream would taste.

That night, for the first time in our whole journey, one of our number became ill. Emil started to complain that he felt "funny." His arm hurt, he said. We rolled up his sleeve, or at least we tried to but couldn't, as it had swollen up. We gave him an antihistamine tablet, but that had no effect. I would have to take him to a hospital.

The nearest was in the small coastal town of Nago. The hospital, high up on a hill overlooking the bay, took an age to find, and I drove around in thickening darkness and growing panic, lost in this strangest of lands with a sick (snake-poisoned?) child and no sense of direction. Emil had started to make wheezing noises, and I was terrified he was having a severe allergic reaction to something and that his throat was closing up.

Eventually, by sheer fluke, I found the hospital. It was in a bedraggled building, not what you would expect from one of the richest nations on earth. The waiting room was half-full; almost all of those waiting were elderly. They looked at Emil and me with some trepidation, and Emil shrank behind me in mutual terror. I smiled weakly at the desk staff, pointing to Emil's arm while gripping my throat. He was looking dreadfully pale, with dark lines beneath his eyes. What on earth was wrong?

Rather embarrassingly, we were given preferential treatment, and after just a couple of minutes' wait we were ushered through into the doctor's office. The doctor, a shy young man, looked as startled to see us as his patients had, and for a moment, the panic in his eyes had me worried that he would simply flee and leave us there.

Quickly, to grab his attention, I rolled up Emil's sleeve. Emil winced.

The doctor examined the arm in a vague, distracted way, then listened to Emil's breathing with a stethoscope. "Don't worry, I can still whistle," Emil told him (he had recently learned, much to his non-whistling elder brother's irritation). He then tried to demonstrate, but he didn't have the breath.

At this point, the doctor walked out, which wasn't encouraging, but he soon returned with an older, female doctor who spoke good English. She said that they were going to give him an injection. Of what, she did not say, but she did ask if he was allergic to anything. I wanted to say, well, yes, clearly, but that would have raised more questions than I could answer, so I said no, not that I knew of.

To this day, I have no idea what happened. Maybe Emil is

allergic to snake (not that easy to test for where we live); perhaps it was one of the tropical fish we ate or more likely some kind of insect bite, but the doctor gave him the injection, and his arm deflated over the course of that evening. By the end of it, Emil was whistling like a kettle.

33. WHO WANTS TO LIVE FOREVER?

Some people have a peculiar approach to mortality. They accept that they are going to die, live with it, and get on with their lives. There are even people—and I have met some—who are perfectly at ease with the fact that one day they will no longer exist, that their heart will stop and they will plunge headlong into an insensible, eternal void.

And then, of course, there are those who would willingly end their own lives in the event of impending infirmity, be it mental or physical; people who embrace the idea of euthanasia and are ready to terminate themselves the moment they start to forget why they went into the kitchen. My father, for instance, used to insist—only half jokingly—that if he ever started to lose his mind we were under strict instructions to take him out into the paddock and shoot him (thankfully, he departed with his marbles intact—which was just as well, as we didn't have a gun, or a paddock). I, on the other hand, think about death—by which I mean whole proper minutes spent staring vacantly into space wrestling with the bitter truth of my own mortality—several times a day. If I only had a dollar for every time someone said, "Cheer up. It might not happen!" . . . But it will! That's why my face looks like this.

I can tell you exactly when this all began: I was at school staring out of the classroom window one sunny afternoon, when I suddenly realized that I would one day die, *and the world would continue without me!* If I hurled myself through the first-floor window and plummeted onto the basketball court below, cars would still drive, people would still watch TV, and, after the school caretaker had administered a pile of sawdust, Miss Weddick would quiet the class down and continue to explain why water goes the other way around down the drain in Australia.

Which is why, as I limp toward middle age, my body and mind slowly disintegrating in ever-more-humiliating displays of decrepitude, I have vowed to cling to life for as long as I can. Never mind that I may become an incontinent, gibbering wreck and everyone will be sick of the sight of me, my liver-spotted claws shall grip the hands of my nurses insistently as they tend to the life-support machine beside my bed. I plan to be a burden to my children as long as I possibly can. A "good innings," as we say in England, isn't going to do it for me, I can tell you, and as for "three score years and ten," five score and then some is more like it.

Gerontologists believe that the human body ought in theory to be able to last until well past one hundred and twenty years—the oldest person ever was a Frenchwoman who lived to the age of one hundred and twenty-two and a half. They say, too, that only around 25 percent of the causes of death and aging is found in your DNA; the rest is within your control. Hence, I am a sucker for all of those health-scare stories that the papers run every day; I lap them up as gospel, worrying over my diet, my lack of exercise, and my stress levels. Only my insatiable gluttony, a susceptibility to addictions, inherent indolence, and a fundamentally weak character have stopped me from becoming a vegan. No, instead of making radical changes to my life, I am on a constant quest for some kind of healthy-living magic bullet, the secret foods and lifestyle tips that will prolong my life and somehow, against all rational belief, keep my tired old body going for another seventy years or so.

So while Lissen and the boys had been dreaming of Okinawa's idyllic sandy beaches and tropical seas, it was in fact my desperate fear of a godless death that had brought us to the paradise islands of southern Japan.

Okinawans, you see, know the secret of eternal life, or at least the secret of living a healthy, active life well into three digits. They live longer than anyone else on earth, and unlike others who claim this title—the people of the Hunza Valley in Pakistan or the Ecuadorian Andes, for instance—they can prove it, having kept meticulous official birth records since 1879. And they don't just cling to life courtesy of expensive medicines and machines that go *ping*; elderly Okinawans are active, independent, contribute to society, and remain healthy and mobile up to and beyond one hundred years of age, into the realms of the so-called supercentenarians. In Okinawa, if you meet an octogenarian, there is a good chance his or her parents are still alive.

The three leading killers in the Western world are heart disease, strokes, and cancer, but the Okinawans suffer from them less than any other people. Out of one hundred thousand people only eighteen a year die from heart disease compared to over a hundred in the United States. Of course, the Japanese in general are world leaders in terms of life expectancy: Japanese women have a life expectancy of 87 years, the highest in the world, while the men have the fifth highest, with eighty years (San Marino in Italy is first, which hardly counts as a country). And Japan has over 40 percent of the world's so-called supercentenarians, aged 105 and over, and has often boasted both the oldest man and woman alive (although, for obvious reasons, these titles change quite frequently). This in itself would be reason enough to look more closely at the Japanese diet and lifestyle—at why, for example, only 3 percent of Japanese are considered obese, compared to 30 percent of Americans—but the longevity of Okinawans is a special case indeed. They have over two and a half times as many centenarians per capita as the mainland. As I write this, there are over 800 centenarians on Okinawa out of a total population of 1.31 million, the highest ratio in the world. (Japan as a whole now has over 60,000 centenarians out of a population of a little over 127 million, compared to 80,000 in the United States, with almost three times the people—and their number has doubled over the last decade.)

The Okinawans are clearly doing something—several things—right. For someone with a morbid fear of death (is there any other kind?), there was no better place to go in search of tips.

The longevity of the mainland Japanese is a fairly recent phenomenon; until the seventies, the Swedes held the record for long life, yet the Okinawans have a reputation for healthy living that dates back centuries, perhaps millennia. The Chinese, who have traded with the Kingdom of the Ryukyus since the third century B.C., referred to it as the "Land of the Immortals." Some even claim that the ancient Chinese myth of Shangri-la is about Okinawa.

On the other hand, there are many factors that mitigate *against* the Okinawans living long. For a start, Okinawans are the poorest people in Japan, thus undermining all conventional wisdom correlating health with income. Okinawa has always been beset by typhoons and famine, its people forever picking themselves up, dusting themselves off, and starving all over again. Periodically, outsiders have invaded and brutally subjugated what was an avowedly nonmilitary, peaceful country where, for a time, all weaponry was banned and guitars took the place of swords. The Japanese Shimazu clan came in 1609, imposing harsh taxes and using the islands as a trading route to China at a time when the country was supposed to be closed to the outside world. In the mid-1850s, Commodore Matthew Perry—hardly barbaric, but still an aggressive outsider—

based his fleet in Okinawa before sailing to Japan with the intention of opening it up like a reluctant oyster. And then, of course, the Americans came again during World War II. Over a quarter—some say as much as a third—of the population died, a large proportion of them having been persuaded to commit suicide by the Japanese rather than surrender (tragically, this happened only some weeks prior to their traumatic surrender when Emperor Hirohito reluctantly conceded, in his first-ever public speech, that "the war has not necessarily developed to Japan's advantage"). And last but very much not least, the place is absolutely infested with poisonous snakes, as testified to by the various puncture marks several locals were to show us during our stay.

The reasons behind the mainland Japanese's longevity are more obvious. After the war, rampant economic growth improved health care immeasurably, stamping out such deadly diseases as tuberculosis. They started to eat more protein and animal fats. The average height increased by three inches. But perhaps the biggest single contributing factor to the improved health of the nation was a reduction in their salt intake in the early seventies. Salt was the single greatest weakness of the Japanese diet, an excessive intake of which was blamed for their high incidence of strokes. They still continue to consume more salt than we do in the West (the Japanese government recommends twelve grams per day; Western governments tend to recommend six grams) but in 1970 the Japanese government imposed reductions on levels of salt in soy sauce. After that, there was no stopping them. Incidents of stroke declined dramatically, and it has really been only their recent enthusiasm for Western fast-food trends that has been attributed to the rise in obesity and cholesterol levels. But what makes the Okinawans so exceptional?

I had made contact with one of the leading experts on Okinawan longevity, a Canadian gerontologist, Dr. Craig Willcox, who lives in Okinawa. Together with his twin brother, Bradley—now based at Harvard—and local gerontologist Dr. Makoto Suzuki, he started the government-funded Okinawan Centenarian Study in the mid-seventies.

A few years ago, the three of them published *The Okinawa Program: How the World's Longest-Lived People Achieve Everlasting Health—And How You Can Too*. It went on to become a *New York Times* bestseller, and the brothers have even been on *The Oprah Winfrey Show*.

One morning a week or so after arriving on Okinawa, I left Lissen and the kids to various beach-themed activities (crab goading, purposeless digging) and drove back down south to the capital, Naha, where the Okinawa Research Center for Longevity Science is based, at Okinawa International University, to meet Dr. Willcox.

Dressed in a Hawaiian-style shirt, with thick, shoulder-length hair and clear, tanned skin, Willcox was a persuasive ad for his own program. I asked how old he was. He glanced at the students working behind us and whispered mock conspiratorially, "Forty-six, but don't tell anyone." I'd be lying if I said he looked ten years younger, but he did at least look a very good forty-six, which was frankly all the hope I needed.

After a brief introductory chat, we decided to continue our discussion over lunch. Willcox knew just the place, a small wooden shack a few hundred yards from the campus. There we ordered some classic Okinawan dishes and got down to the nitty-gritty.

Just how healthy were the Okinawans? "They have low cholesterol and suffer less from heart disease than anyone else, they are not big smokers or drinkers, and they have among the lowest levels of [the amino acid] homocysteine in the world—homocysteine causes at least 10 percent of heart disease deaths," Willcox said, tucking into a plate of *goya champaru*, a classic Okinawan dish featuring stir-fried *goya*—a kind of knobby, bitter cucumber that has been shown to lower blood sugar in diabetics and has also been used to treat AIDS.

"They have a low risk of arteriosclerosis. They have low instances of stomach cancer, which the rest of the Japanese suffer from. The Japanese have also historically had a high rate of strokes, but Okinawans have never eaten as much salt. They have a very low risk of hormone-dependent cancers, such as breast and prostate cancer. They eat three servings of fish a week, on average. They tend to use canola oil to fry with, which is even healthier than olive oil. They eat plenty of whole grains, vegetables, and soy products, too. And they eat more tofu and more konbu seaweed than anyone else in Japan. Squid and octopus, which they also eat a lot of, are rich in taurine, which is believed to lower cholesterol and blood pressure."

I was scribbling furiously at this point, so Willcox paused to let me catch up and take a few mouthfuls of the goya champaru. I had tried to eat some goya earlier in our trip, in Kyoto. I'd picked one of these gnarly cucumbers—some call them "bitter melon"—out of the vegetable section in the supermarket and taken it home to give to the kids in their daily midafternoon raw fruit and veggie snack. Asger had taken a tentative bite before spitting the entire mouthful out into my hand. I had tried it and also found it impossibly bitter, consigning it to the "What are they thinking of?" category of unpalatable Japanese foodstuffs. But here, fried with egg and pork, its bitterness was subdued and helped cut through the fattiness of the dish.

Dr. Willcox continued, "They have strong bones, from the fish they eat, and, of course, they get lots of sun, plus more vitamin D from soy products. They have low dementia rates, which might be linked to the ginkgo nuts they eat, or it might be the sweet potatoes."

Ah yes, the Okinawan sweet potato. I had tried these the night before at a restaurant across the street from our hotel. Okinawan sweet potatoes, while looking from the outside essentially like the orange variety we get at home, are the most extraordinary deep purple inside, the kind of color, almost artificial in its intensity, that you rarely find in nature. It is the color of a bishop's miter, or Prince's underpants—very, very purple. And they taste sensational, particularly as tempura, which is how I had tried them—not too sweet, and with a pleasant, flowery aftertaste and soft, almost creamy texture. I had also tried sweet-potato ice cream, another Okinawan specialty. As ice cream, it loses its potato-ishness, and the floral sweetness comes to the fore. It went straight on the "things to export from Japan to make the world a better place" list, just below soft-closing toilet seats and above disposable umbrella bags.

The Okinawan sweet potato—called *beni imo*—was introduced to the islands in 1605 by a man called Sokan Noguni. Noguni is revered to this day as a local hero, the "Imo King," for bringing this miracle vegetable to the islands. "Since the sweet potato came here from China via South America, Okinawans have eaten pretty much nothing but that, along with fish. At one point in their history they were getting 60 percent of their calories from sweet potatoes," enthused Willcox. Complex carbohydrates are an important part of the Okinawan diet, contrary to several current Western diet fads. Willcox guffawed loudly when I asked about the Atkins diet. "Of course you lose weight with Atkins at the start, but you lose water and lean muscle. You actually increase body-fat percentage.

"Sweet potatoes are high in flavonoids, which are antioxidants and hormone blockers. Okinawans consume more flavonoids than anyone else in the world, up to fifty times more than we do in the West. They [the potatoes] are also rich in carotenoids, vitamin E, fiber, and lycopene, which is a carotenoid that has been shown to help prevent prostate cancer." In fact, one beni imo contains four times the daily vitamin A and half the vitamin C requirements of an adult. Recent research has also indicated that they help stabilize blood-sugar levels and lower insulin resistance.

Of course, what the Okinawans eat is only part of the explanation for their remarkable longevity. As far as Willcox is concerned, what they don't put into their mouths is as important. In his view, calorific restriction—in other words, not eating very much—is the key to a long life. "Calorific restriction has been shown to work in all other animal species, including primates, so I'd be very surprised if it didn't work with humans," he said. "There are so many connections to obesity and health."

"So, what kind of restriction are we actually talking about?" I asked, now slightly nervous.

"Well, back in the 1960s, a study showed that Okinawan children were consuming almost 40 percent fewer calories than other Japanese children, so you can imagine how that would compare to the children in the West. At the same time, Okinawan adults were eating more than 10 percent fewer calories than the normal, healthy recommended level." On average, Okinawans eat 2,761 calories per day, compared to 3,412 in the UK and 3,774 in the United States. Of course, part of this is explained by the fact that they are physically smaller than we are, but personally, I have quite some scope for cutting back.

Eating less is deeply ingrained in both the Okinawan psyche and quite possibly their genes, too. Typhoons, disease, poverty, and their geographical isolation have meant that Okinawans have endured frequent famines. They have adapted accordingly, eating what we in the West would consider emergency-ration quantities on a day-to-day basis. They even have a phrase to describe this philosophy: *hara hachi-bu*, meaning "Eat until you are 80 percent full."

It is said that the three words that have earned more money for the beauty industry than any other promotional or advertising strategy are *rinse and repeat* on a shampoo bottle. Well, here are two and a half words that could wipe out the entire health, beauty, diet, and exercise industries in a trice. *Hara hachi-bu* could transform the health of the entire world, if only we could all find the self-control.

It is based on the simplest of physiological principles—it takes your stomach's stretch receptors twenty minutes to tell your brain you are full, so if you eat until you feel 80 percent full and just wait twenty minutes, you will feel properly full. Try it. It works. (It also explains my confusion at the discomfort I always feel after being allowed near all-you-can-eat buffets.) In the course of our evolution as a species, it is only in the last century or so that a large proportion of the human race has been in the position of having a surplus of food, but our bodies are still physically attuned to having far less.

This got me thinking about diet fads. For the last decade or so in the West, we have been brainwashed into thinking the Mediterranean diet is best. "It is also good," said Willcox. "Sardinians, for example, tend to live long, but there is perhaps too much dairy [in their diets] still."

Usually, when a group of two or more people are gathered and the talk turns to how healthy the Japanese are, someone will confidently assert that osteoporosis rates are much higher in Japan than in the West "because they don't get enough calcium because they don't eat dairy." This is a myth. "Osteoporosis rates are actually lower in Japan," Willcox told me. "They get more exercise and vitamin D. Smoking is a problem, though; lung cancer rates are increasing. That's a problem now because it can take twenty or thirty years for the cancer to appear, and if you look twenty or thirty years ago, to the 1980s, 80 percent of Japanese men were smoking."

The Willcoxes and Suzuki have a great deal to say about fat in their book, too, mostly negative. "Really, less than 10 percent of your calories should come from fat, but a little pork is a good addition for the protein," Willcox said. And guess which meat the Okinawans have traditionally eaten more of than any other? In fact, they are renowned for their pork cuisine and have a saying that they claim originated with them: "With a pig you can eat everything except the oink."

So even when Okinawans are eating bad stuff, it's doing them good. The same goes for the famous (in Japan at least) Okinawan black sugar, a dense, malevolent-looking cane sugar called *kokuto* that tastes wonderfully rich, like molasses or muscovado. "It is true; their sugar is much better because it isn't processed or bleached. It also has more iron in it. But as with the salt, you still want to stay away from sugar if you can," he said.

But dietary and medical factors are still only part of the secret of Okinawan longevity. The improved postwar health care eventually trickled down to Okinawa at a time when those who had endured the war—by definition the most resilient of their generation—were entering middle age. Yet they still ate the traditional Okinawan diet, and so this "survival of the fittest" factor, combined with modern health care, proved to be a potent longevity tonic for a specific demographic, which is now reaching—and flying past—the century mark.

According to Willcox, the fact that they appear to be the least-stressed people on earth plays a role, too. The Okinawan concept of time pays scant regard to the tyrannies of the clock, which makes it difficult ever to be late. He also believes their supportive localized social structures—called *uimaru*—are immensely important to their longevity. One aspect of this is the *maoi*, or local "people's banks," where around a dozen or so friends meet and contribute a small sum to a kitty, then each month vote to decide who gets the money. Meanwhile, their health care systems incorporate both traditional medicines and healers—called *yuta*—and tai chi is widely practiced. Interestingly, one of the reasons given for the superior longevity of Okinawan women in particular is that they are more likely to practice a religion—a belief in a higher power supposedly giving them a greater sense of ease and contentment.

And there is no word in the Okinawan dialect for *retirement*. Many of the centenarians Willcox and his team have interviewed continue, if not to work in full-time jobs, then at least to tend their gardens, grow vegetables, and even have part-time jobs. So while in the West there is growing concern, a resentment even, that people are living longer and becoming a burden on public health care finances, the centenarians of Okinawa are more of a boost than a burden.

In Okinawa, it is usual for the elderly—including centenarians— to live in their own homes. In his book, Willcox describes his centenarian subjects' "youthful glow" and "sharp, clear eyes, quick wits, and passionate interests." They don't suffer from "time urgency," he writes; they are very self-confident, self-reliant, optimistic, and easygoing but also stubborn.

"What about . . . you know . . . ?" I raised my eyebrows.

"What? Their sex life?" He laughed. "Now, that would be an interesting area of research. We do know that Okinawan centenarians have higher levels of sex hormones, and we do know that some of our centenarians are sexually active, but I don't think we could really get away with asking them about that."

Sadly, Willcox told me that it looks like the age of Okinawan longevity is coming to an end. The next generation is unlikely to last much beyond eighty, as they have embraced the American fat- and sugar-rich diet with gusto—young Okinawans are eating twice as much meat as their parents, for instance—with the result that Okinawans aged fifty and below have the highest rates of obesity in Japan, with, inevitably, the highest rates of heart disease and premature death. The last few decades have seen Okinawans go from being some of the leanest people in Japan to having the highest body mass index. Lung cancer rates are on the up, too. Nagoya is about to overtake them as the prefecture with the greatest longevity.

By now, the restaurant owner was starting to clean up in preparation for dinner. I had one last question of urgent personal import.

"I have a friend—not me, you understand, but a friend—who is having a slight problem with hair loss," I said. "I can't help noticing that Japanese men do seem to tend to hold on to their hair pretty well. What's their secret? Is it the seaweed?"

Willcox, who I had long ago noted was blessed with an impressively thick head of wavy brown, lustrous hair, laughed. "Well, they do say konbu is good for [preventing] hair loss, as is perilla, too, but I am afraid you'll have to tell your 'friend' it's more along the lines of folk advice than scientifically proven."

I would just have to settle for eternal life, then.

As I drove back up the coast road, past the vast, razor-wired U.S. military base, I reflected on our conversation. Willcox had described the health of elderly Okinawans as being due, in essence, to a balance between four factors—diet, exercise, spiritual well-being, and psychosocial factors, such as friendships and social support systems. As a misanthropic nonbeliever, I couldn't do much about the spiritual and psychosocial elements in my life, but I vowed to start drinking jasmine tea (I had never as much as tasted tea until Mrs. Shinobu's ceremony in Tokyo, so this was a major life decision), which Willcox claimed was even better than green tea for lowering cholesterol, and to up my intake of vegetables and fish. Willcox took turmeric supplements every day, too, as do many Okinawans: it is thought that turmeric might help prevent cancer and gallstones.

"Eat as low down the food chain as possible," Willcox writes in *The Okinawa Program*. The notion of man as a hunter-gatherer is misleading, he continues. Gathered produce has always far exceeded hunted food in the human diet. Willcox told me that we in the West eat far more protein than we need; we ought to eat only an amount the size of two decks of cards—around three and a half ounces—a day. Perhaps I could start adding a little bit of MSG to my meals to trick my body into believing it is getting more protein than it is, and start eating more tofu, of course. Seaweed is also clearly important.

But you have to eat the real stuff; dried is fine, but supplements aren't nearly as good, apparently.

Recently, Okinawan products like black sugar, the local *hirami* lemon (thought to have anticarcinogenic properties), and sea salt have become popular "longevity produce" on sale in mainland Japanese cities. It can be only a matter of time before you see them in chic health-food stores in London and New York.

All that remained for me was to see for myself the benefits of healthy Okinawan living. I had to bag me a centenarian.

34. THE OLDEST VILLAGE
IN THE WORLD

The best place to find a centenarian on Okinawa, perhaps in the world, is the village of Ogimi, in the northwestern part of the island. Over a third of its 3,100 residents are aged over sixty-five, with a dozen or more centenarians among them—the highest proportion in Japan and most likely the world.

Lissen, Asger, Emil, and I drove there along a coast road of dazzling beauty, the East China Sea glittering in the sunshine. We arrived in time for Sunday lunch, having made a reservation at the village's only restaurant, specializing in longevity food.

Just outside Ogimi, we passed a stone marker on which was written: "At seventy you are but a child, at eighty you are merely a youth, and at ninety if the ancestors invite you into heaven, ask them to wait until you are one hundred, and then you might consider it."

The village itself was just a single, poorly made street with small, low-rise houses, most of them wood, all of them with immaculate, lush gardens. In some of them elderly men and women tended their flowers, fruits, and vegetables—surveys have shown that gardening is good for longevity, and elderly Okinawans are keen gardeners. Only a passing funeral procession put a damper on the idyllic atmosphere.

The restaurant was a simple, open-fronted place with a corrugated plastic roof and bare wood tables and chairs. Above the entrance there was a large cactus loaded with freakish pink dragon fruit. Before we ate, I asked the owner, Emiko Kinjyo, if she might afterward be able to introduce us to a centenarian.

A few minutes later, she returned and beckoned us to follow her down the high street. We came to a dark, wooden, traditional open-fronted Okinawan house, essentially a large living room–bedroom with a small, neat garden surrounding it.

An elderly lady walked slowly out to meet us, smiling at Asger and Emil. We all smiled back. The woman's name was Matsu Taira. She moved with grace and ease, her face exuding a fragile radiance. She smiled again and beckoned us to sit beside her as she knelt on the wooden veranda of her house (without a single knee crack, I might add). She was extraordinarily thin with thick gray hair swept back Don King–style. Her face was weatherworn but serene. She lived alone in the house, she told us, but was visited by her family daily. She still tended her garden, where she grew goya and potatoes. She ate little food, but it was fresh and mostly from her garden or the gardens of her friends. Her only vice was the occasional piece of Okinawan black sugar. She offered some to Asger and Emil, who had been standing some distance away eyeing this extraordinary woman warily, but now approached shyly.

We talked for a while, and I asked her about the war. She said she had hidden in the hills with her mother and sister for many weeks during the fighting. Her father had not survived. It struck me that perhaps this generation of Okinawans, the generation that had survived the war, really was unique. I was reminded of something Willcox had said to me about how impressed he had been by the strong will, the sheer stubbornness of many of the centenarians he had met. Of course, to have survived when a third of their number had perished must have taken astonishing levels of resourcefulness. Surely that will to survive had played an intrinsic role in their longevity.

Emiko explained that the Okinawans don't in fact consider one hundred to be the big milestone we do in the West. Instead they celebrate the ninety-seventh birthday with a public party called *kajimayaa*. She recalled hers with a smile. All her family came, and there were pinwheels, she said, toy windmills that are always used to decorate a kajimayaa to symbolize a return to the youthfulness that Okinawans believe comes with age. The government gives them a lump sum, too.

Taira-san looked calm, then, slowly, tiredness crept across her face, and Emiko quietly suggested we should think about going.

Back at the restaurant, we ate rice and tofu, bamboo shoots, seaweed, prawn tempura, pickles, small cubes of braised pork belly, and a little cake and ice cream for dessert. The seaweed was especially remarkable—Okinawans call it *umi-budo*, or sea grapes; others call it sea caviar on account of its tiny pods arranged around an edible stalk like a DNA helix. The pods pop in your mouth, just like caviar, releasing a flavor of the sea.

Emiko explained that Okinawans differentiate between *kusuimun*, which are foods with medicinal benefit, and *ujinimun*, which are those with nutritional value. She tried to blend the two, she said, offering us a traditional Okinawan dish called *tofuyo*, or fermented tofu (similar to the Chinese *chou doufu*, or "stinky tofu," which is most likely where the Okinawans got the idea). The tofuyo was an evil-tasting, dark red tofu served in small cubes with toothpicks. The idea is that you are supposed to nibble the tiny morsels, but no one explained this to me, so I stuck a toothpick in one and ate it whole. The effect was instant and involuntary. I gagged and spat it out onto my plate.

Emil made a *See?* face, remembering only too vividly his experience with the dried scallop. "Oh my god, ugh, ugh, *pfttcht*.

That is disgusting!" I said, desperately gulping down water. My mouth was burning. It was like Roquefort mixed with Korean fermented chili sauce, but apparently it is good for you. The Pharmaceutical Society of Japan did some research into tofuyo and came to the following conclusions:

Spontaneously hypertensive male rats at eight weeks of age were fed a diet containing lyophilized tofuyo for six weeks. At thirteen weeks of age, the systolic blood pressure of rats in the tofuyo group was significantly lower than that in the control group. After feeding them the experimental diets, the ACE activity of the kidney was significantly lower in the tofuyo group than that in the control group. Total cholesterol in the serum in the tofuyo group was significantly lower while the ratio of high-density lipoprotein (HDL) to total cholesterol in the tofuyo group tended to be higher than that in the control group.

Given the choice, I think I will take my chances with high cholesterol.

35. HEALTHY SALT

I f my insatiable, neurotic fretting over the health pages of women's magazines has taught me anything, it is that conventional dietary and health advice is based on the demonization of three substances: salt, sugar, and animal fats. Salt causes hypertension and strokes, sugar makes you fat and gives you diabetes, and animal fats are not much better.

On Okinawa, however, things are rather different. We have already heard mention of their sugar, called kokuto—an unrefined, dark brown, almost black sugar made with all of the cane plant. Relatively unprocessed, it is packed with minerals, potassium in particular. In terms of animal fats, the Okinawans traditionally eat very little meat, but the one exception to this has been pork, which they have always eaten more of than the mainland Japanese. Pork is a relatively lean source of protein, and is also abundant in other such useful substances as iron, zinc, vitamin B6, riboflavin, and niacin.

And then there is the salt. Gourmet salts have been a fashionable larder accessory for some years; none of our kitchens are complete without a box of Maldon or a little tub of Fleur de Sel de Guérande. The Japanese make some of the most renowned salts in the world, most famously the Red and Blue Label salts of Oshima—but no matter how prettily packaged or expensive, it is still salt, and salt, we are told, is a killer.

But not in Okinawa, at least not if Masakatsu Takayasu of the Nuchi Masu salt company is to be believed. Okinawa is famous throughout Japan for the quality of its salt, and several top chefs I spoke to used Okinawan salt in their kitchens.

Takayasu had recently opened a new, cutting-edge salt-processing plant, which used a new method of harvesting sea salt that produces a salt that actually helps *reduce* blood pressure, as well as offering more minerals—mostly magnesium and potassium—than any other salt in the world. Healthy salt? Was that possible? Could it be the solution to the world's hypertension?

There is more than a hint of a Bond villain's lair about the Nuchi Masu factory. It is located in Uruma, on Henza Island, which you approach across a causeway flanked by an extraordinary rocky seascape. A road takes you around the eastern side of the island, climbing up to wooded cliffs high above the Pacific. There perches a startlingly white, modern salt refinery and visitors' center complex.

Takayasu-san is a physics graduate and, he told me as we sat in his cluttered office, also an expert in evolutionary theory. With his plaid shirt and trouser top rolled over his belt, he looked more like an imo farmer, but he had some fascinating things to say about salt.

"Think about it like this," he said, sitting forward in his chair and resting his elbows on his desk. "Life was created 4 billion years ago from the ocean. We have only spent 400 million years on land, which means for 3.6 billion years we evolved in the ocean salt, living from ocean salt minerals. The first amniotic fluid was seawater; still today, amniotic fluid is salty. How could it not be good for you to still eat those minerals?"

This seems reasonable; after all, Ringer's solution, which is used in intravenous drips, has a similar composition to seawater. But following that theory, wouldn't all salt, even the salt mined on land, still be good for you? "No, because to refine salt, you must heat it, and in that heating you make it more difficult for the body to take in those minerals, because they stick together. But here we have devised a system that harvests the salt using only natural temperatures and an instant evaporation technique. The minerals remain separate and when dissolved in the intestine become ionic and so can be absorbed easily by the body. In fact, because it retains so much potassium, thanks to our special system, our salt *reduces* blood pressure because it helps the body to expel sodium via our urine better. It has all the minerals of seawater—zinc, iron, copper, and manganese. It's pure."

It took almost ten years to develop what Takayasu-san calls the "room temperature, instantaneous, vacuum-crystallization process"—which, in essence, extracts the salt from seawater by turning it into an extremely fine spray directed at a "reverse osmotic membrane," a kind of fine netting. Takayasu-san got the idea when, in a former career running an orchid nursery, he observed the way the flowers were watered using a fine spray mist. He showed me where they do this. We peered through a porthole into the spraying room at an amazing snowscape with salt cascading over every surface. The air was thick with it, like an Arctic blizzard, as a warm-air fan turned the seawater into an ultrafine mist and vaporized it, separating out the minerals, which accumulated just about everywhere else in the room.

There are other salt-spray systems like this, Takayasu-san explained, but they dry the salt at a high temperature. Nuchi Masu uses low temperature. The result is a salt containing twenty-one minerals, including potassium, which is good for reducing blood pressure and, apparently, has a much lower level of artery-hardening sodium nitrate. But you would surely also have to eat an awful lot of salt to have any effect—I mean, we usually eat only about, what, ten grams a day?

"Listen," he said, avoiding the question like a skilled politician. "Why do you think Okinawans live so long?"

"Diet," I replied. "Plus the climate, exercise, good health care . . . oh, come on, you aren't saying it's the salt, are you?"

"Exactly! Yes, it is! You know Okinawa has the most typhoons of anywhere in the world? Well, because of the typhoons Okinawan soil is constantly soaked by seawater. That seawater is full of minerals, which enter the soil and then the fruit, vegetables, grasses, and animals raised in Okinawa. Everyone says Okinawans live so long because of the konbu they eat or the weather, but no. They play just a small part, and anyway, the pork is so good here because their feed is so full of minerals. In Okinawa, all our soil has all the minerals."

This sounded plausible. Perhaps that explained the superb quality of the cows that are raised on Okinawa before being sent to Matsusaka, but, hold on, don't other places get lots of typhoons? What about Florida? He had a simple answer to that: "They don't grow things in Florida. Listen, for many years, Okinawa had no choice; it had to grow its own food. People here say typhoons are our enemy, but now I call typhoons good! If it weren't for typhoons, I would have died at age fifty [he is sixty], so I say to people, what would you prefer, no typhoons and die young, or typhoons bringing goodness to our soil and live to one hundred?"

Though he had skillfully avoided the question of just how much benefit was to be had from something we eat so little of as salt, his argument was still fascinating. Could Okinawa's regular saltwater saturation be the reason for its inhabitants' longevity? The islands are surrounded by coral, which is, of course, rich in a variety of fundamentally important minerals, some of which end up in the soil after each typhoon. I thought back to the magical Okinawan sweet potato—it was the only crop that had flourished on the islands for centuries; it must have acted like a sponge for all the sea minerals that washed the land. It clearly wasn't the only reason for Okinawans' longevity, as Willcox's research has so effectively detailed, but Takayasu's argument had a logic, and he had a good deal of scientific research to back his claims.

He told me that Nuchi Masu is even planning to remove the sodium chloride from its salt to leave just the seawater minerals. "I am going to market it as a health food—a 'sea supplement.'"

It all sounded fantastic, I said. Could this be done anywhere? "Everyone should eat salt produced like this, but people just haven't recognized the value of this system yet. You can use it anyplace the ocean is not polluted. As long as the ocean is clean, you can harvest clean salt. But I do have the patent on the system, of course."

But what about the flavor? Is that better than other salts as well? (I knew the answer to the question even as I was asking it.) "Yes, yes," he enthused as he led me to the factory shop and restaurant, all tastefully decorated in a modern Scandinavian style with gorgeous views over the aquamarine sea. Jazz tinkled in the background as lovely young assistants guided other guests to their tables and around the shop. "I have commissioned research into its umami profile that has shown that it has much more umami flavor than normal salt. It is the ultimate umami salt."

Takayasu-san showed me a book he had recently published entitled: *Salt: Health Revolution to Rescue Modern People*, subtitled *Miracle Salt That Doesn't Cause High Blood Pressure to Say Good-bye to Diabetes and Dry Skin*. Close by were various bath and massage products made from the salt, salt caramels, and elegant nine-ounce plastic sachets of the salt itself, on sale for ¥100—less than a dollar. I bought a packet to try at home. It was extremely fine and soft, like powdered sugar, and as far as I could make out, it does have a slightly milder taste, milder even than the other Okinawan salts I tried, like those from Aguni and Ishigaki. It lacks the textural interest of French marsh salts or Maldon, but is perfect as a dipping salt for tempura or just to finish off meats at the last minute, as it dissolves quickly and evenly.

Nuchi Masu is currently producing around 8.8 tons of salt a month, but capacity is set to ramp up to 33 tons. Takayasu-san had begun exporting it to Germany as "Life Salt" a month earlier, and in 2007, it won a Best Gold at the Monde Selection, a major food produce show held in Brussels. Kamebishi, the company that makes the superb soy sauce on Shikoku Island, also uses Nuchi Masu salt, and top chefs are following suit throughout Japan.

Now, if they could just manage to develop fat-free foie gras and french fries, I need never buy another women's magazine as long as I live—which would, of course, be well into three figures.

36. THE RESTAURANT AT THE END OF MY UNIVERSE

We flew from Okinawa back north to Tokyo the next day just in time for my dinner date with destiny at Mibu, the restaurant Yukio Hattori had said was the best in Japan. Mibu, you'll recall, was the place that made Joël Robuchon weep and humbled Ferran Adrià. It is what the Japanese call an *ichigen-san okotowari* place, meaning "entry by invitation only." Hattori was allowed to dine once a month with seven guests, and this month I was to be one of them.

On the flight, I stared down once more at snowcapped Mount Fuji passing by slowly below, yet I was feeling anything but serene. I was racked by anxiety, working myself up into a proper maelstrom of anticipatory angst. What was expected of me? Why had this rich, powerful, and influential man extended this remarkable invitation? More troubling still, would the food live up to the billing, and even if it did, would I be able to tell? Mibu had no website; in fact, there was no mention of it at all on the Internet. I had absolutely no idea what to expect, what to wear, or how to behave. Was I expected to pay, or at least offer to pay? Or would that cause offense? Whom would we be dining with? Just how many ways were there for me to disgrace myself with some oafish breach of etiquette?

Emi, who had helped me with some of my research, came along to act as interpreter. She tried to assuage my fears when we met that evening in Ginza, the heartland of Tokyo's lavish, high-rolling dining and nightlife scene.

Ginza is home to some of the most expensive restaurants in the world. During Japan's extraordinary economic rampage in the 1980s, this was where you came if you wanted to eat gold leaf–wrapped sushi off the belly of a naked woman—a style known as *nyotaimori*—or spend an average annual salary drinking rare single malts. Today, Ginza, with its redbrick grid of broad avenues and tree-lined side streets, originally developed by the British in the early twentieth century as an area for silver minting, still generates more wealth than many small nations and could easily lay claim to being the planet's retail flagship.

Emi had called Hattori's secretary and been told he would be paying and that we would be accompanied by a couple of food writers and three chefs from Hattori's cooking school.

By the time we arrived outside one of Ginza's best-known landmarks, the Sony Building, at six thirty in the evening, Hattori-san was already waiting, dressed in his customary deep black silk Mao jacket and rimless glasses, together with three men in dark suits and ties—the chefs—and two women dressed for the office in pencil skirts and white shirts—the food writers. We all chatted briefly, making introductions.

Hattori led us down a side road and around a corner to an anonymous building whose open front led to a strip-lit staircase. It looked more like the entrance to a multistory parking lot than a restaurant, but we followed him up two flights of stairs.

We were greeted at the entrance by the chef's wife, Tomiko Ishida, an imposing woman in her late sixties dressed in a magnificent dark kimono, a glossy black crest of hair crowning her cherubic face. Mibu has but one small, low-lit, windowless dining room, given over to the member and his guests each evening. As we were shown through from the entrance, I looked down at the floor. The flagstones had recently been dampened—a Japanese custom intended to express hospitality. Inside the dining room, the pale clay walls were timbered with *hinoki* wood, the most luxurious and costly paneling you can get in Japan, used for the coffins of emperors. But Mibu was neither glitzy nor ostentatious, far from it. The room was very simple, decorated in a Zen style with just a scroll and a vase—both, admittedly, priceless.

We sat at tatami-covered tables, not on the floor, which was some relief. I sat across from Hattori, with Emi on his left, the journalists to my right, and the chefs, who remained silent throughout the evening, taking assiduous notes and photographs, on my left.

Chef Hiroshi Ishida has run Mibu for over thirty years, his wife explained as she offered us sake from a pot with an unusually long spout. She poured it from a height, as you might ouzo. "This is the ancient way," she explained. "When there was a risk of poisoning, if you poured like this, the oxygen would mean the sake was less acidic and there was less danger." The pot was worth ¥1 million ($9,000), apparently. She drew our attention to the scroll on the wall. It was of a dancer. "This is seventy years old. See how she is drawn with one unbroken line." I imagined the decades of study that had led to the point at which the artist was able to create something of such simplicity. "We get power from art," the chef's wife said quietly, almost to herself, as she left the room.

When she returned with the first course, she introduced the flowers that were the only other decorative feature of the room; they were *hamagiku*, or white beach chrysanthemums, representative of the autumn festival period and a celebration of the countryside—the theme of that evening's meal.

The first course was a clear dashi with a fan-shaped ginkgo leaf floating on the surface. Beneath was a ginkgo fritter—chewy, nutty, and bitter—and a sliver of poached *gobi* fish. It was an elegant, refreshing start to the meal. "Eat the ginkgo leaves, too," advised Ishida's wife. "They are very good for vitamins against dementia."

"The chef has a real appreciation of the four seasons," Hattori said. "I have been coming here twelve times a year for sixteen years, and every time is an evocation of the month we are in. You have to eat food in season; that's the only time you can enjoy the moment. It has to be fresh every day."

Tomiko-san brought some grilled ayu, a seasonal river fish. "It goes well with sake. Note the bitterness of the guts," said Hattori.

The fish, caught by fishermen using trained cormorants, had been grilled whole, including the innards, and was served in a plain paper cone. She showed me how to pinch the flesh on the tail together to release it from the bones, and then eat around the spine.

"This is the time when the ayu fish return down the river fat and pregnant. Her life is finished. The fisherman prayed all day and asked the ayu to be medicine, so we appreciate it," she said.

The oily saltiness of the fish went perfectly with the chilled sake, while the bitter aftertaste from the guts of the fish was a welcome challenge to the palate, just lifting it from a complacent comfort zone. Shizuo Tsuji writes of the ayu that it is "the *pièce de résistance* of Japanese grilled foods and one of the few Japanese dishes in which the bitterness is meant to be enjoyed." While it is the least employed of the five tastes in the West, bitterness is an interesting element of Japanese cuisine. The ginkgo nuts, too, had a bitter aftertaste that helped cut through their chewy, cloying texture.

"I could see you were getting hot," Tomiko-san said, returning with a plate of sashimi. It was bonito, a rainbow of purple and red, and below that, beneath a layer of crushed ice, sashimi of gobi fish.

Was it the greatest sashimi I had ever had? No question. This was properly fresh bonito that had never been frozen. Unlike the bonito or tuna I had eaten before, whose flesh had so often been colored and degraded into a soft, sometimes mushy mass, this required ef-fort to chew. It had texture and flavor.

Eggplant was next. Often, Tomiko-san said, chefs reject fruits and vegetables late in their season, thinking they are past their best, but her husband realized that late crops were full of flavor. Indeed, he relished working with vegetables that other chefs might discard. The eggplant we were about to eat, for example, was at the *nagari* stage of the season, the end (the other two stages are *hashari*, the beginning of the season, and *sakari*, the ripe stage).

"We enjoy very much the end of the vegetable's life; we take care of it. It is a principle of our cooking. These vegetables are with us only for three or four months of the year, then they are gone. We won't be able to eat them again, so we celebrate them until they have gone."

The eggplant was slippery and fall-apart tender; I had never ex-perienced such an intense eggplant taste before. Eggplant is often just a sponge for oil and other flavors, but this one, which I assumed had been gently steamed, had not only retained its flavor but inten-sified it. It was served with tiny, soft yams the size of marbles.

Until now the meal had been fascinating, revelatory, and deli-cious, but things took a turn for the transcendent with the next course, hamo, or pike conger, served in a dashi scattered with yel-low chrysanthemum petals.

I took a sip of the gently steaming dashi—thickened with kuzu or arrowroot, which gives body without tainting the flavor in the way that conventional Western thickeners like flour, butter, or corn-starch do—and literally convulsed with pleasure. Hattori saw my reaction, smiled, and nodded to himself.

"You see, I really wanted you to try a proper dashi," he said.

"Now you know what I was talking about. This is the number one dashi in Japan. Usually, restaurants prepare dashi in the morning, but here it is prepared right at this very moment; the katsuobushi is shaved at the last minute. The smell of dashi evaporates quickly, so usually there is only a faint trace, but here you get the full flavor."

My embarrassing shudder of pleasure was involuntary, like a mini-orgasm. Every hair on my body had stood on end. It was as if the chef had found a taste receptor I never knew I had, some kind of palate G-spot, and performed a kind of culinarylingus. The soup had a deep meatiness, an addictive, savory foundation above which danced teasingly tangy notes of the sea. It was impossible to divide its flavor from its aroma, which I suspect is where the great power of this dashi, of any good dashi, lay. I would give anything to experience it again.

"You know," said Hattori, "Ishida just came up with this dish this afternoon. In ten years, I have never eaten the same dish twice. That is almost one and a half thousand dishes, all different."

"But, but . . ." I stammered, incredulous. "I don't believe it. It is like this dish has always been around. This dish must have existed before; it is so good."

"That is just what Ferran Adrià said when he ate here," said Hattori triumphantly. "He said it was like Ishida-san's food must always have been with us. If you really want to experience the core, the fundamentals of Japanese food, this is the place. Much cooking destroys the essential flavor of ingredients, but he makes the most of them."

As always in a Japanese meal, the arrival of the rice signaled the end of the savory courses, but this was not the usual bowl of plain rice to "fill a hole." Instead, we were served exquisite, soft, warm sticky rice studded with chestnuts from Tamba.

Dessert was a *kogyoku* apple from Gunma Prefecture, cooked in thin slices and as light as a communion host. It was served,

Tomiko-san explained, on rare silverware, the only type they could find that could hold perfect droplets of apple juice without them running. It looked like the plate was speckled with Swarovski crystals. "This is the ultimate dessert!" said Hattori.

Ishida-san brought it in to us himself. He was a short, straight-backed, stocky man, with a shaved head and the kindest face, dressed in a single-breasted white jacket and dark trousers—a gentle grandfather.

I stood up to shake his hand, but he gestured, smiling, that I should sit. I asked where he found his inspiration for the constant renewal of his menu. "It is very difficult. But I am always looking to get better at what I do every month," he said.

"He is competing against himself!" said Hattori. "Nobody can cook like him."

Where did he get all of his ingredients? From Tsukiji? "Of course, I do sometimes go to Tsukiji, but mostly I have direct contact with my suppliers, with my fishermen."

If you go to eat at the restaurants of one of the great European or American chefs—Alain Ducasse or Thomas Keller, for instance—the food is generally a direct expression of the chef's personality or ego; there are other top-class restaurants—Nobu, say, or the Ivy—where you go for the ambience, the decor, excessive fawning from the waitstaff, or to spot famous people; and then there are the celebrity chef joints like Anthony Bourdain's Brasserie Les Halles, in New York, or any of the Gordon Ramsay places—to be honest, I am not sure why anyone would go to those, as it is about as likely that the celebrity chef in question will be working in the kitchen as it is that a member of the Ford family has built your Fiesta.

But Mibu was something else. It wasn't really a restaurant in any conventional Western sense of the word. You didn't go for the decor, to be seen, or because it was prestigious or a celebrity hangout. You went for the narrative, for what the food told you about nature, flavor, and texture, perhaps even about yourself. It was dining as a spiritual experience, as an evocation of history, as philosophy, as a path to deeper mysteries of life, creation, death, and nature. Something elemental, in both senses of the word—both basic and fundamental and of the earth. And I am sure I missed around 80 percent of the meaning and references.

"Customers are like patrons of artists for us," Ishida's wife told me. "This food is not something you can buy with money. God gives you the time to enjoy this moment, but you need to have the ability to enjoy it, which is priceless."

It was a seismic moment in my life as an eater. The ingredients were rigorously seasonal. The flavors were pure, representative of the ingredients, subtle but intense when required. Somehow, Ishida was able to overlay different flavors, different intensities of taste within the same dish, yet with each remaining clearly identifiable. How often do we hear the chef behind the latest hot destination in London, Paris, or New York say that his or her food is "seasonal, fresh, local, and simple" before being presented with a plate of foam, gelatin, sous vide this or pureed that; food in towers; food compressed into ring molds; sauces smeared to look, as one critic memorably put it, "as if someone wearing stilettos had slipped in goose shit"? I admit, I spent a year training to make this kind of food, and then worked in two Michelin-starred Parisian kitchens serving it to customers with precision-placed chervil leaves, sticky reduced stocks, and absurdly turned vegetables, but now I knew better. At Mibu, the plating was elegant but without extraneous fuss. The food looked as if it had simply arrived in position.

It was a stark contrast to a meal I'd had a couple of nights earlier, on the thirty-eighth floor of the Mandarin Oriental Hotel. The Tapas Molecular Bar is one of the hottest restaurants in Tokyo, with space at its counter for just six diners. The Japanese American chef, Jeff Ramsay, served us dishes that were part food, part magic trick:

olive oil granita, made by pouring the oil into dry ice; a deconstructed miso soup; and carrot caviar, a classic El Bulli dish made by dropping carrot juice into a calcium chloride solution so that it formed small, soft spheres. It was the antithesis of Mibu—raw ingredients utterly transformed, unrecognizable. Some would dismiss this as too much "messing around" with food, and it is tempting to see Ramsay's style of cooking as a kind of corruption, but personally I feel there is plenty of room for both approaches to the preparation of food, and, once in a while at least, I find the invention and theatricality of so-called molecular cuisine absolutely thrilling. At least there are no airs of "simplicity" and "purity" with this kind of cooking. And I'll never forget the effect of a "miracle fruit" (*Synsepalum dulcificum*), a small, olive-type berry that grows wild in Africa, which, after you chew it a little, turns raw lemon wedges sweet.

But there was a poignancy to our meal at Mibu, an elegiac quality, which, had it not been such a joyous, sensual feast, might almost have been melancholy. The food worked on so many levels: visually, cerebrally, in terms of flavor, and viscerally. Ishida-san cooked with his heart and spirit. He and his food were indivisible. The dishes he had created especially for us that evening—never to be repeated— were born of a lifetime's experience and a depth of understanding of Japanese culture that few Japanese chefs could match and even fewer will attain in the future. There had been around ten courses, but by the end I felt neither bloated nor hungry but perfectly, blissfully sated. "Another good restaurant might manage a couple of courses of this standard, but never be consistent over so many," agreed Hattori.

As we were leaving, we were each given plastic bags with some more of the apple dessert, some foil-wrapped sashimi, and another ziplock bag of some of Ishida's own katsuobushi shavings.

By the doorway, I asked Tomiko-san how old her husband was.

"Sixty-five," she said.

"Oh, he can go on cooking for years yet," I said.

"No," she said quietly so that he couldn't hear. "By cooking he is cutting his life short."

It is only in the last month or so, as I continue to reflect on that evening, that the fundamental lesson of my visit to Mibu has become apparent: that to be a truly great chef, to excel in your métier, surpass your peers, and create something beyond a meal, you must above all else have humility: humility regarding your craft, so that you are constantly striving to learn and are open to new ways and ingredients; humility toward your peers, so that you never rest on your laurels; but, above all, crucially, humility toward the ingredients, because without the produce, without the fruit and the fish, the meat and the vegetables, a chef is nothing. Ishida employed his produce with the greatest respect, allowing its flavors to vibrate with a purity that I could work years to achieve but in reality would probably never even dare to attempt, because as well as humility, that kind of simplicity takes a lifetime's experience. I know that using the word *courage* in the context of a kitchen may sound preposterous, but to serve a steamed eggplant naked and to present this as your best work takes some front.

When Michelin published its first Tokyo guide a few weeks later to a fanfare of publicity and outrage in both the Japanese and French capitals—Tokyo was judged to be worthy of almost twice as many stars as Paris—Mibu was nowhere to be found. It was not even mentioned among the restaurants that had refused to participate in the inspector's assessment.

Sometimes I wonder if it ever existed.

EPILOGUE

Japanese cuisine is deceptively simple. Its key ingredients are but two: a rather delicate stock made from konbu and flakes of dried bonito, and shoyu, Japanese soy sauce.
—Shizuo Tsuji, *Japanese Cooking: A Simple Art*

think the key word here is *deceptively* for, of course, Japanese cuisine is anything but simple. I never for a moment thought I would discover all there is to know about it during just one journey, no matter how action- and meal-packed it was, but, equally, I never anticipated quite how dazzlingly multifaceted, how regionally diverse, how occasionally befuddling it would turn out to be.

On our last day in Tokyo, in one final, desperate box-ticking binge, we did get to sample both *shirako*—cod's sperm, or milt—which I thoroughly recommend, and chicken sashimi, which was also rather lovely once I had surmounted the psychological hurdle. Also, Emil wants it to be known that during a meal later in the day, he ate an entire fish eye and enjoyed it. But there were so many things I didn't get to eat but wanted to, so many cities I wanted to visit but didn't have the time for, and, most important, so many *seasons* of food I wanted to experience. I could spend a lifetime studying just one aspect of Japanese cuisine—as, indeed, my friend Mr. Kobayashi the ramen champion has, or Kikunoi chef Murata-san has with dashi—and still never really find a definitive recipe or perfect my technique. To hope to master it all was, of course, delusional.

I admitted all of this to Toshi on our first meeting after we had arrived back in Paris. I suppose I had hoped for a thawing of temperament, that my conversion to the Japanese cause might temper his argumentativeness slightly. But he merely pouted and shrugged his shoulders as if to say, *This is not news to me.*

"So maybe you won't cook fish so long now, eh?"

"No, Toshi, I won't."

"No more cream. Better vegetables."

"Yes, Toshi."

"One more thing. Say, '*Gochisoma deshita.*'"

I repeated, "*Gochisoma deshita*. What does it mean? 'White men can't cook'?"

"It is from Buddha—a thanks to the cooks who gathered and made the food. Say it every meal."

These days I drink jasmine tea every morning and take my turmeric supplements, as Dr. Willcox advises. I beguile guests with my inside-out maki rolls—which are much better now—and by splashing ponzu and miso over everything. I eat tofu and miso soup, more fish, less meat, more vegetables, and less dairy, and I feel all the better for it, not least because I have shed a few pounds.

My sons still clamor for tempura and sushi on a weekly basis. The Okinawan snake soup is one of Emil's favorite travel anecdotes. He still talks fondly of the Japanese health service and the dead turtle he found on the beach on Okinawa. They remember the Japanese word for dragonfly, *tombo*, too, which they learned back in Sapporo. Asger still talks of the time he felled a sumo and only slightly exaggerates the size of the king crab he was introduced to.

We often look through our photographs, and, of course, over time, memories of Japan will fade, but to have seen it through the eyes of my family was a special experience. And having children in tow opened so many more doors, introduced us to so many more people, and afforded us a far greater latitude for appalling behavior than might otherwise have been the case.

Japan will always be there; we will return, and the food will awe us once more. Perhaps most reassuring of all is that Shizuo Tsuji's fears of a disappearing culinary tradition seem largely unfounded. Japanese cuisine is changing, of course; I don't think Tsuji-san would have wanted it otherwise. Though the worrying trend toward a Western diet continues and is bringing with it all the health problems we are facing in the West, with people like Kanae Okada at the Kamebishi soy company, Hattori-san, or Tony Flenley with his pungent miso, Masakatsu Takayasu and his healthy salt, and, of course, Yoshiki Tsuji, I think the traditions and future of Japanese cuisine are in safe, passionate, and capable hands.

ACKNOWLEDGMENTS

I owe a significant debt of thanks to my researcher, Emiko "Emi" Doi—not just for her amazing ability to get me into places I might otherwise never even have known existed but for her warmth and generosity to me and my family while we were in Japan.

So many people gave their time to help me in the research for this book and displayed remarkable patience when dealing with my innovative scatter-gun interviewing technique. Most are already mentioned by name, but I would again like to express my sincere thanks for their time and generosity: to Toshi, of course, although I doubt anything in these pages will come as news to him; Yukio Hattori, whose Tokyo Taste event I later attended and much enjoyed; Yoshiki Tsuji, a generous host during my visit to Osaka; miso expert Tony Flenley, who tells me the smell from his drains has much improved; Etsuko Shinobu, the Tokyo housewife whose tatami floor I besmirched with my borrowed red vinyl slippers; Yoshio Ando, the wasabi expert; Takahiko Sasaki, the konbu expert; Philip Harper and Akira Toko, the sake experts who shared their knowledge and enthusiasm; Kanae Okada, the remarkable soy revivalist; Shuichiro Kobori, the fu expert; Ikuko Uda, the wasabi cooking supremo; salt revolutionary Masakatsu Takayasu; master chefs Hiroshi Ishida,

Yoshihiro Murata, Yoshifumi Mori, Takamitsu Aihara, Eiji Hayashi, and Jeff Ramsay; Osamu, the peerless sushi chef who kindly and with great forbearance showed us around Tsukiji; Junko and Sasha in Kyoto; Chiaki and Hiroshi for their incredible hospitality in Osaka; centenarian Matsu Taira; Ramen World Champion Takamitsu Kobayashi; our friends at the Onoe sumo stable (congratulations to Sumo Monster and Baruto, who since I wrote this book went on to great success and have now retired); Tamie Kosaki and Kayo Kosaki, the ama divers; Kurt, my Koya-san guru; gerontologist Dr. Craig Willcox; the renowned Osakan food writer Takeshi Kadokami, who gave generously of his time in order to help me understand the nature of Osakan cuisine; and the people at Fuji TV, the Wadakin cattle ranch, the Yaizu fish-processing center, Ajinomoto, and Kikkoman, all of whom received me with great generosity and kindness.

There are also some who aren't mentioned explicitly in the book but were a tremendous help and inspiration, such as Kylie Clark at the Japan National Tourism Organization in London (a true Japanese food fan, and kindred spirit—go to www.seejapan.co.uk to have all your questions answered about visiting) and the helpful assistants at the various tourist offices around Japan, particularly in Mie Prefecture and Osaka.

And then there was the woman who politely tapped me on the shoulder while I was on my phone at a crossroads in Ginza and *apologized* for interrupting me to say, did I realize I had dropped a large banknote on the sidewalk? For me, she epitomized the decency and helpfulness shown to us by virtually every single Japanese person we met during our journey through their astonishingly beautiful, endlessly exciting, and thoroughly civilized land. (I like to think I sent the karma onward when, later, I found a wallet filled with large banknotes on the backseat of a taxi one evening in Kyoto. Perhaps in no other country in the world would I have judged it prudent to pass the wallet to the taxi driver, safe in the knowledge that he would hand it in to the police.)

Practical travel assistance was very generously given by the Japan National Tourism Organization (see above), the Mandarin Oriental Hotel (www.mandarinoriental.com/tokyo), and Oakwood serviced apartments (www.oakwood.com), which are fantastic if you are traveling with a family.

I am deeply grateful for the continuing support and sound advice of my agent, George Lucas at Inkwell, as well as the skillful and sensitive editing of Anna deVries at Picador. Sincere thanks also to my U.S. publisher, Stephen Morrison, and the original publisher of this book, Dan Franklin at Jonathan Cape in London.

Finally, to Lissen, in particular, I want to express my unbounded gratitude for your incredible support and patience during this journey. I know that sometimes there appeared to be precious little method in my madness but hope that in reading this you will see that there was at least some point to the many hours spent trying to entertain two young, restless boys alone in a strange land. (You can now see just how absolutely essential it was that I visit two cattle ranches, for example.)

One day we'll go back and eat at Kikunoi together, I promise.

GLOSSARY

Ainu Indigenous people of Hokkaido

ama Female divers who dive for shellfish and seaweed in waters off the easterly Pacific coast of Mie

anime Japanese animation

aonori Dried seaweed flakes

awamori Okinawan distilled liquor

ayu Seasonal freshwater fish, typically grilled whole

bata-kon ramen Hokkaido-style butter-corn ramen

beni imo Okinawan purple sweet potato

bonito/katsuobushi Oily, red-fleshed fish related to tuna/smoke-dried fillets of same fish

Bunraku Traditional Japanese puppetry

Burakumin Oppressed social minority group in Japan

butsukari-geiko Sumo training exercise where one wrestler attempts to push his opponent across the ring

cha-kaiseki Original, simple form of kaiseki multicourse meal devised to accompany the tea ceremony

chanko nabe Traditional hot pot prepared and eaten by sumo wrestlers

chikuto Fine-quality sugarcane

dai ginjo Exclusive type of sake

dankon Penis

deba Triangular knife for filleting fish

dengaku Skewered tofu coated with miso and grilled

depachika Department store food hall

dohyo Clay ring in which sumo wrestling takes place

engawa the frilly edges of a flatfish

enoki Long, thin, white mushrooms

fu Type of dough made from wheat gluten

fugu Puffer fish or blowfish

fugusashi Sliced raw puffer fish or blowfish

gaijin Outsider or foreigner

genshu Undiluted sake

goya champaru Okinawan dish featuring stir-fried bitter cucumber

gunkan maki "Battleship" sushi, where a block of rice and topping is
   wrapped in nori seaweed in the shape of a boat

gyoza Chinese-style dumpling filled with meat or vegetables

habu Type of snake

hamagiku White beach chrysanthemum

hamo Pike conger

hangiri Wooden rice bowl used for cooling sushi rice

hara hachi-bu Okinawan expression meaning "Eat until you are
   80 percent full"

harusame Transparent noodles made from potato flour or mung bean
   flour

hashari Early-season crops

higuma Grizzly bear

hirami Thin-skinned flat lemon

hiyamugi Thick noodles made from wheat flour

hoko nabe Charcoal-heated samovar
honoki Non-resinous wood

ichiban dashi "Number one" basic stock infused with dried konbu
seaweed and katsuobushi flakes, used as a base for many Japanese
dishes, sauces, soups, etc.
ichigen-san okotowari "Entry by invitation only"
ichigo ichie "One encounter, one chance"
irabu-jiru Snake stew
izakaya Japanese-style pub-diner

jizo Statues erected as memorials to children and infants who have died
junmai ginjo sake Premium sake

kabuki Dance drama
kaiseki Elaborate, ritualistic, formal dinner of up to nine courses,
inspired by the passing seasons
kaiten sushi Conveyor-belt sushi
kajimayaa Public party held to celebrate the ninety-seventh birthday of
an Okinawan resident
kakiage tendon Scallop fritters (tempura)
kamaboko Fish cakes made from steamed fish paste
kami-sama Gods
kanji Chinese characters used in Japanese writing
katsuobushi Smoked and dried, fermented fillets of bonito fish, which
are shaved on a special plane and used as a seasoning
katsuobushi kezuriki Upside-down carpenter's plane used for shaving
dried blocks of bonito fish
katsuramuki "Column peel"—a technique used for peeling
vegetables
kimchi Korean pickled cabbage
kimo Liver of the fugu fish
kito piro Ainu mountain vegetables

kogyoku Japanese apple

koji Fermenting agent used in sake brewing, as well as to make miso and soy sauce and as a marinade/pickling ingredient

konbu (or kombu) Seaweed, dried for use most notably in making dashi; variations include rishiri konbu—konbu laid down and dried for two years to deepen its glutamate flavor; shio konbu—salt konbu; and tororo konbu—konbu soaked in vinegar, then dried and shaved

konnyaku Jelly-like substance made from the "devil's tongue" root and used to add texture to dishes

koromo Enrobed

koshihikari Premium-quality, short-grain rice that has been dried naturally in the sun

kuidaore Osakan expression meaning "Eat till you go bust" (physically and financially)

kura-gakoi Method of preserving konbu using a temperature- and humidity-controlled drying process

kushikatsu Deep-fried breaded skewers

kusuimun Medicinal foods

kuzu Thickening agent

kyo ryori Kyoto cuisine

kyo yasai Kyoto vegetables

kyo-kaiseki Kyoto-style kaiseki

machiya Historic wooden town houses found in Kyoto

maki Sushi roll

makisu Bamboo mat for rolling maki

maoi Okinawan local "people's banks"

matsutake "Japanese truffle"—a rare, rich, woody mushroom

mawashi Loincloth worn by sumo wresters

meishi Business card

miora MSG-laced flavoring added to rice

mirugai Geoduck clam

miso Fermented soybean paste for flavoring soups and stocks; variations include kome miso—made with rice and beans; mame miso—made with beans only; mugi miso—made with barley and beans; and sendai miso—salty miso

mushiro Method of maturing fermented soybeans for making soy sauce

mochi Japanese dessert made with rice-flour dough

modori Bonito fish, or katsuo, returning from the north in the autumn

moromi Koji mixed with brine to form the mash used in making soy sauce

mukkur Wooden Jew's harp—a traditional Ainu instrument

nagari Late-season crops

natto Acquired taste, fermented soybean dish

negi Japanese-style baby leeks

nigari Coagulant used to make tofu

nigiri Edo, or Tokyo-style, sushi, in which body-temperature, hand-squeezed blocks of rice are topped with chilled seafood

nikiri Sushi dip made with dashi, mirin, sake, and soy

ninjitsu Technique for making nigiri that mimics the secret signal of the ninja

Nishiki Ichiba Kyoto's main market

noren Traditional restaurant door curtain

nori Thin, dried, edible seaweed sheets used for wrapping around sushi rice

obanzai ryori Home-style Kyoto cuisine, largely vegetarian, centering on tofu and yuba

oden "Lucky-dip" stew containing any combination of tofu, meat, fish, and vegetables

oishii Delicious

okonomiyaki Japanese-style thick pancake with various fillings/toppings; variations include monjayaki—made with a runnier dough than okonomiyaki; and modanyaki—with fried noodles (yakisoba) mixed into the batter

omachi The original sake rice

omakase "I'll let you decide" (meaning the chef will choose your meal for you)

omurice Rice-filled omelet

onsen Hot springs

o-toro The fattiest part of the tuna belly

pachinko Type of Japanese gaming machine, part pinball, part video game

ponzu Sauce made from dashi and yuzu juice

ramen Iconic noodle dish served in a meat-based broth with meat and vegetables; variations include Hakata ramen, a white, pork-bone (tonkotsu) broth; miso ramen, a thick, nutty, and slightly sweet broth seasoned with miso; and shio ramen, a clear, yellowish broth seasoned with salt

rikishi Professional sumo wrestler "strong men"

robata Open charcoal fire used for cooking

sakari Ripe-season crops

sakoku "national seclusion"

sashi Branches of fat in beef

sashimi Raw fish

senshu mizu Kyoto eggplant

shabu-shabu Boiled escalopes of beef

shiitake Chinese mushroom

Shingon Buddhism "True Word" Buddhism

shirako Cod's sperm

shirataki Low-carbohydrate, thin, translucent noodles

shiso Leaf and flower used in salads, sushi, and sashimi dishes

shochu Japanese spirit distilled from wheat, potato, buckwheat, or black sugar

shojin ryori "Pure food"—the vegetarian cuisine eaten by Buddhists

Shokuiku Food and health education program run by the Japanese government

shoyu Soy sauce

shukubo Zen Buddhist religious hostel

soba Thin brown noodles made from buckwheat flour; variations on serving include kake-soba, noodles served in a large bowl of soup; wanko-soba, white, flour-based noodles served in mouthful-sized portions; and zaru-soba, cooked, chilled noodles served with a dipping sauce

sogi giri Technique for slicing vegetables

somen Ultrathin noodles (At a nagashi-somen restaurant, the noodles are cooked then dropped into a fast-flowing mountain river, from which diners, sitting on wooden platforms, pluck them—supposedly.)

sudachi Small, green citrus fruit similar in appearance to a lime

sukiyaki Quick-fried beef dish served with sugary, raw egg sauce

Tajima-gyu Black-haired, short-horn cows known as "Japanese blacks"

takoyaki "Octopus balls"—small doughnuts filled with octopus chunks

tamago Japanese rolled omelet

taro Edible plant root cooked as a vegetable or ground into paste or flour

tempura Deep-fried vegetables or seafood

tenkasu Cooked flour dough used for tempura

tenugui Headscarf worn by Japanese chefs

toishi Whetstone

toji Master sake brewer

tokonoma Small raised display alcove

tombi hawk Black kite hawk

tonkatsu Breaded pork cutlets

udon Thick, white flour–based noodles; variations include kama-age-udon—served with a cold dipping sauce; and kitsune udon—soft, squidgy udon noodles served in a slightly sweet dashi with deep-fried tofu skin

uimaru Okinawan social groups

ujinimun Nutritional foods

umami The fifth basic taste

umi-budo Seaweed with tiny pods arranged around edible stalks, sometimes called "sea grapes" or "sea caviar"

uni Sea urchin

ura maki Inside-out sushi rolls where rice is spread over dried nori sheets

usuba Rectangular bladed knife for cutting vegetables

Wagyu beef Japanese beef, typically tender and marbled with creamy white fat; often mistakenly called Kobe beef

wasanbonto sugar The "king of sugars"

yakuro Medicinal hunting

yakisoba Fried noodles

yanagi Sashimi knife (with only one beveled edge)

yatai Fukuokan street-cart food stall

yokozuna Highest rank in professional sumo

yoshoku Westernized Japanese cooking

yuba Tofu skin

Yubari Orange-fleshed cantaloupe

yuka Wooden platforms over water

yukata Short cotton kimono

yuta Okinawan healer

yuzu Citrus fruit resembling a small grapefruit

INDEX

ABOUT THE AUTHOR

Michael Booth is the award-winning, bestselling author of five works of nonfiction. He is a broadcaster and speaker, and his writing has appeared in numerous newspapers and magazines around the world, including *The Guardian*, *The Washington Post*, *The Times*, *The Independent*, *The Telegraph*, *Condé Nast Traveller*, and *Monocle*, among many others.

In 2015, this book was adapted into a much-loved twenty-five-part animated TV series called *British Family Eats Japan* by Japanese national broadcaster NHK. It is now available on DVD in English and Japanese.

www.michael-booth.com
@themichaelbooth